The Wealth
Creators

The Wealth Creators

The Rise of Today's Rich and Super-Rich

by

Roy C. Smith

TRUMAN TALLEY BOOKS
ST. MARTIN'S PRESS
NEW YORK

www.stmartins.com

Library of Congress Cataloging-in-Publication Data

Smith, Roy C.
    The wealth creators : the rise of today's rich and super-rich / Roy C. Smith.
        p. cm.
    ISBN 0-312-27259-6
    1. Wealth—United States.   2. Rich people—United States.
    I. Title.

HC110.W4 S614 2001
305.5'234'0973—dc21

                                                    00-064938

First Edition: February 2001

10 9 8 7 6 5 4 3 2 1

To my Mother and Father:
Ann and Roy Smith

CONTENTS

The Wealth Creators

A Shining City
on a Hill

In 1982 *Forbes* first published its list of the four hundred wealthiest Americans. This was a fitting thing to do in the first real year of Reaganomics, that is, after the bull market had begun and the gloomy days of the 1970s were drifting behind us. In the bright new world of Reaganomics it was okay to be rich, and *Forbes* launched its rich-list to much curiosity and acclaim. It may have been seen as tacky by some to flaunt information about how rich people were, but Americans loved it, and each year's release of the *Forbes* 400 became a much-anticipated event. What neither *Forbes* nor its readers knew at the time was just how rich these rich, and others like them, would become over the next two decades. For these two decades—the 1980s and 1990s—have turned out to be the greatest years of wealth creation the world has ever known.

The almost continuous bull market that began during

the administration of Ronald Reagan and ran until the end of the century rose faster and soared higher than during any other boom period in our history. In the 1920s the Dow Jones Industrial Average increased three-fold, the record for any single decade prior to the eighties. The 1920s, however, were concluded by the Crash of October 1929 and followed by the Great Depression. It was not until 1954 that the Dow passed the 381 high level it had reached on September 3, 1929, eight weeks before the Crash.

In August 1982, after Reagan had been president for about eighteen months and his first economic plans were understood, the market stood at a Dow low of 821. Despite a significant but relatively short-lived interruption five years later, in October 1987, the stock market continued to rise. It tripled during the Reagan years, added another 1,000 points during the Bush administration, and strained at its leash thereafter. The Dow passed the 11,000 mark in May 1999 and ended the year at 11,500, a record level and 27 percent ahead of its close in 1998. Altogether, from the recovery in the summer of 1982 through the end of 1999, the DJIA experienced nearly a *fourteen-fold increase*, or an annual compound growth of 16 percent for seventeen years, an all-time record by far. This was an extraordinary achievement, one that made many Americans rich.

Indeed, American household wealth at the end of the twentieth century was about $37 trillion, up from $8.2 trillion in 1980.[1] This was an increase in individual wealth (all financial and real estate assets less all consumer debt and mortgages) of more than four and a half times what it had been just before Reagan became president. It was what a generation of Americans had set aside after paying taxes and tuitions, taking vacations, and improving their homes, and it had compounded at a rate of 8 percent for twenty years, more than twice as fast as the real growth rate of the economy. Adjusted for inflation, household wealth in 1999 was two and a half times what it was in 1980. And as large as these wealth numbers are, they almost certainly understate the true value of holdings in privately owned businesses.

By the end of the twentieth century, there were approximately 5 million millionaires living in America, only a small fraction of whom were millionaires in 1980, when there were fewer than 200,000 of them in the entire country.

THE BIG RICH

Most of us were astonished to learn in 1982 that there were twelve American families worth more than $1 billion. There were also twenty-five between $500 million and $1 billion; nearly 100 between $200 and $500 million; and 267 others among the richest 400 families with net assets (at approximate market value) above $100 million. In those days, billions were numbers that only governments dealt in.

The richest American then was D. K. Ludwig, an international supertanker tycoon whom virtually no one had heard of. He put together the world's largest fleet of oil tankers by borrowing money in Japan to place contracts with shipbuilders there on the strength of long-term bareboat charters with major international oil companies that would go into effect when the ships were delivered. Ludwig put up very little money of his own and simply collected rent on his ships for twenty years at a time. He was worth about $2 billion in 1982, but later lost about half of it in a huge, disastrous wood-pulp investment in the Brazilian jungles. He was very reclusive and had no children. He died in 1992 at the age of ninety-five and left all his money to a medical foundation.

The next ten or so families on the 1982 list included several more oil people. That is, people who had inherited from the estates of John Paul Getty, Sid Bass, and H. L. Hunt, all early Texas wildcatters, or independent oil drillers. David Packard, cofounder of Hewlett-Packard, was twelfth on the list; Walter Annenberg, the publisher of *TV Guide* was fourteenth. Altogether, 115 families on the list (38 percent) were people still working in manufacturing or other businesses that they had started. Those who had inherited their money from others represented 32 percent of the four hundred families. Those in real estate were 15 percent of the list, those in natural resources 10 percent, and those thought of as financiers less than 4 percent. Some of the many names new to *Forbes'* readers included entrepreneurs Sam Walton (founder of Wal-Mart and later to become the richest American), Donald Trump (a brassy New York real estate guy), Ross Perot (Electronic Data Systems); Ray Kroc (McDonalds), Philip Knight (Nike Shoes), Steven Jobs (Apple Computer), and Fred Smith (Federal Express). Other interesting characters included J. R. Simplot, the Idaho potato king; Bob Hope; Robert Guccione (*Penthouse*); Yoko Ono (widow of Beatle John Lennon); and George Lucas (*Star Wars*). Also included were a number of the rogue rich: Meyer Lansky (mafia gangster), Marc Rich and Robert Vesco (fugitives), and Ivan Boesky (inside trader).

The list told us something about our economic and financial culture in the United States. Using the top four hundred families as a sample, we could conclude that about a third of sizeable American personal wealth was inherited, much of it from roots that were not very deep. About a third was tied to industrial activities involving an endless variety of business ideas and technologies, and about a third was associated with entrepreneurial, proactive investors in real estate and finance. Many of the names that surfaced were of extremely low-profile people; others were much more visible—controversial folks who had earned reputations as ruthless competitors or highly idiosyncratic individuals, as well as much-admired founders of popular businesses.

Just how unique American wealth creation is was revealed when *Forbes* published its 1999 list. In the seventeen years since the first list, some staggering things had happened. The number of billionaires had grown from twelve to 268, and the estimated wealth of the four hundredth family had also grown, from $90 million to $625 million. In 1999, 251 names were classified as "self-made," as compared to 159 in this category in 1982. Three of the four richest Americans in 1999 were Microsoft billionaires: nerdy Bill Gates, forty-three years old ($85 billion, the world's largest fortune); his obscure cofounder Paul Allen, forty-six ($40 billion); and the company's current CEO, Steve Ballmer, forty-three, ($23 billion). Stuck in among the Microsofts, in third place was Warren Buffett, sixty-nine ($31 billion), the investment guru of Omaha. Gates was nowhere to be found on the 1982 list and Buffett was well down it. Michael Dell, thirty-four, founder of Dell Computer Corp., was ranked fifth in 1999 with $20 billion. Gordon Moore, seventy, an Intel founder, was among the top ten with $15 billion. Further down the list, among those with net worths between $5 billion and $10 billion, were Jeff Bezos, thirty-five, founder of Amazon.com; Abigail Johnson, thirty-seven, CEO of The Fidelity Group; media tycoons Ted Turner, sixty-one, and Rupert Murdock, sixty-eight; and discount broker Charles Schwab, sixty-two.

Of the top fifteen families on the 1999 *Forbes* 400 list, only one (the Rockefellers) represented old oil money. Ten or so other families also traced their fortunes to the nineteenth century, but there were an equal number of families whose large inheritances were only one generation old. Sam Walton, for example, had died since the first *Forbes* list was published and left his money to his wife and children (the Walton family, with $85 billion between them, was the richest family of all).

By 1999, the percentage of the top families' wealth that was from inheritance declined to about 25 percent (from 32 percent in 1982), and the portion represented by industry increased to more than 50 percent (from 38 percent). Real estate declined to 6 percent (from 15 percent) and finance increased to 12 percent (from 4 percent). Most of the names on the 1999 list were new to those reading the list from 1982. These included Ralph Lauren of Polo; Michael Bloomberg, the rising media industry star; and technology wunderkinder Joseph Liemandt, thirty-one, founder of high-tech Trilogy Software; Mark Cuban, thirty-one, cofounder of Broadcast.com; and Pierre Omidyar, 31, founder of eBay. There were also Craig McCaw, cellular telephones; John Malone, a cable TV king; Donald Tyson, the Arkansas chicken man; and Mark McCormack, the sports agent. Financial and investment people on the 1999 list included George Soros, the foreign-exchange trader; Peter Kellogg, the New York Stock Exchange specialist; mutual fund operator Michael Price; and Michael Milken, the former junk bond king. Also on the 1999 list were nonfounder managers of big businesses Michael Eisner, chairman of Disney; Maurice "Hank" Greenberg, chairman of the AIG insurance group; Lew Gerstner, CEO of IBM; and Sanford Weill, then cochairman of 1998's merger-of-the-year, Citigroup. Jack Welch, legendary CEO of General Electric, did not make the first four hundred cut; neither did John Reed, Weill's cochairman at Citigroup.

The 1999 list also included sixty people (15 percent) who were making their first appearance in the *Forbes* compilation, thirty-five of whom were from Internet or related new technology businesses. There were dropouts to make room for them, mostly deceased entrepreneurs or inheritors of old money (in 1984 the list included twenty members of the DuPont family, in 1999 there were none). But not all the new money was from high tech. There were also a considerable number of low-tech entrepreneurs on the 1999 list, including Monroe Carell (parking lots in Nashville); Bradley Hughes (rented storage spaces); Summerfield Johnston (Coca-Cola bottler); James Moran (car dealerships); Leslie Schwab (tires); and Glen Taylor (printing). It would be hard to imagine a more diverse compilation of sources of wealth than those in the 1999 list. "How typically American," some would say: "big, new, and showy; constantly changing and scattered all around." That's us.

THE REST OF THE RICH

The wealth reported by *Forbes* far more than doubled between 1982 and 1999, when the four hundred combined were worth more than $1 trillion. To make this list was to be among the biggest of the big hitters, surely a group that was not really representative of what was going on in the rest of the country. However, the increase in American wealth in the 1980–1999 period was far more extensive than throughout just the top four hundred families. It penetrated well down into the country.

In 1996, according to William Danko and Thomas Stanley, authors of the bestseller *The Millionaire Next Door*, there were 3.5 million millionaires in the United States, whose families represented about 3.5 percent of the population. By 2005, these authors estimate, there will be nearly 6 million millionaire households. Not to be outdone, *Forbes* estimated that there were 5 million millionaires in 1999, and that there would be 20 million of them by 2010.[2] (A millionaire household is a family with assets the market value of which, less all financial liabilities, equals or exceeds $1 million. The key word is *market* value; not book value, or the historical cost of the investments held. Market value is the price you can sell an asset for. For publicly traded investments such as stocks, bonds, and mutual funds, usually all you have to do is look up the prices in the newspaper. But the market values of nontraded assets, such as land, real estate, and privately owned businesses, are more difficult to value, and are often underestimated by economists. As a result, the true value of wealth in the hands of households is probably significantly greater than that which is reported.)

The substantial increase in the number of millionaire households indicates that wealth is now somewhat more widely distributed than before. In March 1998 the Internal Revenue Service issued the results of a study of tax-record data which showed that the richest 1 percent of Americans owned 21.4 percent of the country's wealth in 1995. Though this ratio reflected a slight increase from 1992 levels, it was just about the same as it had been in 1989, so the rich were not getting richer at the expense of the poor, at least not during the 1990s. The report also noted that there were 4.1 million people in 1995 with gross financial assets of $600,000, up from 3.7 million in 1992.[3] Making allowances for the substantial appreciation of asset values since then, we can arrive at the Danko and Stanley estimate of 3.5 to 4 million millionaires in the country as of the end of 1996. By contrast, there were only about four thousand millionaires in 1900, at the end of the gilded age of robber barons, when the population was 75 million. That would mean a millionaire density then of less than .01 percent of all Americans. Today the per-capita density of millionaires is about twenty times greater.

The existence of so many millionaires invites further classification of them. Years ago there were only old money and nouveaux riches. In 1982 if you made it onto the *Forbes* four hundred, you could be sure of being among the Big Rich. In 1999 *Forbes* suggested that those with more than $100 million should be called "superrich," while those with less than $100 million but more than $10 million would be "just rich." Below $10 million and you were cast by *Forbes* into the unhappily indistinct "upper middle."[4] *Barron's*, on the other hand, had a different classification. If you had more than $35 million you were among the "very, very rich." Below that but above $20 million would make you "yachts and limousines rich." Below these categories there were two more—"filet mignon and champagne rich" and "beer and pretzels rich," which tipped the scales at a net worth of $2 million.[5]

The United States has often in its history been a country of tremendous wealth creation. What's extraordinary about the last twenty years of the twentieth century is how much more wealth was created then, and, because the stock market was its principle medium of transmission, how much more widely spread it became. Such developments, of course, beg the question of why.

WHY US? WHY THEN?

The simplest answer is that America is a land, more than any other, that is devoted to free enterprise, hard work, and a willingness to take risks. We have been nourished by free markets, democratic capitalism, and upward mobility longer and more extensively than any other large industrial nation. Not only that, we developed the business culture and gave it respect. We invented business schools at the turn of the twentieth century, provided the first executive training programs, and perfected market research and advertising. We harnessed the country's commercial and financial instincts and energies, making the most of them. So we come by success in business and finance honestly. We have paid our dues.

But the last twenty years have been truly special. Things

came together in ways they may not again to provide an unusually fertile environment for wealth to develop. To begin with, this period of two consecutive decades is the only one of the twentieth century in which the United States was not at war, or in economic crisis, or just recovering from one or the other. Wars and economic crises inhibit wealth building, at least for most people. Even so, or perhaps *because* the country has been free to pursue the business of business for an extended period of time, some special conditions did come together during the last two decades to significantly accelerate developments.

The special conditions that shaped the period were the effects of major political-economic changes, the release of new competitive market forces, and the introduction of new technologies that accelerated changes. These were powerful events that made much of what happened in the past twenty years possible.

New Economic Policies

A new set of economic policies emerged in the 1980s and 1990s, the essence of which was that the government's intervention in the economy would be less than in previous periods. The private sector was recognized as the principal source of job and wealth creation, and the free market was selected as the best mechanism for allocating resources within the economy. These policies have now been accepted by both of our major political parties—mainly because people believe they worked. Unless some large problems requiring intervention by the government arise (and they do periodically), the consensus appears to be that our present system of arms-length government involvement in economic affairs works well, so let's leave it alone.

But it was not always so. The 1960s were a period regarded by many economists as a golden age, when growth averaged over 5 percent for nearly a decade, and productivity and family incomes increased at rates not since equaled. Unemployment declined to a record 3.4 percent in late 1968, and the economy expanded for 106 consecutive months, the longest uninterrupted period of growth in the century. These exceptional results were stimulated by major tax cuts in 1962 and 1964, designed to increase the output of the economy to its full capacity. But the role of the federal government in the Kennedy-Johnson years was still very large in American economic life, and very hands-on. The government's role, it was thought then, was to promote balance and fairness in the economy by interventions that would assist and encourage some sectors (e.g., labor, the poor) while restraining or constraining others (business, finance). This was intended to make society more democratic, but it didn't necessarily make it more efficient. Such policies, moreover, resulted in large government budgets that were extremely difficult to manage. Accordingly, economic policy initiatives were almost impossible to fine-tune. Toward the end of the decade, the government had become committed to a war in Vietnam and a wide range of expensive new social policies at the same time. It struggled hard to control inflation and defend the value of the dollar, but ultimately without success. The stock market, which enjoyed the first half of the decade, was much less confident during the second. Despite outstanding performance in some sectors of the economy, the Dow Jones Industrial Average did not quite double during an eleven-year period encompassing a low of 536 in June of 1962 and a high of 1,053 in January 1973. During this time the index flirted with 1,000 on several occasions, only to fall off again. The age may have been seen as golden by economists, but to investors the gold never amounted to all that much.

But things were worse in the 1970s, a period of economic disaster not experienced in the United States since the Great Depression. Inflation, now out of control, rose into double digits for the first time in anyone's memory. This kicked interest rates up to corresponding growth-killing levels and caused the Richard Nixon-led government to try totally un-Republican-like emergency solutions, such as wage and price controls, protectionism, and devaluation of the dollar, to get the economy going again. None of it worked. During the 1970s we had the worst part of the Vietnam War, the quintupling of oil prices, Watergate and the resignation of the President. Later we had Jimmy Carter and the Ayatollah Khomeini, more oil price increases, more inflation, lagging corporate productivity and competitiveness, a continuously sinking dollar, and gold climbing to over $800 an ounce when the Russians invaded Afghanistan causing America to withdraw from the Olympic Games. An investor purchasing a share of the Dow Jones index in January 1973, just before Nixon's second term, would have to wait eleven years, until December 1983, just for it to get back to where it started from. In real terms, however, after the effects of inflation averaging about 8 percent for those eleven years, the investment would have lost more than 40 percent of its value. And there was no tax deduction for wealth lost to inflation. If the U.S. economy had behaved in the 1970s according to just ordinary, even lackluster standards, in which stocks might grow at an average rate of, say, 7 percent, then the Dow would have ended the decade at about 2,100, not at something less than 900.

Ronald Reagan ran for the presidency in 1980 at a time when the country had lost confidence in the government's ability to manage the economy and to maintain its important position in the world. He was elected because of the appeal of his old-fashioned values and a well-communicated, popular platform of economic renewal, a decreased government role in the personal and corporate lives of Americans, and a tougher, more confident stance against the Soviet Union. Reagan's skillfully conducted campaign offered images of a better "morning in America," and it was successful. In 1984 he was elected again, proclaiming a dream of America as a "shining city on a hill," in which presumably all would be safe, rich, and happy. The reference was to a sermon by John Winthrop to his fellow Puritans in 1630, in which he observed that for the dream to be achieved, they all must (among other things) be bound by a common faith. Reagan's simple economic ideas appealed strongly to those faithful to the conservative school of Nobel Prize–winning economist Milton Friedman, the reigning prince of monetarism and laissez-faire. His supporters believed that governments were incapable of managing the economy to maximize growth and prosperity because the political arena required too many compromises and economically wrong-headed detours. The country should leave growth and prosperity to the private sector, a natural marketplace, they maintained, and everyone would be better off, even the poor who would benefit from more jobs and other opportunities that would "trickle" down to them. This was a very different way of thinking about the role of governments than had been conventionally accepted for nearly fifty years. During this time, Big Government was to be looked upon as all-wise and all-powerful, and relied upon to act in the best interests of the people. The government, of course, had not been up to the task, especially during the 1970s. The group of Friedmanites foresaw a profound economic revolution occurring in America, if only Reagan, "the great communicator," could persuade his countrymen to change their ways and declare the end of Big Government. He was unusually successful in doing so.

Reagan came into office with a landslide victory and a powerful mandate for economic change. Much of his work, however, had already been done for him by the Federal Reserve Board, which, under Jimmy Carter appointee Paul Volcker (a Democrat who was reappointed by Reagan), had already turned inflation around by an extraordinary, Friedman-like tightening of the money supply in 1979. Without Volcker, the Reagan economic revolution would likely have gone nowhere. But the country was still in recession in 1981, so the first action of the new Reagan economic team was to offer an economic stimulation program that included a major tax cut, not unlike the Democratic Kennedy-Johnson plan that had worked so well twenty years before.

The tax cut was a large one, and it was accompanied by an increase in defense spending, and no appreciable reduction in the rest of the budget, so a large deficit was unavoidable. (The Reaganaughts apparently never thought the deficit would get to be as large as it did, but, anyway, they blamed it on the Democratic Congress' unwillingness to cut spending.) However, the first effect of the 27 percent personal income tax cut enacted in 1982 was a sudden burst of consumption, which, combined with a steady lowering of interest rates, enabled the economy to grow at real rates above 4 percent for four years. The early Reagan years were heady ones, creating conditions that pushed the stock and other financial markets into sudden, joyful recoveries. The economic success would last for several years until the stimulus wore off and the heavy burden of the deficit started to take hold, by which time Reagan's time in office was about to end, and George Bush's was about to begin. However, professed conservatives Reagan and Bush were criticized by Ross Perot and others as being recklessly unconservative (worse than the Democrats) for having wrecked the country's financial position by over-borrowing, and putting the burden for repaying the national debt on their children and grandchildren.

The economy briefly fell back into recession as Bush was running for re-election in 1992. A lack of confidence in Bush's ability to regain control of the economy surfaced, and Bush was beaten by Bill Clinton, who, of course, promised to get the economy moving again and to undertake significant spending programs that were popular with the voters. Clinton was easily able to ride out the recession, which ended before he was inaugurated, but he had no convincing mandate and soon found his legislative ideas blocked by Congress. But he made a significant contribution to the economy by focusing on interest rates, not the budget. "You've got to worry about what the bond traders think," Wall Street veteran Robert Rubin, then chairman of the National Economic Council, is reported to have said to him early in his administration, "because they really are the people who set interest rates." He probably added, "And what they think is that if the deficit starts to go down, interest rates will too, and you can tell everyone how much he or she will have saved on mortgage payments. Everyone has a mortgage. Besides, falling rates will encourage growth and help the stock market, which folks are going to like, no matter what they think of other things going on around here."

Bill Clinton had never known a bond trader in his life, but he followed the advice anyway, and it worked. All he had to do was stay away from all the temptations that had beset Democrats from the days of Franklin Roosevelt. With reducing the deficit being seen as the necessary and patriotic thing to do (thanks to Ross Perot's convincing rhetoric in the 1992 presidential campaign), there was no room for new social programs or reforms, even if the Republican Congress would allow them, which was doubtful. Indeed, New York Democratic Senator Daniel Patrick Moynihan claimed that Reagan's real strategy in creating the larger federal deficits was to bankrupt the Democrats politically by forcing the end of their spending programs.[6] Clinton did narrowly pass a tax increase for further deficit reduction, and reappointed conservative Republican inflation-hater Alan Greenspan, Volcker's popular successor as Chairman of the Federal Reserve, on whom Clinton had relied to keep interest rates down. But mainly he just waited for the deficit to reduce itself as economic growth, responding to the check on the money supply, began to resume. Economic value popped back into the system and helped to fuel strong growth and profit results late into the 1990s. It was a brilliant strategy, and resulted in a continuous period of growth in the economy even longer than the 106 consecutive months of the golden years of the 1960s. But unlike the earlier growth period, the Reagan-Clinton expansion was not accompanied by a prolonged war or ambitious spending programs that would release the demon inflation. The Clinton stock market (1993–1999), which nearly tripled the Dow, was able to do so well because no such big spending programs loomed ahead and, in any case, Clinton's position with Congress was stymied. To many, Clinton's economic policies (not his other actions) seemed to be about what you would expect from a steady, mainstream Republican. The market felt it had nothing to fear from the Clinton administration.

Releasing Market Forces

Beyond the budget, a fundamental belief of Reaganomics was that government should get out of businesses and functions it had no reason for being in. The idea, originally called deregulation, actually began with the Carter administration, when airline rates and routes, and a number of other industrial sectors subject to government approval, were set free. Reagan's policies went further and were more vocal. America would participate in privatization efforts, just as Margaret Thatcher was beginning to do in Britain. Unlike Europe, however, the United States owned relatively few commercial businesses that could be privatized. (Conrail was one, and it was privatized in 1988.) Americans instead settled for reregulating a number of industries that had to be regulated but not quite so tightly. Such reregulatory efforts were directed at the transportation, telecommunications, and defense industries, but foremost among the industries affected was the financial services industry, which, following crises, restructuring, and changes in regulation, is now an entirely different industry from what it was in 1980. These regulatory changes released decades of pent-up market forces, which soon left their own mark.

After being prohibited for more than seventy years, interstate bank branching is now permitted; after more than sixty years, the Glass-Steagall Act has been repealed, permitting banks and securities business to be joined. Savings and loan organizations, long a favorite of states and local municipalities and their political representatives, are now run like other banks. The changes enabled healthy banks to grow into much bigger, more powerful businesses by entering new markets in different areas of the country, and permitted many of them to capture cost savings by merging with other large banks in their principal markets. Others have been permitted to enter previously prohibited businesses, as was demonstrated by the landmark merger of Citibank, Salomon Smith Barney, and Travelers Insurance into the financial conglomerate Citigroup. As a result of finally being permitted to do just about anything, and because of serious competitive threats in their industry that many felt required banks to be bigger and more streamlined, the banking sector began to consolidate in the early 1980s. Indeed, the banking industry has been the most active of all U.S. industries participating in mergers and acquisitions and general corporate restructuring since then. As a result, the banking industry was able to offer one of the highest returns to investors since the Reagan market began. Citicorp, which was trading at $8.25 per share in December 1991, was valued at $168 when its $74 billion merger with Travelers Group was announced in 1998. Chase Manhattan, a veteran of several large mergers since the 1980s, which traded at a low of $3.50 per share in 1991, reached a high of $160.75 in 1999.

Deregulation did not make these results happen by themselves. But it did remove barriers to growth that had stultified the industry for many years before the bad loans and poor management problems caught up to them in the 1980s. Altogether, $558 billion in banking industry mergers took place in the United States from 1985 through 1999. There was a further $187 billion in mergers in the insurance industry, and $57 billion in mergers in the (global) investment management industry. Altogether, the eighties and nineties saw more than $800 billion in mergers in the U.S. financial services industry. As a result the firms that survived were bigger, stronger, and are now competing with each other to offer the lowest rates and newest ideas to customers and to find ways to accommodate new customers who might have been excluded before. The massive shift of wholesale banking to the capital markets is one example of this, but another is the increase in consumer credit facilities being extended by banks and other providers. The result: access to capital has expanded enormously, and the cost of capital has declined significantly, relative to that provided by the financial services industry in 1980. Needless to say, a large, low cost, flexible capital market is indispensable to changing the performance of an entire economy and fueling future growth. As interest rates declined and stock prices rose during the 1980s and 1990s, the corporate cost of capital dropped to historically low levels.

The Reagan administration also extended its deregulatory reforms to accommodate a significant relaxation in antitrust enforcement actions by the federal government. For the previous thirty years or so, even during robust Republican years, the government's view of antitrust violations was much more broadly drawn than it has since become. Bigness was bad in itself, because it *might* restrict competition. This forced companies that wanted to grow by acquisition to become conglomerates instead, mostly inefficient ones, by buying a large variety of small companies in vastly different businesses, because these would not have any competitive effects (until the conglomerates became big companies themselves). In the early Reagan years, however, the government reset its antitrust positions, and substantially reduced its objections to business combinations on the grounds of restricting competition. And when it did intervene, it allowed companies to negotiate a solution based on selling off businesses in overlapping sectors. This policy was eroded a bit during the Bush and Clinton administrations, but not substantially. Huge transactions involving direct competitors with large market shares (Exxon and Mobil, for example) were allowed to go ahead all through the 1990s, although the government did pursue the break up of Microsoft and the Visa-Mastercard combine. Nevertheless, the lessening of antitrust policy restrictions on corporate combinations created many restructuring opportunities for larger companies in the 1980s and 1990s, undoubtedly to a far greater extent than they might have imagined at the beginning of the period.

In 1980 a great many American companies were in a sorry state and in need of serious restructuring. Yes, they had had to live through the 1970s, when it was difficult to make any money, let alone grow their businesses, and the markets were especially cruel to their shareholders. Many top managers of large companies, a conservative group adapted to the special habits of working inside large, stable, bureaucratic structures, became paralyzed by these events. Domestic economic conditions were worsening every day, and they were losing ground. They were encountering tough competition in home markets from Japanese and other foreign manufacturers. They did what they could in the context of the management model they were used to—in bad times, you reduce debt and hunker down. You don't take big risks or initiate major changes in the business unless you absolutely have to. Corporate debt as a percentage of total capitalization dropped in 1980 to its lowest level since the Eisenhower years. At many companies, executive stock options had not been worth much for years, and the guys in charge, who didn't own much stock anyway, were not thinking like aggressive institutional investors looking for high returns on investment. The managers were trying to *protect* their great, old American companies, and the environment they knew (including their own jobs and perks), from external dangers such as "unfair" foreign competitors and corporate raiders seeking to rip apart and destroy them. Many such companies were thought to be cheap in 1980—the price-earnings ratio of the S&P 500 composite of publicly traded companies then ranged between a high of 9.5 and a low of 6.6. (In 1970 the S&P 500 P/E ratio had ranged between 18.2 and 13.5. In 1990 it would return to and exceed these levels.)

But a company could be considered cheap only if the investor knew how it might be returned to fair value. Otherwise, maybe it was cheap because it was no good. A company could be undervalued only if there was a plan for changing things so significantly that it could trade at a maximum valuation—that means at a level reflecting what it would be worth if the best reorganization plan imaginable was adopted, and effectively and completely implemented. The trouble was existing management groups were not about to undertake such drastic reorganizations without being absolutely sure that the best plan had been identified and that it could be implemented without hurting the company or the managers. Such plans were the subjects of endless meetings and debates that were often left unresolved or subjected to debilitating compromises. Indeed, little might have happened to change things if the raiders hadn't appeared.

The raiders were a group of opportunistic capitalists— bright, insolent, cocksure individuals responsible only to their financial backers—who didn't care much if corporate America liked them or not. They bought stock in companies they thought could be improved, issued press releases criticizing management, made threats and trouble at annual meetings, and sometimes launched tender offers to achieve control. The idea was that the targeted companies had been badly managed in the past, and if new management was brought in, the company could be completely restructured in the interest of increasing shareholder value. By restructuring they meant selling off divisions and other assets that no longer fit into a highly focused, back-to-basics strategy. They also wanted to increase leverage, run companies for cash (not just accounting profits), milk all possible tax benefits, and provide substantial incentives to management to work their butts off to make all this happen. And they insisted on layoffs of unnecessary personnel, a process later called downsizing.

At first the business establishment reacted very negatively to these ideas, suggesting instead that stockholders accept that management knew best, and criticizing the motives, reputations, and integrity of the raiders. Then the raiders launched the first wave of greenmail in the early 1980s. This was the purchase of a minority interest, accompanied by threats of takeover or continued harassment until the targeted company gave in and bought out the greenmailer at a profit. Greenmail evolved into fully financed takeover efforts, supported by bank loans or standby credits and junk bonds. Stockholders were usually bought out for cash at a substantial premium over the market value of the company before the offer. Institutions saw the value in these deals right away, but it took longer to convince the general public. Finally people began to see the raiders as actually doing some good, even if they didn't want to bring them home to dinner. Before long, the expectation was that all companies needed to examine shareholder value issues and either initiate self-restructuring measures themselves or otherwise expect a hostile group, with shareholder support, to come after them.

The activity levels in the mergers-and-acquisitions field were extraordinary in the 1980s, and constituted a merger wave of its own, only the fourth in the twentieth century. From 1982 through 1988 more than 10,000 merger transactions, valued at over $1 trillion, took place in the United States, including in 1988 the then-largest-ever acquisition, that of RJR Nabisco by KKR for $25 billion. About one in four of the merger transactions during this period was initiated by a hostile bid, and one in six was in the form of a leveraged buyout. Obviously, the majority of transactions were neither hostile, nor leveraged, but all this combat going on around them made managers and their boards of directors nervous. This led to an increase in self-initiated actions to cure the problems that made companies attractive to others. Some close observers of the scene, such as Harvard's Michael Jensen, believe that more overdue restructuring took place during this time as a result of management's own efforts than happened as a result of takeover attempts.[7]

Another development assisted the ease with which large merger transactions could go ahead. This was in the law, as it applied to takeovers and the protection of shareholders. In the United States, takeovers are a matter of state, not federal, law (except for antitrust law, which was relaxed during the 1980s). They involve corporation law, and, as most major corporations are incorporated in Delaware, Delaware corporate (or chancery) law applies. During the decade of the 1980s, the Delaware Chancery Court adjudicated hundreds of cases involving the processes of mergers and the rights of managers and shareholders. The court issued influential opinions allowing the poison pill, an extremely effective antitakeover device introduced in 1984, deciding when it could and could not be used, and determining the general appropriateness of a variety of takeover defenses. The work of the court was often controversial, but it resulted in guidelines as to what would be permissible behavior in takeovers, and alerted the business and financial communities to the importance of shareholder rights. By the end of the 1980s, management cadres, even of large companies, knew they could not entrench themselves in office and had to be fully accountable for the company's performance. Such attention to accountability for performance (i.e., shareholder returns) had a lot to do with improving the returns. A number of market observers hold the view that the strong stock market performance during the 1990s was a direct result of the large-scale corporate restructuring (and increases in productivity) that began during the 1980s. Improved corporate profits had certainly been a major result of the struggles of the 1980s. By the 1990s, it was understood that companies were required to produce returns on investment that would be acceptable to investors or face the consequences. The stock market, in fixing new price levels, was in fact capitalizing future earnings improvements, which many companies hoped to turn into a permanent, systematic recurring event. In 1980 the return on equity of the S&P 500 index of companies was only 11 percent; by 1998 it had increased to 18 percent.

During the first few years of the 1990s, the pace of mergers-and-acquisitions activity fell off sharply. The junk bond market collapsed in 1989, financing for deals became scarce, and the financial entrepreneurs who were buying so many of the companies up for sale quit the scene. It may also be said that there were no longer low priced, easy restructuring deals to be found in the market. By 1994, however, the merger market was back in business, at an even faster pace than before. This time financial entrepreneurs played only a small role. The big deals were being done by companies seeking strategic partners, or a major repositioning of their business for the future. In the five-year period from 1994 through 1998, $2.6 trillion of U.S. domestic and cross-border M&A deals, involving more than 36,000 companies, took place, making it the most merger-intense period of all time (in terms of five-year combined merger value per unit of GDP). The activity in the 1994–1998 period eclipsed the much-acclaimed merger intensity of the 1898–1902 period, which had never (even during the heyday of the 1980s) before been even closely approached.[8] The merger boom continued to expand in 1999; $1.7 trillion of announced deals involving American companies occurred in that year alone.

Wealth from New Technologies

The bull market of the 1990s occurred during times of great change in technology, which greatly improved productivity in large sectors of the economy (finance, education, manufacturing) and also created entire new industries and applications. Three new industry groupings in particular have emerged as a result of these changes: the computer electronics and related fields (hardware, software and applications), the new telecommunications field (embracing wireless systems, cable, and the Internet), and the reconfigured health care industry (drugs, biotech, and health care delivery systems). Together, these industries comprised about a quarter of the stock market capitalization of all of American industry at the end of 1998.

The computer industry was especially expansive, particularly in terms of new companies, products, and services being introduced to the market. There are a number of separate sectors within the industry, such as hardware, software, and connectors, and they overlap considerably. A Goldman Sachs study of the industry in June of 1998 by Abraham Bleiberg demonstrated that fifty-six companies in this industry group accounted for almost $1 trillion of market capitalization.[9] Of this, less than 22 percent was provided by eight companies that had been major players in the industry in 1981 and were still independent (including IBM, Hewlett-Packard, Unisys, and Texas Instruments). The rest of the group's market capitalization was provided by new companies such as Cisco Systems, Compaq Computer (which acquired 1980s star, Digital Equipment, in 1998), Dell, Gateway, Micron Technology, Microsoft, Oracle, and Sun Microsystems. Of the thirty largest computer/communications companies by market capitalization in June 1998, only five were listed on the *Fortune* 500 list in 1981. (The smallest of these companies was Intel, ranked 363rd in 1981.) Intel in 1998 was the thirty-eighth largest company in America, with a market capitalization of $190 billion. IBM was the leading computer-technology company in 1981; its market capitalization at the end of 1998 was $170 billion. Microsoft's was $343 billion. Dell Computer's was $93 billion. Since the Bleiberg report the new technology companies have seen their market valuations soar even further (Microsoft was valued at $550 billion, Dell at $141 billion as of December 31, 1999). In 1999 the NASDAQ index (the market on which most tech companies trade) rose by more than 80 percent.

Similarly the Bleiberg study noted that in the high-tech sectors of the telecommunications industry (leaving aside the traditional telephone businesses) thirty-one companies contributed $340 billion of market capitalization. This did not include another $133 billion of market capitalization of MCI WorldCom, which came together in 1998 in an exchange of shares, and subsequently attempted a merger with Sprint in 2000. Of the market capitalization of the thirty-one companies, more than three-quarters was contributed by companies that were nonexistent or insignificant in 1981, such as America Online, Ascend Communications, Comcast, Netscape, TCI, and Yahoo!

Similar high-tech communications companies were sold (and passed their market capitalization on) to larger, long-established companies not included in the Bleiberg report. Some examples include the purchase of McCaw Cellular Communications by AT&T in 1993 for $12.6 billion, Time Warner's acquisition of Turner Broadcasting for $6.7 billion in 1995, and U.S. West's acquisition of Continental Cablevision for $5.3 billion in 1996. Lucent Technologies (the former Bell Labs part of AT&T) acquired several high-tech companies in 1997 and 1998, including Octel Communications ($1.8 billion) and Yurie Systems ($900 million).

The main point of the Bleiberg report was to call attention to the fact that the urge to merge had hit the technology sector. A great many deals occurred within the sector during 1997 (accounting for approximately $50 billion of transaction value). Later even larger mergers between both high- and less-high technology companies in the global telecommunications industry occurred as competition for market share and coverage heated up, and the trend continued over the next two years. In 1999 Bell Atlantic merged with GTE in an $89 billion transaction, and AirTouch Communications, the West Coast wireless company, was merged into the British communications company Vodaphone in an exchange of shares valued at $58 billion. Olivetti, an Italian manufacturer that had converted into a telecommunications company, acquired control (for $60 billion) of the much larger Telecom Italia.

Later in the year, Vodaphone AirTouch made a surprise hostile takeover attempt to acquire Mannesmann, a German wireless company, which finally agreed to a friendly merger for a price of $180 billion, the world's largest deal to date. In January 2000, America Online organized a friendly merger with Time Warner in a transaction valued at $165 billion. America Online, one of the country's first Internet portal companies, had already acquired Netscape and Compuserve, two star performers of the Internet era. All of these mergers, of course, were effected at high valuations, reflecting very high price-earnings ratios by ordinary standards. Accordingly they created and released a great deal of personal wealth to founders, key employees, and initial investors of the companies involved. They also provoked a substantial amount of post-merger restructuring, management changes, and asset sales. The merger wave of technology deals continued unabated into 2000, with dozens of deals completed in the first quarter alone.

The health care industry was another to grow enormously in the 1990s. At the end of 1997, this industry, which was loosely defined as comprising pharmaceutical companies and health care service providers, aggregated more than $900 billion of market value. The eleven pharmaceutical companies among the *Fortune* 500 contributed most of this value, but in 1997 there were also 13 health care service companies, such as hospital management companies and HMOs, among the *Fortune* 500 worth more than $60 billion in market capitalization. None of these companies were among the 500 largest American companies in 1981. In 1999 and 2000 there were massive mergers between the leading pharmaceutical companies, such as the $93 billion combination of Pfizer and Warner-Lambert, and the $75 billion merger of Smith Kline-Beecham and Glaxo-Welcome, along with rumors of several other large pharmaceutical company deals. This industry, like the other technology-based industries reported on by Bleiberg, and like the financial services industry and many others in the United States, had shown few signs of slowing down by the end of the twentieth century.

The potent mixture of policy shifts, released market forces, and technological change has made an enormous difference to our economy and society. Without their potent effects, the environment in which we all work and invest would have most likely remained much more normal; that is, ordinary and unexceptional. Because of them, however, we have enjoyed a special time, one that has permitted many things to happen that might not otherwise have done so. One obvious consequence is in the wealth building that has occurred. Part of our understanding of this has to do with the large environmental changes. But the major contributors to the wealth-creation were the human beings on the scene who took advantage of the opportunities presented. Without these men and women, who responded to what was available to them, not much would have happened.

The rest of this book focuses on a number of these special individuals who were among the most successful during the past twenty years in creating wealth for themselves and their families. What did they do to create so much of it? And how did they, and others like them, do what they did? Some—our entrepreneurs—did it from nothing; they created, or are still creating, businesses that they hope will become large, permanently established businesses of the sort that are today's household names. Many made their money as financial entrepreneurs, or deal makers, locating and pursuing a succession of different business opportunities over a considerable time. Others were professional investors, who succeeded beyond almost all others in turning opportunity to profit. A few were managers of big businesses who took advantage of rising markets and generous stock ownership plans provided by their companies to get rich. Finally there were those who mastered the arts of the entertainment business to make themselves into financial stars. These individuals are not normal at all, at least in terms of their individual achievements or their dreams. But individuals like them, and the types of business activities they pursued, were plentiful and generally typical of their time, the great wealth-creating period at the end of the twentieth century. Their stories are presented to comprise a portrait of one of the most economically significant periods of our history.

During these twenty years I was a partner of Goldman Sachs & Co., investment bankers in New York. Toward the end of the 1980s, I resigned my position as a general partner of the firm and became a limited partner (a retired partner who's money is still in the firm), to accept an offer to join the faculty of the Stern School of Business at New York University. There I became a professor of Finance and International Business. After years of deal-doing and traveling about the world, I was delighted to be asked to explain what had been going on to my students, even while whatever it was, was changing still. Later I began to study smaller, riskier businesses and ventures, and in time I became a professor of Entrepreneurship also. In that capacity I ventured myself, as an investor and an observer, to learn more exactly what entrepreneurs were and did. Out of all this came an understanding that the world was going through something very different from what I had become used to since going to work on Wall Street in the mid-1960s.

These times were different, and extraordinary things were happening. Market values of American assets had shot through the roof, enriching more of us than ever before. At first, neither the extent of the wealth-creation, nor its sources, were clear. Much of what developed appeared to be the result of one-time improvements in policies and technology that would run off over time. Other things appeared to be more lasting, reflecting basic changes in attitudes and benchmarks of how private-sector economic performance was to be measured and judged. Many of these latter characteristics are now being inculcated into our long-term business and financial practices (and those too of companies in Europe and Asia), suggesting that in the future the world of business will become even more competitive. For someone with my background, these were interesting fields to study. This books attempts to capture what I learned from the effort.

CHAPTER I

The Entrepreneurs

The 1999 *Forbes* 400 list includes 251 individuals whose source of wealth is described as "self-made." These include founders of businesses and others who have not relied upon a salary or inheritance to make their fortunes. Among them are the greatest creators of new wealth in the country, the most successful of our living businessmen. But most of the individuals on this most exclusive list of self-made entrepreneurs are not well known and their business activities are varied beyond belief. They include billionaires whose money comes from medical devices, computer software, railroads, testing laboratories, real estate, home building, stock market investments, trading stamps, oil and gas, computer assembly, direct sales organizations, retailing, health care, mobile phones, music and records, newspapers and media, insurance, cable TV, public storage, plastics, garbage recycling, video tape rent-

35

als, sunglasses, sports shoes, credit cards, movie special effects, car dealerships, entertainment, potatoes, and auto rentals. If you add those on the *Forbes* list worth less than a billion, the number and spread of businesses is much larger and more diverse. The self-made are inventors, manufacturers, financial investors, real estate guys, hole diggers, entertainers, and hundreds of other things.

They are what we think of today as entrepreneurs, though the word itself means little more than businessman or investor. In the parlance of the late 1990s, however, entrepreneurs are not just ordinary businessmen—hired hands and administrators—they are something more, something much more. They are, first of all, owners, who work for no one but themselves. They can be extreme risk-takers and colorful, self-confident persons of strong character and personality. Some get a lot of attention, and many have become celebrities and heroes in our complicated society, in which traditional hero types are in extremely short supply. Some are nerdish, some dull, some mischievous, and some roguish. Think of Bill Gates, Steve Jobs, Michael Dell, Richard Branson, Ted Turner, and Donald Trump. There are also many you never heard of. But stripped of all the hype, entrepreneurs are simply people who, as individuals or in small groups, have started or acquired businesses and attempted to grow and/or alter them to a point where they could cash in on the rewards. (Not all of them are successful, of course, but the image is projected by those who are.) They are founders of enterprises that have made it through the difficult years and been able to profit handsomely. Some are more akin to the dealmakers described in the next chapter. We have always had entrepreneurs, though the times have not always been good to them. Today, after two decades of good times, rising markets, and thousands of entrepreneurial success stories, everybody wants to be an entrepreneur.

Academics have been studying self-made businessmen for a few decades, looking for the keys to success and a methodology to teach to young, would-be entrepreneurs. The literature is rather thin, however, as there really are not a lot of data to study about privately held companies, and the field is endlessly diverse. Most of what we know is anecdotal, and serious scholars are unwilling to conclude much based on anecdotes. We have not yet found, of course, a simple, repeatable formula for turning small or substantially restructured businesses into gold mines. Indeed, many academics believe that great entrepreneurial success is usually a random event, influenced as much by luck as by skill, or by fortuitous (if unwise) risk-taking as by any other quality, in which case there is not much to write about. Accordingly, most of the academic and professional literature about entrepreneurship involves macroeconomic analyses of the role and importance of small businesses in the economy as a whole, or emphasizes the practical how-tos of small business: such things as how to develop a good business plan, how to prepare financial forecasts, how to attract venture capital, or how to go about an initial public offering of stock. These are useful, no doubt, to people who want to carry out these exercises but don't know how to, but for those seeking gold mines, well, they won't learn much.

But we haven't given up entirely. There is something to be learned from studying what the successful entrepreneurs actually did to become successful. As a result there is a steady supply of increasingly high-quality case studies and biographies of such individuals. There are some patterns that can be recognized when we study their careers, and by analyzing the patterns we can learn something about what seems to work or would seem to increase the probabilities of success. Or, to put it another way, we can look for the sine qua non of success—those things without which great success probably cannot happen.

The Bloomberg

The two best things that ever happened to him, Michael Bloomberg believes, were "getting hired by Salomon Brothers and getting fired by Salomon Brothers." Bloomberg, now in his late fifties and chairman of the Bloomberg Group, which he founded in 1981 after being fired, is one of the many self-made entrepreneurs among the *Forbes* 400 who, in 1999, made up more than half the list.

Bloomberg graduated from Harvard Business School in 1966 and joined Salomon Brothers as a trader. He became an equity block trader, and a partner of the firm in nearly record time. His boss was a colorful but highly controversial character named Jay Perry, who was removed from his position in 1973 following a fistfight with one of his partners.[1] Bloomberg then became the head of all of the firm's equity businesses. But he, too, was (in his words) "pushed aside" six years later in another of Salomon's periodic palace coups. It was all very Wall Street, and Bloomberg was not especially upset by it. He found himself, however, pushed pretty far away from the trading desks he loved and which were the source of all power and fortune at Salomon. He was put in charge of the firm's backoffice computers, something he knew next to nothing about. It

38

was clearly an undisputed transfer to oblivion. The computers were mainly used for operational purposes, to keep track of settlements of traded securities and of the firm's books. All the Wall Street firms used computers to speed up their backoffice activities, but nobody who was anybody at Salomon even knew where they were.

Bloomberg wondered why the computers couldn't be used to assist traders more than they were, to gather up and provide the information they really needed to do their jobs, particularly information about how one security with particular characteristics compared to another. If two essentially similar securities were trading at different prices, a clever trader could buy the cheap one and sell the expensive one and have a position free of market risk that would be profitable when the market recognized that the two securities were slightly mispriced.

About this time, however, he was fired. Salomon had agreed to be acquired by Phibro Corporation, a large commodities trading house. Salomon's partners would get cash for their capital in the firm and a new convertible debenture for an equal additional amount to reflect the intangible values of the firm's franchise. Seven partners, however, would not be asked to join the new company. Mike tells of how he was ushered into the office of Salomon's chairman, John Gutfreund, and bluntly told he was to be one of those not continuing on. Mike was surprised and hurt, but also he knew he was rich. His capital and premium were to be paid out to him in cash—$10 million—more money than he had ever imagined having. At Salomon all partners were required to retain their share of all earnings in the firm as a part of its ongoing capital. They were paid 5 percent interest on their money, and could make withdrawals for taxes and charitable contributions. But otherwise the only way a partner could actually get his hands on his own capital was to die, resign (and then be paid out over ten years), or to be fired. If what you wanted was to take your capital out of the firm, of the three options being fired was the best.

Mike immediately knew that he didn't want to recycle himself through another Wall Street firm and maybe get fired again. Besides, he now had too much money to go work for somebody else. He wanted to be on his own, and he had his own capital to back a business venture. So he set up a new firm in a small office on Madison Avenue and went to work trying to think through a business plan. He had been a trader and knew what traders needed. He had been a computer executive and knew what computers could do. Why not put together the ultimate desktop black box for traders, he figured, one that could provide live market data and could call up from a database all frequently traded public securities, letting the traders compare the various characteristics and prices. The only problem was, such a machine did not exist.

So he set out to design, manufacture, and sell one, and to do so in competition with all the major computer makers and software suppliers that serviced Wall Street plus the now burgeoning technology departments of the firms themselves. And, as he was convinced that the traders on the Street were warming up to what they needed quickly, it would only be a matter of time before someone came up with the black box that everyone would want. This window of opportunity, Bloomberg figured, would only be open to him for a couple of years.

Mike hired some former Salomon colleagues and got to

work. Before long he had a pretty good idea of what could be done and what couldn't. Then he went out to make some sales calls to Wall Street firms that he thought would be interested. The critical moment came when he went to pitch his yet-unbuilt machine to Merrill Lynch. He had done some consulting work for Merrill and was easily able to set up a meeting with the head of capital markets, who brought his information technology man with him. Mike delivered an impressive performance, solidly making a case for his machine (and inventing it as he went along). "We can give you a yield curve analysis updated throughout the day as markets change," he said, among other things. He pointed out that no one else had these capabilities on their desks, and it would be a big advantage for a leading trading house like Merrill to have it. The Merrill capital markets head then turned to the technology associate and asked what he thought. "I think we should build it for ourselves," said the technology man. "Well, when could it be ready?" asked the capital markets head. The computer guy, confronted as all Wall Street technologists were by a huge backlog of uncompleted work orders submitted by desperate operating departments, grimaced and said, "We could probably start working on it in about six months." Mike immediately saw his opportunity and went for it.

"Your traders will want this capability long before you can build the machine yourselves. If others have it and you don't, your guys will be at an expensive disadvantage in the market. And, if your technology people are at all like the ones at Salomon, you shouldn't take their promised get-started date at face value. They mean well, but they don't know what other demands, some legitimately urgent, will be put upon them over the next year. Every department of every firm on Wall Street wants to be upgraded to state-of-the-art computer capability as soon possible. The demands on your guys will be incredible and deadlines are going to get missed."

So, he said, he would make Merrill Lynch an offer it couldn't refuse. "I'll get it done in six months and if you don't like it, you don't have to pay for it." The capital markets man accepted on the spot.

The team at Bloomberg now had a problem—they had to meet their commitment or eat their costs and perhaps all their plans for the future too. But they also had an advantage. They could focus all their efforts on one thing without being distracted by other requests. They could also work around the clock if they had to—they had nothing more important to do—to accomplish their goal. But still they had to pull it off, and right up until the last minute it was not clear that they would be able to deliver a model that would work well enough. But they did, and "the rest," says Mike, "is history."

Merrill not only ordered a lot of machines, it offered to buy 30 percent of the company. Mike was ecstatic. In only three years he had invested over $4 million of his own money in this venture, and now he had gotten it back and more. Plus he had had the world's biggest securities firm as a confirmed customer. This relationship would help just about everyone else sitting on the fence decide to buy a machine as soon as they could.

Mike named the machine *The Bloomberg*, and soon traders everywhere had to have one. Just as he had predicted, the traders could not bear to be unequipped with something their rivals were using successfully. They didn't want a similar machine, they wanted the real thing—*The Bloomberg*. So orders poured in.

His next breakthrough was to realize that he was not just supplying a trading machine with historical data on it to the securities market, but indeed providing all the real time information needed by traders and other businessmen operating in an environment that could not wait for tomorrow's newspaper. So he redirected his focus toward becoming the equivalent of CNN for all fast-moving business and financial news. He would supply the information—the blades, not just the razors. Thus the Bloomberg Group became a media business unconstrained by its history or vested interests. Bloomberg TV runs twenty-four hours a day and includes interviews with newsworthy company officers, ratings agencies, and Wall Street analysts to present investment information continuously. Bloomberg Radio is a twenty-four-hour news-only radio station. Bloomberg.com gives you all this information in extremely user-friendly form on the Internet. There are also the Bloomberg Forum, the Bloomberg News Magazine, and other forms of multimedia information delivery, all of which are available throughout the world. The business, though still heavily dependent on the cash flow from *The Bloomberg*, is self-financing. Mike has since bought back a third of the stock he originally sold to Merrill Lynch, leaving Merrill with 20 percent, and he still owns virtually all of the rest of the company himself. He has no desire to go public, he says, reflecting his continuing disinterest in working for other people (i.e., independent shareholders). In 1999, seventeen years after forming the company (and two years longer than he spent at Salomon Brothers), *Forbes* estimated his net worth at $2.5 billion.

SELF-MADE MONEY

For those who, against long odds, succeed as entrepreneurs in building a business that becomes highly valuable, there are special rewards: wealth, power, and (if you want it) fame and the right to be a bit eccentric.

To do this, though, first requires that you quit your day job, the one that has been providing you with a paycheck. When you do this, you start to appreciate the risks that entrepreneurs take from the first day, including the risk of not having any money to support yourself with. You may also have ruined an otherwise promising career by quitting it abruptly without any assurances of being able to return. And for years into the future, you must live with the knowledge that all that you have gained, or hope to gain, could amount to a lot less than what you walked away from, or could be lost tomorrow on a misstep or a sudden change in the market. No matter how else you measure entrepreneurial characteristics, this first, primordial requirement must be present—the willingness to step off into the void, risking most of what other people think of as security and well-being.

Entrepreneurs usually must beg, borrow, and scrape every barrel to collect enough money to get started, and then to meet payrolls and to continue to invest in expanding the enterprise. Years may have to go by before you can take anything out for yourself. The Business becomes an obsession; disproportionately important in your life—your main reason for being—and it extracts a heavy price from other, more normal relationships. Entrepreneurs worry a lot and maybe become a bit paranoid, but underneath there is a feeling that it's all worth it; a passion is being satisfied—the satisfaction of having done things your way, for having succeeded in the real world largely as a result of your own vision, follow-through, and leadership and organizational skills. Achieving entrepreneurial success may be the greatest challenge available to anyone in business. And being a founder of a successful business is certainly the best way to make the greatest amount of money, if all goes well, which, of course, often it does not. Indeed only a very small percentage of entrepreneurs are able to see their efforts culminate in big money.

Today's business entrepreneurs may have become the cultural replacement for the famous American rugged individualists of the last century, the ones who tamed the West and built great industries from nothing. Most of these entrepreneurs own and operate small businesses. According to the Small Business Administration, there were about 6.6 million corporations in the United States in 1996, the vast majority of which were small businesses. This total swells to about 23 million when sole-proprietorships and partnerships are included, 57 percent more than in 1982, the first year of the Reagan bull market. These small businesses are engaged in the most humdrum and mundane of all human commercial activities as well as the most exciting, such as the latest biomedical and computer software enterprises. Small businesses collectively accounted for 64 percent of all job growth in the country in the period 1990–1996. Because of this, and the large number of them, small businesses are popular with politicians and attract support from federal and state governments for financing and start-up assistance. In 1996 842,000 new small businesses were formed, but there were also 72,000 that failed.[2] Most survive the many hazards of the first few years of existence but do not reach the point of becoming a publicly owned company, when significant wealth may first appear to be within reach.

Only the most promising of small businesses are able to effect initial public stock offerings, but in good stock markets there is a great deal of demand for them. In 1999, for example, the most recent record year for IPOs, there were 571 offerings, valued at $71.4 billion. In December 1999 there were approximately 9,000 publicly traded companies in the United States (5,100 on the NASDAQ, 3,100 on the NYSE, and 770 on the AMEX). Twenty years ago there were 4,900 publicly owned companies in the United States. Most of the new companies now traded in the market arrived there through an IPO (there have been about 9,500 IPOs valued at more than $500 billion since 1978). Of course the total number of companies has also been reduced by several thousand mergers and acquisitions and many bankruptcies during the twenty-year period.

In the last several years, since the development of the Internet and the vast interconnected world of electronics, telecommunications, entertainment, and other things, the cycle time of companies from birth to IPO has been shortened considerably. This has been partly due to a market eager to buy stock in small, promising companies in new industry areas, and partly because the companies have grown so quickly that many of them have reached the IPO stage sooner.

After an IPO, founders can sell some of their stock or borrow against it to create cash for other diversifying investments or money for some long deferred extravagance. Alternatively they can cash out entirely by selling the business to another company when they are ready to give up control of it. In 1999 alone there were about 4,000 sales of domestic companies that did not involve the reporting of a transaction price, usually meaning that the seller was not a publicly owned company.

Most small businesses do not go public. They lack either the profitability or the growth to do so, but nevertheless they can provide a generous cash flow to their owners. When the owner decides to retire, the business is either liquidated or sold (often through small business brokers). The new owner may run the business just as before or try to change it into something that could go public. Meanwhile other entrepreneurs are setting up new businesses. The organism regenerates itself, and, at least for the past twenty years, has been expanding, much to the benefit of the American economy as a whole and to the millions of individuals associated with the small business sector as owners, investors, or employees. Indeed the small business and entrepreneurial sector is responsible for most of the personal wealth in the country. This is the area of the American economy where most of the five million millionaires reside, where most of America's wealth is concentrated and has been growing most rapidly.

HOW DO THEY DO IT?

In this chapter, however, we are mainly interested in remarkably successful entrepreneurs; those who, like Bloomberg, have created something fantastic from nothing, making themselves and others quite rich in the process. Can we look at such a level of entrepreneurship as a profession, something that by training and application we can expect to duplicate? That is a question to which serious students of the subject do not feel quite ready to answer but are certainly inclined to study. What is it that sets the most successful apart from the rest?

The Vision Thing

When an entrepreneur decides to enter a business, an equilibrium already exists between those products and services that are in circulation and those that could be but aren't. Unless a new product or service can overcome the existing barriers to entry into the market, it has no chance. This is normal market economics at work—unless existing products and services can be priced and marketed in such a way as to create some level of competitive barrier to entry, too many new products will get in and destroy the profit opportunities.

The entrepreneur is looking for a way around this equilibrium by finding something new or different that will reset the equilibrium more advantageously. What is sought does not have to be an entirely new product or idea (like Edison's electric light, which took a long time to introduce and required expensive power plants and transmissions lines), but it has to be new enough to change the current configurations of the market. This is the central idea, or vision, of the business. Once it is identified and fixed in the entrepreneur's mind, the rest of the process is just making it happen by whatever means that seem to work.

Rockefeller did not invent the oil lamp, but after the Titusville discovery in 1859, he saw the opportunity of producing large quantities of kerosene from petroleum to be sold as a cheap, efficient fuel for illumination. Prior to kerosene, whale oil was the principal source of lamp illumination, but it was expensive and not available in the large quantities that surely were to be needed as the American economy expanded.[3] He was not in the illuminants business before Titusville, but he saw an enormous potential for kerosene and decided to focus on refining and distributing it. The market was totally new at the time, and there were no barriers to entry, so a large number of small refiners and oil producers entered the business. They cut prices and conspired with or against each other to try to make progress, so business conditions in the industry became chaotic. As a result Rockefeller changed his central idea—instead of just refining crude oil, something for which he had no particular comparative advantage, he would focus on consolidating the refining, transportation, and marketing components into a new industry. This decision, a vision of opportunity and a wholly different way to develop it, played to all of Rockfeller's organizational and administrative strengths—his comparative advantages—that enabled him to become the success he was.

Sam Walton once worked for J. C. Penney. Walton didn't conceive the low-price, general merchandise chain store, or the more recent discount department store, but he did see the value in bringing these retailing ideas to places where they had never been introduced, the rural South. The population in this area was scattered and low-income, and the retail stores available to them were limited to relatively high-priced local shops and the occasional small variety store, or five-and-dime. In 1962 Walton opened his first store—Wal-Mart Discount City—in Rogers, Arkansas. His idea was that the bigger retailers avoided the rural areas because it was too expensive to ship goods to them, and the goods would take too long to sell. Walton designed a system of large central warehouses that could service daily a group of high-visibility stores circled around them. He purchased in bulk and passed on some of the savings to his customers, but what he really offered them was a much larger assortment of good-quality, low-priced goods for everyday use. In 1970 the company went public, and only ten years later, as a result of Wal-Mart's continuing success from its hub-and-spoke system of rural retailing, Sam Walton headed the *Forbes* 400 list as America's richest man. He died in 1992, leaving a fortune estimated at more than $22 billion.[4]

Steve Jobs didn't invent the microprocessor, but he saw the potential for an easy to use desktop personal computer and made the Apple. It was an instant success and Steve Jobs became very rich. Bill Gates was not the first computer programmer, but he, too, saw the market for personal computers, so he dropped out of Harvard in 1980 to join his friend Paul Allen in developing software for them. Soon afterwards IBM called to ask for help in developing an operating system for its new personal computers, which were designed to compete with Apple's. Their operating system, called MS-DOS, rode the rising popularity of the IBM personal computers to become the dominant operating system for all PCs, which had to be IBM compatible to attract serious business buyers.[5] The Apple computer, however, was not IBM compatible, and despite substantial consumer loyalty to the product, it fell behind the others that were and lost its way.

Ted Waitt (Gateway) and Michael Dell (Dell Computers) had the same big idea—to manufacture customized, fully assembled and operational personal computers that could be ordered by customers directly on the phone or the Internet. They could do this by establishing a central assembly location and shipping all orders from it. Their competition was established brand-name manufacturers who sold through independent retail stores and discount houses with negligible customer service or assistance. Before long they were assembling computers for customers all over the world.

Ralph Lauren captured a new (old money) look in men's fashion; he called it *Polo*, and it caught on. Philip Knight conceived of a new kind of sports-shoe company, and Nike was off and running. Backed by prodigious advertising campaigns, both companies quickly gained market share at the expense of their long-established competitors. And so on. There are lots of distinctive ideas among our entrepreneurial companies, and every successful entrepreneurial business is inspired by one, however simple the idea may seem in retrospect.

Starting a business with an idea that is *not new* at all, something that just presents another choice for the consumer, can be a very tough grind for the entrepreneur. Another bank branch on the corner, a new videotape recorder, or even another version of an IBM compatible personal computer may take forever to gain any kind of market share and could divide the total profits available in the market into increasingly smaller pieces. Something *somewhat new*, however, can capture the market's attention without having to completely reeducate it. It can quickly change market dynamics, increasing total demand for, say, tennis shoes because they are not tennis shoes any longer but performance enhancing footwear favored by professional athletes with a different shoe for every sport. In changing the dynamics of market demand, the relative market shares of the different competitors go up for grabs, giving you a shot at establishing a solid place for yourself relatively quickly. Of course your idea has to be strong enough to alter the dynamics, but it is clear that many of the most powerful *new* business ideas have not been all that new. Not *that* new, perhaps, but different enough.

In March 1998 Walt Minnick, then fifty-six years old, became a plant man. That is, he and some partners bought seven stores selling nursery products in Silicon Valley, California, from Woolworth, which was getting rid of them, and a larger store in Phoenix. Altogether the group of stores had sales in 1997 of about $20 million but barely broke even. Walt and his partners would have to raise $25 million to acquire the properties and make some necessary improvements in them. About half of this money would be in the form of equity, the rest in debt from a high–interest rate finance company lender. His plan was to put together a group of profitable, full-service, up-market re-tail home-and-garden centers into a large, category domi-nant company, and then take it public. He would do this by an aggressive acquisition strategy called a roll up.

Walt hardly knew a tulip from a twig. Before becoming a plant man, equipped with business and law degrees from Harvard, he had been chairman and CEO of TJ In-ternational Corp., a NASDAQ traded specialty building products company with $700 million in sales. The com-pany was based in Boise, Idaho, where he lived for about twenty years. The company was subsequently sold, and Walt, a longtime moderate Republican, accepted an invi-tation to run as a conservative Democrat against Larry Craig, the incumbent U.S. Senator from Idaho, who was up for reelection in 1996. Walt had very little chance to defeat the popular, deeply conservative Idaho politician, but still he ran a race that was called a "toss up" by *The New York Times* on election eve. But he lost, and when it was over, Walt had to decide what to do with himself.

He could have retired or taken an appointment in the Clinton Administration. But he decided he wanted to go back into business and make some money. (He hadn't been paid in two years and his campaign was costly.) He was bored with big business, he said, and wanted to have the sort of fun you can have only when you are deeply immersed in something that is very much your own doing. He started to look around for a business to buy and decided it had to be something simple enough for him to be able to learn quickly, a business that would need the basic, general management skills he had accumulated over a lifetime. Something he could get hold of, and organize and drive along at a steady pace to create long-term value for himself and his investors. He also wanted to stay in the northern Rocky Mountain region that he loved, with its outdoor lifestyle and friendly small town people.

His research acquainted him with roll ups. These involved acquisitions of numerous small businesses in fragmented, low-tech industries that had little history of regional or national consolidation. Businesses that would benefit from some sort of centralized organizational structure, economies, and cost-discipline. Real estate and insurance brokerages, funeral homes, auto repair shops, even car washes had attracted attention from venture capital investors as roll up possibilities. They were not franchises (like McDonald's) that were all stamped out of the same cookie cutter, but pre-existing independent businesses often operating under local brand names. The roll up strategy depended on being able to buy the businesses cheaply (which meant they were often in need of fixing up), then apply practical, hands-on management improvements, centralized control of purchasing, good financial management, and focused marketing and advertising expenses. It meant finding good people to fill the operational jobs, and it also meant using leverage to increase stockholder returns. After a few years of wrestling with all sorts of little details, the businesses could grow and, before long, blend into a sizeable company that could be offered to the public through an IPO or put up for sale to one of the big national chains.

After his Senate race, Walt and his wife went on vacation in the South Pacific. The idea of buying up family-owned nurseries came to him, and by the time he returned to Boise he had a draft of a business plan. He began calling around to his friends for information and began a fact-finding tour of Western cities with populations of more than 100,000, camping out in cheap motel rooms. In Phoenix he met Mike Bergland, who had owned the Desert Winds Nursery for fifteen years. Mike, a chemical engineer who managed chip factories before becoming burned out with Silicon Valley, was enthusiastic about the idea of a roll up. Together they learned about the sale of the Woolworth stores in California. Minnick negotiated a ninety-day option to buy the property for $22 million. Immediately he began to call on fifty or so of his old school friends, former business associates, and anyone else he could think of for the seed capital. He got his new company, SummerWinds Garden Centers, going in 1998. Before he had been able to do much of anything with the stores he had bought, he encountered an opportunity to acquire from a bankruptcy auction an eight-store company in Phoenix that was losing major amounts of money. He snatched them up, for less than the cost of their inventory, and later added another profitable store in Vancouver. Then he started to get everything organized. By the end of 1998, he estimated that on a full-year basis the stores he owned produced sales of $33 million, and, despite a loss of $700,000, was running a positive cash flow (earnings before interest, taxes, depreciation and amortization, or EBITDA) of over $1 million. Positive cash flows are very important to leveraged business investments. It was a good start. The next year sales rose to $40 million. He raised some new capital, created an e-commerce venture, and watched the company come around into the black. His target, Walt said, was $100 million in sales and cash flow of at least $10 million by 2002. At $10 million of EBITDA the company could be worth $60 or $70 million, which would represent a six- or seven-fold return for his investors in four years. And this return, of course, had almost none of the risk of a new business start-up, especially a business with a new product or technology to build a market for from scratch. Everybody likes plants, and lots of people want to buy them. Why do it the hard way?

Making It Big

The new thing, though, to be a big success, ought to lead to a business with a large potential market. The national market for kerosene must have seemed enormous to the young Mr. Rockefeller, who became a billionaire long before the automobile assured the future of the oil business.

Ray Kroc, a traveling milkshake-machine salesman, became a billionaire because he realized that a small hamburger stand could be cloned into thousands of McDonald's stores nationwide through a franchising process. To become big, there has to be a national, or, even better, a global market for the idea.

Ted Turner, the founder of CNN, saw that the value of cable television ultimately depended on what went through the cables. He knew there would be many new channels made available through the cable hookups, and these channels would be offered to subscribers who would pay to get certain kinds of programming. Turner was interested in what the subscribers wanted to watch. Turner already owned some sports teams and WTBS, an Atlanta-based UHF broadcasting station. (UHF was tuned to a different set of frequencies than the traditional VHF channels used by all the networks.) In 1976 he pioneered the superstation concept by arranging to transmit his UHF signal by satellite to content-starved cable system operators all over the country. The idea worked. In 1980 Turner introduced the all-news channel for his system. This was thought of as a bit crazy, because most people could not imagine tuning in to just news all day long. That would be true for the networks, each of which was but a single channel trying to capture as much of the viewer's time as possible. The cable operator, however, was selling a package of several channels for a fixed cost. You could watch what you wanted, when you wanted to watch it. You paid for it to be there, and many people wanted to be able to check on the news periodically during the day without having to wait for CBS or NBC to put it on. By 1985 the Turner Broadcasting System cable packages reached 80 percent of American homes equipped with cable, and one item in the package that was almost always in demand by subscribers was Turner's cable news network, CNN. Before long Turner had tens of millions of subscribers paying to have a few minutes each day of CNN in their house (especially after the Gulf War, which demonstrated the effectiveness of the CNN coverage). Later he proved he could do it also with old movies and cartoons.

Making It Happen

Marc Josephson is an engineer, a specialist in making data communications work. He worked in the computer field for ten years, helping to design and build data communications networks. In 1985 he formed a small consulting firm serving both the telecom industry and its clients. In 1995 he formed a new company to connect New York City's new Information Technology Center at 55 Broad Street in the Wall Street area to the Internet backbone network, which operates at unprecedented speed. This building was to become the focal point of New York's effort to create a new information technology industry that would, of course, be dependent on efficient utilization of the Internet. Marc's role was to connect the building to the Internet so that tenants of the building would have all the access they needed to conduct their high-tech, multi-media publishing, and other businesses. These businesses were already flocking to New York's Silicon Alley, and they didn't want to be just connected like everybody else using the Internet, through a modem and a dedicated phone line. They needed to be connected to big-time bandwidth (a measure of Internet flow-through capacity) to accommodate their products and services and to have the fastest possible connection speeds. They also wanted it to be cheaper than other services, more reliable and quicker to install. After all, this was New York, so they weren't shy about asking for what they wanted, even though no one offered all of this in a single package.

Marc thought he could do it, however. Years before, New York City had been encircled in fiber-optic cable in anticipation of the day when everyone would want it. Several of these cable circuits (backbones) were essentially idle inventory, and they contained bandwidth ample for any known purpose. Marc figured out how to connect the building at 55 Broad Street to the cable circuit directly and was able to pass on the bandwidth advantages—virtually instant connection speed and low costs to the building's occupants. To capitalize on his discoveries, he set up a small company to make the investment in the connection and to lease the Internet access to the tenants directly, which he could do at much less cost than the regular access providers.

It all worked like an Intel chip, so Marc offered to wire up the Jacob Javits Convention Center, the next big building to go on line. Then he persuaded Rockefeller Center to let him wire up the whole complex, which he then had to lease to the tenants, one office at a time. Marc was ecstatic. All his engineering know-how was coming together. His idea worked and people liked it. But he had to think about how to make the most of his success.

Marc had to build out his business as quickly as possible so some other Internet access provider didn't figure out what he had done and offer the same service. Once a competitive service was installed in a building, it would be very difficult to get tenants to change. He wanted to exploit this advantage, rather than be exploited by it. To do so he had to expand rapidly. The problem was doing it right while still doing it fast and doing it all over the country. Marc's high-value service was only as good as his ability to execute the buildout.

For this he needed a team of competent engineers, and he needed capital. Through a lawyer friend he met some small-scale venture capitalists who invested a few million dollars of seed capital. By the end of 1998, two years after finishing 55 Broad, Marc's company, now called Intelli-Space, had wired fifty customers for its on-line services in New York City; there would be 140 a year later. The building space wired by the company was growing at 400 percent per year, and Marc was shaping up plans to replicate his business in Philadelphia, Boston, and Washington D.C. For this he needed more capital, which proved surprisingly easy to attract. In 1999 IntelliSpace completed a $35 million second round of financing, all of which was to be used to accelerate the expansion of the business. Marc was able to attract the investment largely because his investors had confidence in his engineering skills and executive ability to carefully plan out a step-by-step program for building out the business. Marc's ability to do this may, in the end, prove to be his real comparative advantage.

To act on a big idea means having the ability to execute it effectively. To distribute product to the national or global market quickly, and in such a way as to gain a strong share of the new or different market that has been established, is a very complex and difficult undertaking.

Think of Gordon Moore and his cofounders at Intel. Their idea was that the expanding world of computer technology would require a continuous stream of ever more powerful internal circuits, printed on silicon chips. They recruited top engineers to design these state-of-the-art circuits and sold them readily to all the main manufacturers. But they had to make them in huge quantities. Intel was just a little company then, but it had bet its entire future on being able to deliver the chips they sold on time and without defects. They had to set up assembly lines to do this, raise the money for them and insure that the reject rate didn't put them out of business. And they had to do this year after year. Making semi-conductor chips is a crazy business that was in a constant state of high-level innovation ("throw out batch six over there, it's obsolete now") as well as being in a viciously cyclical business in which customers suddenly changed from wanting millions of chips to wanting none. Without the ability to deliver the chips on schedule, and to stay ahead of dozens of powerful competitors, Intel would never have been heard of.

Bernard Marcus, Arthur Blank, and Ronald Brill founded Home Depot. They had worked for years at Handy Dan's, a hardware chain that was sold to Daylin Inc. The parent company faltered and brought in a turnaround specialist to straighten things out. The men clashed with their new boss and soon left to start their own business. They knew the hardware business and had observed the successes of Sam Walton and some of the specialized large retailers, such as Toys 'R Us and Circuit City, and decided to apply them to the do-it-yourself home improvement market. They, too, organized huge retail stores that could sell thousands of items cheaply, but unlike the others, they had a different idea. They offered professional how-to services—advice and instruction in how to do things—to customers in the store and on the telephone. Their competitors didn't have the equivalent of a master plumber available to discuss your project with you—but to make the idea work, they first had to accomplish a number of very basic things. They had to set up hundreds of stores, warehouses, and suppliers all over the country, and, more important, recruit and train thousands of store personnel who could offer the technical services they advertised.[6] And they had to do it quickly, before their many competitors in the off-price hardware businesses caught on. And, they did. You have to wonder, though. Were they so successful because their idea was a good one, or was it mainly in their ability to execute it?

Margins Matter

The best and the biggest ideas will certainly fail if the economic fundamentals are not there and adequate margins cannot be earned. Selling into a huge market means small margins can still be very profitable, but larger margins are even better.

Henry Ford's mass manufacturing of Model T's was an operation designed to exploit economies of scale so his cars could be sold as cheaply as possible to get the entire country to shift to internal combustion automobiles as quickly as possible. Although the cars were sold cheaply, the volume was large enough for him to capture healthy operating margins. These permitted Ford to pay generous wages to increasingly skilled assembly line workers he wanted to retain, and to invest in facilities to make almost everything that went into the cars at Ford's huge central factory at River Rouge. These were new ideas in business economics at the time—providing long-term employment for an increasingly valuable work force and investing heavily in productivity improvements. The investments increased his margins further, permitting even more investments to improve and expand the business. His competitors were still building many different models of cars in small quantities before they noticed that Ford had sewn up more than 50 percent of the market.

Ted Turner bought obsolete inventories of old movies, discontinued TV series, and cartoons, then offered special channels to his cable carriers that would carry only these old shows. The carriers then marketed the Turner Classic Movies and the Cartoon Channel as part of the optional package they offered to millions of subscribers. For a few cents a day, cable fans could have available to them an unlimited supply of old Humphrey Bogart and Ingrid Bergman movies or *I Love Lucy* reruns. But a few cents a day is a lot of money if it's being paid by millions of subscribers, and the margins captured by Turner were very attractive.

One small business called MaxFlight, founded in 1994, makes aircraft flight simulators for amusement parks. The founder of the business, Frank McClintic, is a former helicopter pilot and a natural tinkering mechanic. He was familiar with aviation training simulators and thought he could improve on their motion characteristics. He did, but decided that to sell it to the military or the airlines would involve obstacles he might not be able to overcome, which might destroy his margins. Traditional simulators are sold to a small number of conservative buyers with longstanding suppliers to whom they are loyal. These buyers were more interested in advanced avionics training than in reproducing cockpit motions accurately, especially through extreme maneuvers. So instead he decided to change his product to make it into a cheaper, glitzier model for the amusement business, where it could be sold by the ride. The product became an enclosed audio-visual-enhanced aircraft cockpit that rotated on all axes, every which way. The rider would be treated to dramatic virtual carrier take-offs and landings, dogfights, or space flights that were very realistic because of the precise coordination between the controls, the visual display, and the cockpit motions. Big park operators thought they could sell a lot of rides. The machines could be big revenue generators for both the park operator and the manufacturer, providing it worked and the public liked it enough to pay up to $10 for a five-minute ride. Frank was confident he could get some of his machines in the big parks, where he would have to compete against other manufacturers of similar rides.

But he also knew the operators would be squeezing him as others came into the business. If they did so, his profit margins would be under pressure. He knew he had to keep his costs down to control the firm's future. Indeed, if his costs could be kept lower than his competitors, he might be able to create an attractive barrier to entry that could protect his profits into the future. Mostly his costs were in the sophisticated parts that the machine required, which cost much more than the labor to assemble them. He focused on lowering these costs, working personally on the problem, after hours and whenever he could. He scoured every technical publication available in search of lower cost replacements for his parts. He found several, including some surplus government equipment that he could buy at distressed prices and substitute for one of his more expensive components. These efforts substantially lowered his costs and maintained his margins well into double digits. But, like Mike Bloomberg, he knows he has to continually reengineer his machines and improve their performance capability to keep ahead of his competition, all bigger companies than his. MaxFlight, in many ways, is a business designed from the outset to have attractive and defensible margins.

Without paying attention to such details, of course, things can go wrong. The Anglo-French alliance to build the supersonic aircraft Concord was a failure because the aircraft was too small to ever be profitable. It could not carry enough passengers or fuel to ever amortize its development costs, even if there had been no objection to supersonic flights over land areas. It had negative margins from the beginning. D. K. Ludwig's billion-dollar commitment to growing cheap pulpwood for paper mills in Brazil failed the basic economics test because the local costs became uncontrollable and could not support the planned scale of the operation.

In today's climate of dot-com start-ups and Internet IPOs of companies with no earnings, it might be tempting to think that successful entrepreneurs can bypass the requirement to produce regular profits like everyone else. This is not so, though in the hot markets of the past few years the real economics of some of the favorite stocks has been obscure. Russ Planitzer, a venture capitalist in New York, says he sees dozens of business plans every week. What he wants to know right away is how does "the thing" (the product or service) produce economic value, and how long is it going to take to reach breakeven? "I don't care so much about immediate profits," he says, "but if the thing can do its job five to ten times better than what's already out there, then the profits will come along soon enough. But if it only does 20 percent or 50 percent better than what's already in the market, I'm not too interested."

Timing

Michael Bloomberg stepped into the market with his *Bloomberg* machine just at the right moment. He understood the business well enough to know of the machine's coming importance and that his competitors might be slow to develop a similar product—but only for a while. He moved within his two to three year window and successfully launched his product. Bill Gates's introduction of MS-DOS was a similar story. Indeed he almost sold his business to IBM, but IBM backed away. Dr. Thomas Frist was one of the first on the scene with his Columbia/HCA hospital management and healthcare business. Wayne Huizenga, who first sensed the need for inexpensive garbage recycling, then saw the potential for a high-grade nationwide videotape rental system and got in with Blockbuster Video early. Now he is trying to figure out a new way to sell new and used cars at retail. Charles Schwab was an early exploiter of the opportunities in discount stock brokerage, and he gained a significant market share and $1.8 billion of net worth in the process.

In early 1998 Greg and Glen Morello, two brothers in New Jersey, decided to expand their Bridgewater Autobody repair business. They already had two shops and wanted to expand to a dozen or more, and they sought to raise capital for doing so. Their idea was to gain some economies of scale by operating at a larger size, but mainly it was to contract with auto insurance companies for bulk purchases of repairs. By gaining the trust of the insurers and working directly with them, they estimated that about 15 percent to 20 percent of the cost of each repair could be saved. The insurance companies wanted to be sure that the repair shops they used were reliable and honest, but as they were also under pressure to lower their insurance rates, they particularly wanted to be able to contract for repairs at a lower cost. Knowingly or unknowingly, the insurance companies were forcing consolidation in the collision repair industry. The two brothers believe they have a year or two to be able to pull their new company together before some other more aggressive or better financed autobody repair chain comes into their market and forces them out. Such businesses already exist elsewhere in the country. Time is critically important for them.

In the late sixties a friend of mine quit his job and started a computer software company. He had worked for IBM before business school and knew the computer business pretty well. He knew, for example, where the software glitches were, and offered a series of products designed to replace the original IBM software. The company was very successful very quickly, and my friend was happily flying all over the world setting up distributorships and joint ventures. The company went public after only a few years in business. It was an Internet sort of business of its day, and my friend became the first millionaire I ever knew. But in the early seventies an economic recession weakened the markets, and the computer business changed to favor minicomputers, and the old mainframe stuff was not as important. IBM changed its software, too, and, well, it all fell apart. A basic trend in the information processing business had changed, and it worked against the interests of my friend's company. To save the business, my friend put back some of the money he had taken out. But he couldn't save the company, which went bust, and my friend went back to selling computers, no richer than when he started only a few years before.

In the fragile world of the entrepreneur, a good idea performed too early or too late is not worth nearly as much as one performed at just the right time. Indeed a good idea may be worth very little if badly timed. But also, a well-timed idea may play to great reviews at first, then fade way if it is not in step with changing market trends. For most hard-pressed entrepreneurs who take one busy year at a time, good timing can mean the difference between being quickly established in a marketplace, or not established at all. Getting established is better than not, but the story doesn't end there. The early market position has to be reinforced and defended against strong competitive efforts, better products, and, of course, trend changes.

The Right Stuff

In 1979 author Tom Wolfe published a bestseller about the first American astronauts, which he called *The Right Stuff*. It is a wonderful book about the experiences, the skills, and the characters of the first Project Mercury team—Alan Sheppard, John Glenn, Scott Carpenter, Gordon Cooper, Wally Shirra, Deke Slayton, and Gus Grissom. These men were combat fighter pilots, many of them test pilots, too, with many hours of flying in dangerous circumstances. Wolfe sensed that as different as they all were from one another, they did have something important in common. They all had something that seasoned aviators knew to be "the right stuff." That meant that they behaved like people think fighter pilots should—they were fearless, of course, and somewhat reckless, though always confidently so. They had extremely quick reflexes, were low key and very cool under pressure, and never showed any concern that they might end up among the gruesome statistics of their profession. They were perhaps not overly smart, but smart enough, not overly disciplined but possessing amazing levels of self-control. Not everyone had the right stuff, but you had to have it to make it to the top in combat aviation or the test pilot business. It was hard to define, but everyone knew it when they saw it.

Wolfe should do a book about successful entrepreneurs. They, too, must have the right stuff, or their equivalent of it, if they are going to make it big. It's the special software inside the product that makes amazing things happen. Big-time managers of large corporations don't have it, though they do have their own different set of special attributes. Neither do professional investors or wheeler-dealers. The quintessential American big-time entrepreneur is a composite of experiences, skills, toughness of character, and self-control that are, as with our astronauts, unique to their profession.

To begin with, they have to have a certain mindset that most business people do not have. They want to bet on themselves and their abilities, even if the odds look pretty long. They are not especially concerned with financial security, or appearances, or creature comforts, as they are always too preoccupied with what they are trying to do. They can stay focused on the tiniest of goals for the longest of times—e.g., to increase sales of bird food products in Bensonhurst—without losing interest. They perform well under pressure and adapt optimistically to even harsh disappointments. They believe totally in what they are doing but are prepared to change things often, so that what they end up doing may not have been what they started out believing. They often demonstrate a disdain for large, bureaucratic working environments and the lines of authority that go with them, at least until they have their own working environment and authority structures in place, which they think are fine. Many are poor delegators, and most have an unusual capacity to absorb details and worry about them. Many seem paranoid about their competition, their suppliers, and their investors, but as Mike Bloomberg says, "Just because you are paranoid, doesn't mean they're not out there." They are absorbed in what they do, and the rest of their life often shows it. They can be hard and ruthless competitors but, when successful, much more generous with their time and money than those who inherit wealth and slowly feed the old money charities. In short they are highly driven to succeed and to do things their way. They have a lot of attitude.

Most real estate investors will tell you that the three most important factors in determining the success of a property investment are location, location, and location. Most investors in small businesses will tell you that for them the three most important factors are the CEO and the management team, in first, second, and third place. Not the product idea, nor the size of the market, nor even the expected operating margins.

In the early sixties a Wall Street broker named Arthur Rock left town to settle in California, where he founded one of the country's first high-tech venture capital firms. He had great instincts and had early success with Apple Computer, Fairchild Semiconductor, Teledyne, and Intel. He likes to know well the companies he invests in and wants them to be within driving distance of the Bay Area. "You have to pay a lot more attention to who is running the company," he says, "than whether the products are right or not."[7]

Other Stuff

But before an entrepreneur has established a track record, it is difficult to tell whether what you might think is the right stuff is the real thing. So investors have to fall back on more conventional criteria to decide whether a proposed new company should warrant their attention.

First the entrepreneur must possess the ability to identify and develop viable plans for capturing an attractive business opportunity. This means coming up with a comprehensive plan that can demonstrate how the economics of the proposed venture can be realized. This is the central idea, requiring some insight or understanding of the opportunity that not everyone else has seen. But it is also the ability to form a team that is capable of putting the idea into action.

Second the entrepreneur must be able to act charismatically, first to attract competent team members largely on their faith in the leader and the business plan, and then to build confidence in the venture by customers, employees, and investors. To be credible, not to mention charismatic, you have to be able to convince people that you know what you are talking about and that you have sufficient experience in business to be believable. Mike Bloomberg tells students eager to form their own businesses to gain solid business experience first, which is what most of our big-money entrepreneurs did before plunging ahead on their own (Bill Gates notwithstanding).

Third an effective entrepreneur has to be good at operating in the field, out there with the customers, the suppliers, and the financial backers. He or she must be able to make things happen, to create the break that makes the critical sale at the right time, to talk the supplier out of cutting him off, to finalize the last bit of high-priced financing without which the business cannot go on. Some of these things may appear to be just luck, and luck is an important factor in all equations for success. But the good field operator helps good luck along by constantly finding other ways to accomplish things and by marshalling talent and resources just where they are needed at just the right time. The effective entrepreneur will maintain a cool-headed demeanor in the face of difficulty, which is constant in a new business, and be able to use these qualities to act as a tactical leader, reacting and adapting effectively to the constant changes in the marketplace. Much of what any successful company does several years out was unpredicted at the time of its beginning. Opportunities continue to change once you get going, and the effective entrepreneur changes with them.

Finally the entrepreneur has to be capable of growing with the business, to be able to create a workable (if idiosyncratic) corporate organization, to handle people well, and to be able to deal with the increasing administrative burden that falls on any successful enterprise. A great many gizmo inventors, super salesmen, or manufacturing geniuses have fallen by the wayside, after getting off to good starts, because of their inability to function as the chief executive of a growing and increasingly complicated organization.

Successful investors in small businesses look for all of these qualities, and background, work experience, and other references to confirm them. They review the business plan endlessly, looking for flaws and vulnerabilities to changing market conditions. When they decide to go ahead with the investment, they know that in most cases they will be proven to have made a mistake. Only a small minority of such investments turns out to be big winners. It's a risky business.

RISKY INVESTORS

Investors in small businesses are different from the standard Wall Street sort of financial operator. They invest in very fragile businesses they do not control, and the securities they own have no market, nor are they likely to for some time. They prefer taking these greater risks because when the investments work out the payoff can be enormous. For every ten investments, they might expect two or three to do poorly, five or six to do no better than the S&P 500, and only one or two to do exceedingly well, producing, say, a return of twenty to fifty times the original investment in about five to seven years. What they hope is that their ability to select winners, to move along the mediocre, and to manage the losers better than otherwise might be the case, will result in a better risk-adjusted return than the stock market itself. On the whole this means being able to turn the portfolio into marketable securities that provide exit, or profit realization opportunities, as quickly as possible.

Most of these investors have their own investors, people who have allocated some of their capital to them in order to achieve a return, over the long term, that is greater than that for publicly traded stocks and less directly correlated to their returns. During the 1990s these investors were looking for gains of 40 percent to 50 percent per year; i.e., a market return plus a premium over that return to account for the extra risk they were taking. This was a pretty high level of return, especially because the S&P 500 market index had been performing so well. For the five years ending in December 1999, for example, the compounded annual increase in the S&P 500 was about 30 percent.[8] Add to that whatever you think the small company risk premium should be (say, at least 10 percent more than the expected S&P 500 return), and you were looking at a required total return of about 40 percent *just to break even*[9]—that is, to give you a reward no better than the market averages after you adjust for the extra risks you are taking. That is a high level of return to realize for a whole portfolio, certainly for any length of time. To do so generally means you have to ask for close to 100 percent annual compounded returns in order to average up with 50 percent after subtracting the losers.

Gazelles

The only way to produce such returns is with the winners. These are companies that, whatever operational problems they have to overcome, nevertheless are capable of growing at something more than 25 percent per year. Such growth can come from spectacular demand for a new product or technology, from a revised distribution system that greatly enlarges its market, or as a result of efforts to consolidate companies within an industry through mergers or acquisitions.

Not all companies, in fact relatively few, are in businesses sectors that have such high growth possibilities. Without the possibility, of course, it can't happen no matter how capable management is. With the possibility, no matter how iffy the company's chances, it *could* happen. This *could* is worth something. Companies with such possibilities are called gazelles by some of the players in the business. They have the spring in their legs that we are looking for, even if the neighborhood they hang out in is a dangerous one, filled with lions and hyenas.

Companies with low growth potential—say, below 15 percent per year—however well managed, are not of much interest to venture investors. They just can't get there from here. These are called lifestyle companies and are generally thought to be appropriate for individuals seeking a suitable income and lifestyle to own, but not for professional investors seeking high returns. Most American small businesses are lifestyle companies. They are capable of providing a good income and satisfaction to their owners, and can sometimes be seen as annuities rather than opportunities for substantial wealth enhancement. Companies with expected growth rates between 15 percent and 25 percent are in the maybe category, and investment in them will depend on a variety of factors, including how much money the investment manager has to put to work. An investor might be inclined to go ahead if the company was less risky (i.e., it was already profitable and closer to an

IPO than the typical gazelle) and it was willing to accept the investor's terms and conditions.

Assembling a herd of gazelles has to begin with finding the animals one by one and, once spotted, capturing them. In theory, all very small, obscure companies are much the same. No one can know for sure which ones will turn out to be winners, so all are looked upon with equal delight and suspicion. In reality this is not the case. Most candidates for venture financing are obscure and have to fight hard for attention. But there are some areas that are densely populated with gazelles, such as certain computer applications, telecommunications, and biotech companies, and more recently Internet dot-com companies. Such companies can be attractive to investors as soon as they become aware of them. Venture capital firms put themselves in the middle of these densely populated areas and look for the best. Firms specialize in particular areas of technology clusters, like Silicon Valley in California, in and around Boston and other university towns, and in the northern areas of New Jersey where so many drug companies have their campus-like research facilities. Newest among these, perhaps, is Silicon Alley in New York City, a center for Internet publishing and multimedia activity. Within these clusters there are people in the know about what's going on, what's being worked on, and who is leaving what firm to start up which new business.

Venture Investors

Some of these investors in the know are called angels. For the most part they are wealthy business owners or executives interested in investing in things they can understand or wish to encourage, or in persons personally connected with the entrepreneurs in some way.

Angels are wealthy individuals accredited by the SEC to invest in unregistered securities, who invest on their own or alongside others. They are a large, informal, unorganized group that does not properly constitute a market. But they are important. A 1996 study by the Center for Venture Research at the University of New Hampshire estimated that there were 250,000 active investors in the United States who invested approximately $20 billion annually in about 30,000 small companies. This is a huge amount of financing (more than twice the amount of money invested in venture capital funds in 1996) for a sector in American finance that gets relatively little attention. Still the study suggests that angels only supply about a third of the annual demand for new capital investments in American small businesses.[10]

The better-known part of the small company financing industry is that of the venture capitalists, or VCs. The original venture capitalists were angels, often entrepreneurs themselves, who funded promising ventures that came to their attention. A number of wealthy families continued to make such investments after their own capitalist progenitor died. The Rockefellers, Whitneys, Paysons, and a number of other families were early venture capital investors. In time some opened up their investment funds to non–family members. In 1946 Harvard Business School professor Georges Doriot founded American Research and Development Co., the first independent firm to enter the VC business. Subsequently a number of other independent firms were formed, especially in the Boston and San Francisco areas, to manage equity investments in promising new sectors of the economy, especially technology. Most of the money given to them to manage came from wealthy families, university and other endowments, and financial institutions. The firms stayed in touch with each other, invested together, and shared information. But the amount of new investment into these venture capital firms was still quite small.

In 1979, however, the U.S. Labor Department, which regulates pension funds in America, declared that the trustees of pension funds were free, as "prudent investors," to allocate a portion of their funds to "alternative investment classes" in order to achieve greater diversification of their entire portfolios. This led to a flood of money into risky, but potentially very profitable, private investments in funds and other vehicles focused on leveraged buyouts, real estate, emerging market securities, and venture capital.

Through their considerable networking activity, venture funds tend to hear first about the most promising new start-up efforts. Promising in the sense of the state of the technology, the prestige and reputation of the team leader and its members, and the early indications about product effectiveness. VC firms are often invited to conduct several weeks of fact-finding and investigation (due diligence) of the companies to determine their investment potential. Such investigations are costly and can tie up key people for extended periods. But they are necessary for the venture investor to decide whether, and at what terms, he or she wishes to proceed to make a financing proposal to the company. Once one firm has been given a go-ahead to commence due diligence, it is unlikely that another firm would wish to do so at the same time. If the first firm is happy with the investigation and makes a proposal that the company accepts, then it will most likely syndicate the financing among a number of like-minded venture capital firms. A firm invited to participate in a piece of business by a prominent venture capital firm rarely refuses, if only to make sure that it continues to receive such invitations in the future. The more prominent the firm's reputation for bringing out winners, the better the access it will have to the all-important deal flow of current prospects being advanced by other firms.

The venture investors usually nurse the company along for some time (originally seven to ten years or so, but perhaps less long at the end of the 1990s) until it can create an opportunity for a merger or a public sale of stock. It will place a partner or two on the board and spend a lot of time offering operating advice and helping to deal with personnel problems. Overall these investors might expect two out of ten investments to produce significant returns, and two or three to go bust or nearly so. Overall, the big winners alone make the difference in whether the firm is successful or not.

One of the most successful venture capital firms is Kleiner Perkins Caufield & Beyers, of Menlo Park and San Francisco. Founded in 1972 by Eugene Kleiner and Tom Perkins, and now headed by John Doerr, the firm has developed into one of the most successful in its field, with a large stable of winners, such as Intel, Cisco Systems, Dell Computer, and Seagate Technology. The firm's fifteen partners have significant operating, as opposed to financial, backgrounds. All have been line managers of companies, with responsibility for bringing new products to market and for their unit's profits. Through their efforts, Kleiner

Perkins has raised over $1.2 billion for its clients and brought over 100 companies public. The firm, like many venture capital firms, believes in nurturing the businesses that it invests in to improve their chances for success. They introduce them to potential employees and directors, to people they need to know to help sell their products, get publicity for them, become customers of other firms that were clients, raise bank loans, and have access to technical or business advisers or board members. They also have formed a business support network that links 175 companies and their executives to help each learn how to succeed by sharing experiences and ideas.

For an industry segment as powerful as it is, the venture capital business is fairly small. Though there are lots of little firms around the country that make venture investments, the greatest successes are concentrated in a couple of dozen firms that all together probably employ, partners included, fewer that 1,500 people. Many of these people, however, have done extremely well during the past twenty years, though often they have had to wait several years for the firms they invested in to break even. The VC firms acquire shares in the companies that they invest in at very low prices. In time the successful companies will sell out or go public at share prices far higher than the price paid by the original VC investors. After the offering the VC firm at some point either sells the stock or distributes it to the principals of the firm, who then may take several more years before they sell it into the market at fully seasoned prices. You can imagine what it would have been like to buy in to Cisco Systems at a nominal price, then watch it rise, year by year, to ever more incredible prices. It went public in 1990 at approximately $0.07 per share (adjusted for splits), and was trading at over $20 per share in early 1999, and at $153 a year later. The VC investors' original cost, in terms of today's price, must have been virtually nothing; their stake today has to be worth a considerable fortune—for just one investment.

Indeed the profits of the business have been sufficient to attract two kinds of newcomers. One of these is the large pension fund that invests in the limited partnerships and other vehicles that venture capital firms set up to attract assets for them to manage. As new clients the pension funds are, of course, welcomed by the VC industry. At the same time, however, the pension funds have shifted, in aggregate, huge amounts of money into a small, fragile industry. In 1998, for example, a record $14.3 billion was invested in venture capital, up 24 percent from the prior year and a 78 percent increase over 1996.[11] Most of the increase in VC funding over these years went into what the pension funds wanted most, technology investments. (In the third quarter of 1999 alone, VC investments totaled over $8 billion—up 180 percent over the prior year—and 90 percent of this amount was directed into technology investments.)[12] The fear is that all this money coming into the technology sector of the industry will distort prices and spoil the balance that the VC industry has struck over the years between the risks taken and the returns received.

The other new investor is the non–venture capital VC firm, the "private equity" investment departments of banks, brokerage firms, and other financial service players who also try to attract some of the pension fund money. The total number of firms making VC investments has increased by about 25 percent over the past ten years, mainly to accommodate this new group of participants. However, the amount of money to be invested is many times greater, and much of it is being invested by firms that have little VC experience. Accordingly the size of new investments by the firms has increased significantly. Now many firms look for deals in which they can invest $15 million to $20 million at a crack, instead of $2 million to $3 million. And, of course, competition for deals has increased among the investors. In turn these larger investments will have to grow into relatively large companies (with market valuations of well over $100 million) for the investors to make the kind of returns they look for. Companies of this size are not just small companies, and what they require to grow into $100-million-plus companies is different from what a much smaller company needed ten years ago. The industry had shifted to a whole different scale, with many complex requirements that go well beyond the traditional nurturing capacities of the VC firm.

Also, to make the larger investments, the firm began to disregard syndication and make more investments alone. Less syndication meant less cooperation, less networking, and less assurance of participating in the industry's future deal flow. Because the minimum investment size has increased so much, many of the investments are not, in fact, start-up investments at all, but second or third round financings of companies originally backed by others. Angels were bringing their deals to the VCs as feeders, and the VCs were repositioning themselves further down the risk curve. All hoped to be able to achieve an exit, however, in only a few years—preferably an exit through an IPO into an even hotter market that would push the stock price up even higher. Like Cisco.

CANDY'S NEW AMERICAN DREAM

In June 1995 Candice Carpenter and Nancy Evans co-founded iVillage, an Internet media company targeted at women. Both women were designated chairpersons of the board of directors, though Candice was chief executive officer and Nancy was editor-in-chief. Candice, a Stanford graduate, rock climber, and former Outward Bound instructor and all-around overachiever, became a career media person after graduating from Harvard Business School in 1983. She was always starting little enterprises, she said. "At six, I embroidered all my neighbors' pillows and charged them for it. I started a café when I was ten. I designed greeting cards and sold them to stores. I was constantly coming up with ideas."[13] After business school she joined American Express, then became president of Time-Life Video & TV. After that, Barry Diller, the CEO of QVC, Inc., hired her to head up Q2, an upscale version of the shopping channel. She quit QVC when Diller did, and chilled out for a while with consulting jobs at America Online, Inc., and Discovery Communications.

At AOL Carpenter recommended creating a number of upmarket media brand locations to offer to AOL's various "grassroots communities." These communities were really just groupings of AOL customers that shared a common interest and might, if encouraged, collect together at a "community site," where they could chat and share information (and read any advertisements and sales promotions that might be put there by AOL). Carpenter's idea was to offer a variety of branded sites (i.e., advertised to create name recognition and consumer preference) for particular interests (topics), especially interests appealing to the baby boomers who were then thought to be among the most active and affluent users of the Internet. Ted Leonsis, then-president of AOL Studios, apparently replied, "Fine, you start the first one." So she did. Carpenter then recruited Nancy Evans, publisher of *Family Life* magazine, to be responsible for the editorial quality and content of all iVillage products, and their business was launched.

When she started iVillage, Carpenter was a forty-three-year-old divorced single mother of a new baby. She got herself a full-time nanny and cook and coped. Later, overcoming many difficulties and frustrations, she adopted by herself a second child from Hungary. She knew that "women today are so pragmatic and time-pressed that they would use the Web to find out how to get things done." She and Evans soon worked out the concept of an Internet destination for women that would connect them to inter-related websites (channels) that specialized in topics important to working, upscale women, mainly those aged twenty-five to fifty. The hottest topics were health, child care, and financial planning, and the women could use the site to ask questions and make suggestions to each other. From the outset, iVillage's strategy has been to promote the use of its branded website and to expand the number of specific content channels that are accessible from it. It also seeks to promote sponsorships by manufacturers and distributors of products for women.[14]

Carpenter was able to utilize her close connections to AOL to create an important partnership arrangement for the company soon after its establishment. In early 1996

AOL invested about $1 million, then more, and by the time of the IPO it owned 12 percent of the company. In May 1997 iVillage issued shares of convertible preferred stock to several venture capital investors at a price of $1.95 per share, and in February, March, and May 1998, additional shares were issued at $2.50 per share. By the time of its IPO three principal venture capital firms, each represented on the board, together owned a 15 percent interest in the company. Venture capital and private equity investors altogether owned approximately 60 percent of the company. The approximate weighted-average holding period prior to the IPO for the venture capital firms was about fourteen to eighteen months; not long.

In November 1998 the company entered into an advertising, promotional, and stock-purchase arrangement with the National Broadcasting Corp. NBC said it invested through a non-cash transaction and would pay for its equity stake by swapping some of its inventory of on-air broadcast time for advertising. In the period just before the IPO, NBC owned approximately 8 percent of the company.

By March 1999 these various promotional and support arrangements, and the funds supplied by the venture capitalists, diluted management's stock holdings (including their stock options) in the company to less than 6 percent. During the year prior to the IPO, Carpenter, Evans, and three other members of management had been issued a total of about 200,000 options exercisable at $6 per share. It was essential, Carpenter and Evans agreed, that the company be able to offer attractive stock option packages to senior management whom they were constantly attempting to recruit to their small company, one that was just getting started in an entirely new communications industry.

Four years after its founding the company launched its shares onto the market with an initial public offering, which at $24 per share valued the company at $554 million. At the end of trading on the first day, iVillage stock had more than doubled to $55 share, valuing Carpenter's stock in the company at $37.4 million. These happy events occurred despite the fact that iVillage had reported a net loss for the year ended December 31, 1998, of $43.7 million, on revenues of just over $15 million.

The company's business is (working) capital intensive. From the outset the company's business operated at a loss, due to the heavy promotional and other expenses required to establish its brand, create demand for its websites, and fund the acquisition of other women's media websites for incorporation into the iVillage network. Net cash used in operating activities was $8.7 million in 1996, $15.3 million in 1997, and $43.7 million in 1998. Accordingly the company was constantly in a financing mode since its inception. In 1996 it raised $11 million, in 1997 $24 million, and in 1998 $65 million through the sale of convertible notes, common stock, and convertible preferred stock. The company had made it clear that its future financial activities would resemble those of its past. It would continue to expend increasingly larger sums for promotion and advertising, and would continue to pursue acquisitions, one of which, iBaby.com, a website devoted to selling baby-related products, would be financed by applying part of the proceeds of the IPO. Future acquisitions, of course, could be accomplished more easily if the company's shares traded at a high stock price relative to its future earnings and net worth. It was a typical Internet company of its time—it had no track record, it burned up capital at an incredible rate, and had losses greater than its revenues. Having any earnings at all seemed well off into the future. Yet its stock went through the roof.

Within a few weeks of its IPO, the stock price soared above $100 per share, reaching a peak of $130 a month after going public. This was the Internet boom at its best, when stock prices shot to euphoric levels. But in iVillage's case, it didn't last. Almost immediately after reaching its high, the stock began to deflate, then collapse. Nine months after the IPO the stock was trading at $22. The company's business had stayed more or less on track during the post-IPO period, though by then it had attracted some new competitors, had some embarrassing personnel defections, and some of its accounting practices were questioned. Its losses were greater but so were its sales and advertising expenses, all more or less what was expected.

At some point the market will require the company to produce some profits, but not, it seems, before having invested whatever it took to secure the best and most enduring market share position that it could. Indeed one theory of valuation of companies like iVillage is to separate out the money spent on business development and technology, and capitalize it rather than expense it as required by accounting conventions. The capitalized amount represents the intangible values of the business, which can be separately evaluated rather like a drug company might do with its patents. Intangibles represent a huge portion of the *potential* of Internet businesses, and this potential is generally worth quite a bit more that the business's otherwise meager current results.

Candice and Nancy and their investors saw the stock price sink to $13 per share by January 2000 and below $8 per share by June 1. It was certainly disappointing to see it shoot up so high (showing so much confidence in their business), only for the market to change its mind almost instantly after such a sharp correction. Still, serious analysts had begun to recommend it again, and the company continued on its regular journey as a public company. This is not an easy journey, and for many companies the post-IPO experience is disappointing. Companies have to compete for attention in the investment community and struggle to keep trading volumes in the secondary market up to minimums required by institutional investors. A number of companies become discouraged a few years after their IPO and seek to buy back stock or look for another company to buy them.

The original iVillage investors were unable (through December 1999) to sell any stock at all. If this condition continues, they may begin to cast around for an exit opportunity to get their money and maybe some modest profits back by selling the business. Management may not wish for such an exit at the time, but with control of the company resting with large investors, it would be almost impossible to do anything about it.

Candice and Nancy are typical of today's new breed of entrepreneurs. In the old days it might have taken a lifetime for a business to be organized, financed, and developed to the point where it could be valued at half a billion. It was a struggle that the entrepreneur was usually not able to share with others except a financial partner or two. It was a long hard slog. The iVillage experience is very different, first in being founded by two women. Indeed these were two well-educated, workaholic professional women who were fortunate to be where they were when opportunity knocked. When the Internet wave began to crest, they put together a feasible idea for a business at a time when everything was chaotic, and found an important player, AOL, willing to back them. With AOL's support and their ideas, know-how, and effort, the women were able to attract substantial additional support from venture capitalists on the look for the newest new thing. These investors did not ask for quick profits or ordinary business results. They were willing to believe in the idea, regardless of its incredible cash-devouring appetite, at least as long as the stock market confirmed their judgement.

Candice Carpenter and Nancy Evans have shared an opportunity that few men or women ever have, that of founding a company *de novo* in a totally new industry with hardly any investment of their own and guiding the company through its early, hazardous years. In their case, the experience must have seemed unreal. It all happened so quickly. First putting the concept together, raising the initial money, going public, and watching the stock price soar out of sight, then watching it come back down again, plunging to a third of the IPO price within its first twelve months of being a public company. The governing notion supporting their business—e-commerce—was coming unstuck, and investors were dumping all sorts of business-to-consumer Internet stocks, including iVillage. Without the support of the market for the company's plans and ideas, it is difficult to attract the money needed to implement them. Without the gilded promise of stock options, it is difficult to attract and hold key employees. These are stressful conditions under which to manage a business, and with management owning only a modest percentage of the stock, the ultimate destiny of the firm may be determined by someone other than themselves. There would be many tough days before things settled down to "normal," a condition Carpenter and Evans had long since forgotten. In the end the old truisms still apply: Internet or no, business is tough enough, but the business of entrepreneurs starting new companies is tougher still, and only the toughest of them survive.

Carpenter once told a reporter that she would really like some day to have about six children and live quietly and securely on a beach somewhere. Maybe iVillage will be the means for her to do this, but not yet. There is still a lot of living through the adventure yet ahead. But the great dream that so many Americans have, and have had over the centuries—of starting and building a successful business—is one that has come true for her.

CHAPTER 2

The Dealmakers

When the Reagan bull market began, so did the era of the modern financial entrepreneur, or what might otherwise be called the time of the late twentieth century wheeler-dealer. Financial entrepreneurs are dealmakers who gain access to transactions through the financial markets and make large, sudden investments for sometimes relatively short periods, manage the position until they can liquidate it at a profit, then pull back and wait for the next opportunity. They usually work by themselves or with a small staff to identify opportunities and formulate a plan to take advantage of them. They don't worry much about what other people think of them. They live by their wits and do what they have to do. Like their late nineteenth century counterparts, they are sophisticated financial players capable of large, opportunistic maneuvers. They are often effective, but also often misunderstood.

Such in-and-out actions are typical of proprietary traders, who see themselves as investing their own capital to profit from a particular strategy they have devised. Financial entrepreneurs use similar methods to follow somewhat different strategies. They look for undervalued companies to either take over or threaten into a deal with someone else. Usually they are called *vulture* investors if they are just swooping down on some bankrupt or distressed company, or *raiders* if they are seeking to gain control of a company through a hostile takeover. In either case the effort frequently is to buy out the old shareholders and then recapitalize the company using a great deal of borrowed money, in a magical process that came to be called the leveraged buyout. They would then restructure the company, run it to maximize its cash flow, and repay the formidable amount of debt they had assumed to purchase control. Afterwards they could either enjoy the surplus, sell the company, effect an IPO, or redo the whole thing three or five years down the road after paying a hefty dividend to the financial entrepreneur who was responsible for the whole process. Sometimes the entrepreneur would instead burrow in and try to manage the company over a longer period but, while doing so, sell off bits and pieces and extract cash for other investments. The longer this process takes, the more these individuals drift away from being traders to becoming investors, a profession listed by more than a few of the *Forbes* 400 in 1999. A lot of big money has been made through dealing: as raiders (takeovers and LBOs), as arrangers of deals and financing (investment bankers and junk bond distributors), and as real estate investors, who in addition lend their skills to developing and promoting projects from scratch.

RAIDERS

Declining interest rates, rising stock markets, dramatically
increased liquidity for financial investments, and a general
tolerance of the aggressive tactics of the corporate raider
all contributed to the great swashbuckling years of the financial deal and the leveraged buyout, the period from
1982–1988. During these years more than 10,000 merger
transactions valued at more than $1 trillion took place, the
first major takeover boom since the 1960s, when conglom-
eration was all the rage. Now the conglomerates and many
large, stodgy multi-industry companies, which had been
raked over the coals during the 1970s, became targets for
aggressive recapitalization and restructuring.

This was a time when almost anyone with a little talent
or some chutzpah could pull a stake together and go off
harassing large public companies with poor operating records. It was a time when unknowns without convincing
signs of financial support could frighten directors of major
corporations into *greenmail*, in which their tormentors (and
only they) would be offered a premium price over the market for their shares. It was also a time when shareholder
rights were publicly asserted by those who actually were
attempting to exploit shareholders by buying their shares
cheaply and to bring down and humiliate established
managers through hostile takeover bids or proxy fights.
But perhaps more than anything, it was a time when market values were out of alignment with their potential. By
paring the large behemoths down, introducing more financial leverage, and changing management and corporate
strategies, much could be done to rebuild them into revi-

talized, far more valuable enterprises. The 1980s were certainly the time of the value investor. They were also the time of the brilliant lawyers and financial engineers who were capable of devising unusual securities and sophisticated market operations that would totally change the tool kit that financial entrepreneurs of the past—particularly Jay Gould, James Hill, and Bernard Baruch—had relied upon in their day. The 1980s launched a series of money wars between the best of the lawyers and engineers that did much to change the American business landscape.

The skirmishes began with greenmail efforts by Saul Steinberg (a surviving corporate raider of the 1960s), Carl Icahn, T. Boone Pickens, and others. They picked on such unlikely targets as Texaco, Gillette, and Disney, and made off with a bundle. They would acquire a modest stake, 10 percent or so, then claim that they had secured financing to fund a full takeover. Frequently the boards of the target companies panicked and bought them off. Institutional investors, who got nothing in these transactions, were furious but impotent. The greenmailers became bolder, and companies were put in play by their threatened takeover efforts, which often prompted the company to seek another, more favorable bidder instead, a *white knight*. In 1984, under attack, the Household Finance Company introduced the first *poison pill*, which radically altered takeover tactics thereafter (and also brought an end to greenmail). Household said it would issue special share-purchase rights to all of its shareholders that would permit the preexisting shareholders to acquire additional shares in the company at about one-half the market price. The rights, however, could only be exercised if any other person or company succeeded in acquiring more than a threshold amount (i.e., 30 percent) of Household's common stock without the approval of the Household board of directors. If that happened, however, the threshold crosser would not be eligible to acquire any of the newly issued stock at half price, so his position would be hopelessly diluted. The court upheld the action, so, after the poison pill, perpetrators would have to get the target board's consent or else hold their fire. This consent, subsequent legal cases decided, could not unreasonably be denied; the directors of the target company had to act correctly in the context of their duties of care and loyalty. Care required that the directors know what they were doing and get outside, expert advice from lawyers and investment bankers before acting. That was good for the lawyers and the bankers. Loyalty required that they not place any other interest, such as their own or management's, over their obligation to look after the shareholders' interests first.

The Beauty Queen

Ronald Perelman rose to fame in 1985 on this issue, that of a board's duty of loyalty to its shareholders. Perelman, the son of a small-time but successful corporate raider, went into business for himself in 1976, after working for his father for ten years. He started with small deals (e.g., a $2 million investment in a New Jersey jewelry chain store that he sold for $15 million) and parlayed these into bigger and bigger deals, keeping some in his privately owned conglomerate, MacAndrews and Forbes (acquired in 1978), and selling others. In 1984 MacAndrews and Forbes acquired Pantry Pride for its huge tax loss carry forward. To put it to use, in 1985 he set his sights on Revlon, the queen of beauty products companies, which had been badly run down since the death of its founder, Charles Revson, in 1975. Revson, knowing he was dying of cancer, hand picked his successor, Michel Bergerac, an elegant, French-born former head of ITT's European businesses, in 1974. Bergerac expanded the company into health care and other businesses and increased sales several fold. Profits, on the other hand, were declining, along with the company's market share. The stock was thought to be cheap relative to its potential, which Bergerac and the Revlon board were thought to be holding back.

When Perelman struck (backed by Michael Milken and the junk bond men from Drexel Burnham), Bergerac and the Revlon board were horrified. They could not bear to see "a great American consumer products company" like theirs being controlled by someone they regarded as an unknown little upstart, who (worst of all) was being financed by Drexel's junk bonds. One of the most bitter defense efforts of the 1980s resulted. Revlon turned to a friendly LBO operator, Forstmann Little, that at first attempted to do a buyout deal in which management would get to own 25 percent of the stock. This was frustrated, however, so Forstmann Little made an offer contingent on Revlon agreeing to (1) sell it two key businesses for relatively low amounts—a feature called a *crown jewel lockup*—and (2) not negotiate with any other party. Whatever Forstmann Little offered in price, however, Perelman would top by twenty-five cents per share. Perelman also challenged the deal in the Delaware Chancery Court. The court decided in Perelman's favor—*Revlon v. MacAndrews and Forbes* is now a classic case in takeover law. It established the principal that once a company has declared itself to be for sale, it has to keep the bidding process open so as to be sure that the company can be sold to the highest bidder. The court threw out the lockup, and Perelman won control of the company, though it was probably the most expensive deal ever done at that time. The Revlon shareholders did very well, gaining about $1.5 billion in increased value of their stock. Bergerac did especially well, as he was able to walk away with $35 million in stock profits and payments due him under his *golden parachute*, a predetermined settlement for losing his job as CEO, the biggest one ever at that time.[1] Lawyers and investment bankers pocketed a total of about $110 million in fees, of which Drexel Burnham earned $60 million for arranging the junk financing and participating in the deal's merger advisory fees.[2]

Perelman began an effort to break the company into effective business units and to revive it, partly by adding new acquisitions in the cosmetics area. According to Revlon, two years after its acquisition by Perelman, operating profits were doubled. He took it public again in 1996, at $28 per share, though a previous effort in 1992 was withdrawn for lack of interest. By mid-1998 the stock had reached $57 per share, but then fell off sharply as a variety of operating and management problems emerged.

Perelman became well known as a predator after Revlon, putting together greenmailing runs on Transworld Corporation (Hilton International Co.), Gillette, and Salomon Inc. In 1988 Perelman hit the jackpot from the S&L crisis. He made a hugely favorable deal with the Federal

Deposit Insurance Corp., which was trying to unload defaulted S&Ls, to acquire First Gibraltar, a group of Texas thrifts. The market quickly recovered, and Perelman sold out for a profit of about $1 billion, plus an additional $3.5 billion in tax loss carry-forwards. He used some of the money to acquire camping equipment maker Coleman Co. in 1989, which he has since sold 17 percent of back to the public. Subsequently Perelman sold his remaining 83 percent of Coleman to Sunbeam Corp. in exchange for a 14 percent interest in the appliance maker, a deal that was worked out despite Perelman's inability to get along with Sunbeam's then-new CEO, hard-nosed Albert Dunlap. Despite his reputation for turning troubled companies around, "Chainsaw Al" was not effective at Sunbeam and was fired, and Perelman's Sunbeam stock dropped from $53 per share to $5.125 by August 1998. To replace Dunlap the Sunbeam board picked Jerry Levin, Perelman's key corporate troubleshooter, and issued Perelman 23 million five-year warrants exercisable at $7 per share. If Levin can just get the stock back to where it was when Coleman was sold, Perelman would stand to earn another $1 billion.[3] By the end of 1999, however, the stock was below $5 per share.

Revlon still serves as the anchor in MacAndrews and Forbes, which owned about forty different businesses in 1999 (including Marvel Comics, New World Communications broadcasting, First Nationwide Bank, Boston Whaler motorboats, and Consolidated Cigar) with no discernible connection except that Perelman liked them. "I love all the businesses we are in," he says. All of his businesses are fully leveraged and run to maximize shareholder wealth. Like some of his nineteenth century predecessors, Perelman, fifty-six in 1999, is known to be a tough, even vengeful, character who is frequently in litigation with customers, investors, former employees, and former wives.[4] Also like some of his predecessors, he is extremely religious and a generous but demanding father who intends to leave all his assets to his children. *Forbes* listed Perelman as its most successful raider-investor in 1997, with a net worth of $6.5 billion. But Perelman proved to be less effective as an operating manager and, caught up in the wrong part of the market, the unglamorous old economy sectors, he had to watch his net worth decline sharply to $3.8 billion by 1999.

The Ugly Ducklings

Being involved in a nationally celebrated, extended takeover battle gave Ron Perelman a lot of public visibility and attention. Almost as wealthy, Larry and Preston (Bob) Tisch, both Flatbush born, have managed their business empire more quietly, although both have become prominent and respected public figures in New York and Washington, where Bob was postmaster general for two years in the Reagan administration. Larry, who was seventy-six in 1999, is known for his more than thirty-year tenure as chairman and CEO of Loews Corp., a publicly owned diversified investment company. He is also known for his philanthropy in New York City. (He was chairman of the board and a large contributor to New York University for many years.) The Tisches (Larry, Bob, and their children, three of whom are active in the business) own about a third of the stock of Loews, which began as a chain of renovated, once-failing hotels. Loews still owns hotels, but also an eclectic portfolio of dissimilar holdings, including 98 percent of Bulova Watch, 84 percent of CNA Insurance, a 50-percent stake in Diamond Offshore Drilling, 100 percent of Lorillard Tobacco, and a large portfolio of stocks and other investments. Loews aggressively bought a 25-percent stake in CBS in 1985, and Larry became CEO a year later, after predecessor Tom Wyman was forced out. He then replaced William S. Paley, CBS's founder, as chairman when Paley died in 1990. Tisch was chief executive of CBS for nine years, during which time he was all business, looking at the bottom line much more closely than at esthetic or reportorial values. Within CBS, Tisch was often criticised behind his back. But Tisch's eye was stuck on the company's profits until he was able to sell CBS to Westinghouse for $5.4 billion in 1995. The sale involved a $900 million profit for Loews. "He'll be remembered," said Ralph Gabbard, chairman of the CBS affiliates group, "as the guy who made the shareholders a lot of money but destroyed the network."[5] Meanwhile Bob Tisch, acting on his own, bought a 50 percent interest in the New York Giants football team for $75 million in 1991.

Loews Corp. has a commendable long-term investment record, with a compounded growth rate from 1973 though December 1998, the stock's peak in price, of about 18 percent. Loews' long-term investment return is comparable to that of Warren Buffett's Berkshire Hathaway, which produced a compounded growth rate since 1973 of 24 percent through 1998. However, according to a December 1997 report by Duff McDonald in *Money* magazine, Loews was trading at the time at a discount of 22 percent from the estimated market value of its individual holdings, typical of many closed-end mutual funds. At that time Berkshire

Hathaway was trading at a 7 percent premium to its underlying value, no doubt because of the magic of the Buffett name. According to McDonald both operated a diversified investment company inside a publicly owned holding company that trades on the basis of investment results. Both have very large holdings in some basic businesses (they have insurance in common) that throw off considerable cash for further reinvestment. Both began as value investors following the best known gurus of the 1930s and 1940s, Graham and Dodd, though Buffett has gone with the flow in recent years and purchased some popular high-priced growth stocks. Larry Tisch has remained where he was, looking for really cheap stocks when there were not many to find.

Tisch is a tough-minded contrarian, plunging into big investments in obscure, down-and-out companies or commodities when he thinks prices are truly low. Loews has backed tobacco when it was considered a horrible bet, bought oil tankers when they were being laid up, and continually since 1996 has taken large (and extremely expensive) short-side positions in cash and futures markets that would pay off only if the market declined.[6] Both Tisch and Buffett step in and control businesses when they have to, but the Tischs do it regularly and without frills of any kind. Larry and Bob, however, are hardly known at all outside of New York City. Compared to Buffett, the glamorous darling of today's portfolio managers, they are the ugly ducklings. Nevertheless, together the Tisch brothers are worth about $4.5 billion.

Babe Ruth

Kirk Kerkorian was seventy-six when he and Lee Iacocca launched a proxy fight for control of Chrysler Corp. in 1994. At the time he owned a 13 percent position in Chrysler, which he had begun to accumulate in 1990. Known for his long involvement in Hollywood and Las Vegas, his appearance as a suitor of the third largest American automobile maker seemed very much out of context. The effort, which had seemed weak and poorly thought through from the beginning, fell apart and Chrysler was declared the winner in the struggle.

For a few years Kerkorian, the son of an immigrant fruit dealer, and a junior-high-school dropout, had been giving advice to Robert Eaton, Chrysler's chairman, about things he thought ought to be done to improve the stock price. These included increasing dividends and repurchasing shares with the company's huge cash horde. Eaton felt that Kerkorian knew very little about the peculiarities of the car business, and tried to pacify him without agreeing to anything. Kerkorian had made a similar pitch to Lee Iacocca when he had been chairman, with a similar result. Now he approached Iacocca, a perennial troublemaker, and asked him to join in an effort to take control through a proxy fight that would call attention to Kerkorian's long-standing grievances. Iacocca agreed, and in April 1995 they told the company of their intentions. The Kerkorian plan was announced and the battle was joined. But Chrysler won, and its independence was preserved. In February 1996 Kerkorian signed a standstill agreement not to purchase any additional stock.

Nevertheless Kerkorian won the war. His secret all along was that he never intended to take the company over, only to force it to do things that would benefit him as a large shareholder. Just about everything Kerkorian pressured Chrysler to do, it did in order to gain market support for repelling him. It raised its dividends 60 percent, split the stock two for one, increased the threshold of its poison pill from 10 percent to 15 percent, and announced a $1 billion stock repurchase. Kerkorian's total cost in acquiring his stake was $1.5 billion, $1 billion of which he borrowed. It was worth $3.3 billion by December 1997 and had earned him $400 million in dividends. After the merger with Daimler Benz, Kerkorian's Chrysler stock was worth another $1.5 billion.

The strategy began in 1990 when Chrysler was still being run by Iacocca. Kerkorian decided he wanted a 10 percent stake, and asked his banker, Michael Tennenbaum, a partner of Bear Stearns, to buy the stock. Tennenbaum did not see the logic in an aging, reclusive, Las Vegas and Hollywood investor jumping into the automobile business without any advice and taking a position large enough to be threatening without discussing it first. "Don't you want to talk to Iacocca first?" he said.

"No, just buy the stock."

"Look, I'll be happy to spend time studying this and let you know what I think," said Tennenbaum.

"I would rather you wouldn't," replied Kerkorian, getting irritated. "Do you want the order or not?"

Tennenbaum did, and bowed to his client's wishes. Later he told Bear Stearns' chairman, Alan Greenberg, about the conversation, adding that "Kirk must be going crazy, he wants to buy 10 percent of Chrylser."

"Well, maybe" cautioned Greenberg, "but don't ever tell Babe Ruth how to hold his bat." Kerkorian took seven years to do it, at an age when most wheeler-dealers would have long since given up caring, but he still hit another homerun, one of many during his long career.[7]

Kerkorian was an amateur boxer and a flyer who trained pilots during World War II. After the war, he purchased surplus Air Force planes and turned them into an airline, which he sold in 1966 for a profit of more than $100 million. In 1969 Kerkorian paid $82 million for a 40 percent interest in MGM, to which he added United Artists in 1981, after which he began to dismantle its assets. He sold historic back lots once frequented by Clark Gable and Katherine Hepburn, auctioned off relics and costumes worn by famous stars of the past, sold the old film library to Ted Turner, and brought the MGM name into the Las Vegas hotel-and-casino business. Then he sold all the rest to Ted Turner for $1.5 billion in 1986. Soon thereafter, however, Turner was seriously wounded by the stock market crash of 1987 and the subsequent drying up of credit for low-quality borrowers. Strapped for cash, Turner sold most of the MGM/UA assets back to Kerkorian for a mere $480 million. In 1990 Kerkorian sold the MGM/UA properties again, this time to Giancarlo Parretti, a slick Italian wheeler-dealer, for $1.3 billion. Parretti soon went bankrupt, leaving the property in the hands of his creditors, principally the government-owned French bank Credit Lyonnais. In July 1996 Kerkorian bought it all back yet again, for $1.3 billion.[8] Maybe he went crazy again, as Michael Tennenbaum once thought, though it is doubtful that Michael was telling him how to hold his bat. *Forbes* identified Kerkorian as being worth $7 billion in 1999. In February 2000 Kerkorian, then 82, surprised his crosstown rival Steve Wynn with a $3.4 billion unfriendly offer for his sagging Mirage Resorts casino empire.[9] The acquisition would create a gambling behemoth that would dominate the industry. This Babe never rests.

The Loner

Carl Icahn was a typical 1980s activist raider who thrived on flamboyant attacks on companies that he regarded as mismanaged and therefore undervalued. Unlike others of that time—T. Boone Pickens, the Belzberg family, Irwin Jacobs, Harold Simmons, the late James Goldsmith and Ronald Perelman—most of whom have retired or picked one principal company to manage, Icahn has continued to do what he did before. He looks for opportunities, takes a position by himself (he doesn't like working with partners), then settles in for a long siege, during which he becomes a highly visible and critical opponent, and attempts to wear down the other side through seemingly endless negotiations. He has had a lot of battles, and on balance made a lot of money (*Forbes* put him at $4.2 billion for 1999), most of it in the 1980s. The 1990s did not produce many of the high-visibility opportunities he thrives on, but, in his early sixties at the end of 1999, he was still looking. The overpriced nineties, he thought, would be succeeded by huge market opportunities when prices collapsed and management mistakes were again revealed. He would be ready.

Icahn comes from Queens, New York, where he was one of the smartest kids in his class and went on to Princeton. In the 1960s he drifted into Wall Street and made enough money in arbitrage there to buy himself a seat on the New York Stock Exchange. He made money, then lost it. In the 1970s he began to take small stakes in undervalued companies that either paid him greenmail or ran into the arms of a white knight. This was easy money for Icahn. There were hundreds of undervalued companies in the 1970s—the grim years before the Reagan market—and management almost always did what the raiders wanted them to. All Icahn had to do was to stick to his game plan, be irritating and troublesome, and wait for the money to come in. Emboldened by his success, he refined the plan for the 1980s, when bountiful supplies of financing became available from Milken's junk bond market and from banks eager to get into the business of financing lucrative hostile takeover deals.

In 1984 Icahn purchased ACF Industries, a railcar-leasing company, in what was probably his most successful deal, the one that has accounted for most of his wealth today. He paid $400 million, mostly borrowed, and quickly recovered his investment by selling off assets. ACF is a huge cash-generating machine that he has used to finance other ventures. In 1996 Icahn turned down $2 billion for ACF. Instead, he leased most of ACF's cars to General Electric, then effected a $1.25 billion, 7-percent asset-backed financing deal secured by GE's AAA lease payment obligation. He used the proceeds to buy back ACF's $800 million in outstanding high-yield bonds, which previously he had been offered a rate of 11.5 percent to refinance. The deal saved him 4.5 percent in interest cost on $800 million, or $36 million a year.

The first venture he undertook with ACF's cash flow was the acquisition of Trans World Airlines in 1985, which was not a success. He loaded the airline up with junk bonds, paying himself a dividend that recovered most of his initial investment, but the refinancing was too much for TWA, which ran into the ground in 1992. The bankruptcy cost Icahn about $30 million, but more important, he became liable for the $1 billion underfunding of its pension fund.

After the 1987 market crash, Icahn came out hunting for distressed companies or wounded entrepreneurs. He found the Australian wheeler-dealer Robert Holmes à Court reeling from the impact of the market collapse. He was able to buy out Holmes à Court's 10 percent stake in Texaco, which Holmes à Court had acquired when Texaco declared bankruptcy following an adverse $10.5 billion judgement against Texaco in the Penzoil case. This was a classic Icahn situation: he criticized, harassed, badgered, and pushed Texaco toward a settlement that netted him a greenmail profit of more than $500 million. He used some of this money to buy up junk bonds in the 1990s when that market collapsed following the indictment of Drexel Burnham and Michael Milken. Working out of these positions kept him busy until 1995, during which time he claims an annualized return of 47 percent.[10]

In 1995 Icahn teamed up in an unlikely partnership with old antagonist Bennet LeBow to launch a proxy fight against RJR Nabisco. This was to force the company to spin off its food businesses, an idea the company had considered but did not regard as feasible. The partnering effort foundered a year later, leaving Icahn more convinced than ever that he should stick to operating on his own. So he pursued an abortive proxy fight in 1997, but the deal didn't work as he received virtually no support from other shareholders. He did, nevertheless, manage a profit of $130 million on his investment. Then, a year later, he made another effort to use his 8-percent stake in RJR to force the spin off of the food units. He lost this fight, too, but made another $130 million on the stock he owned. Then he drifted off briefly into high-tech investing and an effort to take over a bankrupt hotel in Atlantic City, but in March 2000 he was back with another offer (his third) to take control of RJR Holdings, the holding company that owned 80 percent of the food group. He persisted as usual without much support, but this time his efforts paid off. In June 2000, Phillip Morris offered $55 a share for Nabisco Holdings, the food group owned by Nabisco Group Holdings, topping a rival offer from a consortium of European companies. This was a very complex transaction in which the food group would be sold for cash to the holding company, which would be subsequently sold to R. J. Reynolds Tobacco Holdings, which Nabisco had previously spun off to its shareholders. In the end, the company was broken apart cleanly, and the stock price of the food group was double, and that of the holding company triple, what they had been before Icahn reentered the fray in March. Icahn's ownership of the holding company stock would be worth $930 million, a $590 million profit for an investment span of only nine months. "It's a pleasant way to lose," he said. Ironically, this deal, which dissolved the landmark transaction of the 1980s, enabled Icahn to claim the role of the big winner in the twelve year history of the company, one which had frustrated Kohlberg, Kravis & Roberts, the buyout organizers, and dozens of others of the best financial engineering talents available.

Those who have written about Icahn claim that he has

thrived for years on a self-image of a Clint Eastwood–style of loner tough-guy who perpetually challenges established authority, never gives up, and in the end wins against heavy odds because of his strong character and unwillingness to compromise. Or something like that. A more realistic picture might be that Icahn owes his success to being very street smart and having a very difficult personality that loves confrontation as if it were a sport. He is very good at spotting value-investment opportunities, which have been scarce since the middle 1990s. Of course he hopes that other big opportunities like Nabisco, which the market had driven down, will appear. Some others think that the times may have passed Icahn by. Dealmaking by confrontation and maneuver may no longer be a workable approach, they say. Too many antitakeover developments have occurred in the courts, too many managers have toughened up and are no longer afraid to fight back, and too many institutional investors have turned their backs on the large-company, multi-billion-dollar, junk-bond-financed takeovers of the 1980s, like TWA.[11]

But in the Nabisco case, Icahn wasn't trying to finance a leveraged acquisition of a broken-down company, he was trying to force one to be broken up. He had stayed in the game by changing with the times, though most of the others of the 1980s deal-doing gang had settled for lower profiles. Richard Rainwater ($1.2 billion) has become an investor who focuses on one or two out-of-favor things at a time, such as health care, oil, and real estate. David Murdock ($1.1 billion) and Nelson Peltz ($890 million) continue quietly to manage their portfolios. Alfred Checchi, whose LBO of Northwest Airlines made him rich, recently lost an expensive contest to become the Democratic Party's nominee for governor of California in 1998 (he was no longer on the *Forbes* 400 list in 1999). These men were among the most celebrated of the new faces of finance in the 1970s and 1980s, who made their money aggressively and are now in the process of transitioning it into the sorts of prudent, well-balanced portfolios held by the old capitalists they once displaced.

ARRANGERS

Generally, among deal people, the ones with the most money are those who took the risk and financed the transaction with personal funds or credit. Since the early 1980s, however, this model has changed to admit a new species of deal-doer to this special community: the intermediary or middleman. In the past such arrangers worked on commission, taking a small piece of all the deals that were done but rarely making it into the big rich. J. P. Morgan did, but his time was very different and long ago, and even so, he often took his fees in stock and frequently invested the bank's capital in deals he wanted to do. Nonetheless Morgan was much less rich than many of his clients and adversaries.

The Reagan bull market triggered a nearly twenty-year period of merger and dealmaking activity that was a paradise for middlemen. The merger wave of the 1980s and 1990s made many of them rich, especially those working for large investment banks. Felix Rohatyn, a senior partner of Lazard Freres who had first made his name in the 1960s, was dean of the profession until retiring to become ambassador to France in the late 1990s. His firm did little else but merge companies in the U.S. and Europe. As the 1980s were such a dramatic time of sensational raids and defenses, the merger business became glamorous and leading figures were given a lot of publicity. Merger men Bob Greenhill and Rick Gleacher of Morgan Stanley, Bruce Wasserstein and Joe Perrella of First Boston, and Steve Friedman and Geof Boisi of Goldman Sachs were among the superstars of their times. By the nineties, however, most of these people had moved on and were replaced by no-name professional teams that never attracted the limelight, though the deal volume in the nineties was much greater than during the 1980s. Still some big-time deal arrangers are still celebrities today.

Herb Allen, of Allen & Co., is one of these; a certified *Forbes* billionaire ($1.6 billion) in his own right and a quintessential deal man for the entertainment industry. Michael Orvitz ran a Hollywood talent agency but still brokered Matsushita's disastrous acquisition of MCA and Sony's of Columbia Pictures and later went on to serve a short time as president of Disney, for which he received separation pay of about $100 million. There are more deal men out there than anyone can imagine; most of course, playing in lesser leagues but still actively suggesting transactions and schmoozing them along.

In the early 1980s the world of the arrangers was changed significantly with the introduction of large-scale leveraged buyouts into the takeover stimulated financial markets of the times. The public attention was first drawn to them in 1983, when former Treasury secretary and Salomon Brothers bond salesman, the late William E. Simon, was reported to have made $250 million over a period of only eighteen months. This was on the occasion of an IPO for Gibson Greeting Inc., which Simon and his partner,

Raymond Chambers, had bought from RCA in 1982 for $80 million. Simon and Chambers invested only about $330,000 of their own money and borrowed the rest from banks and finance companies. They were going to reorganize how the company was run and operate it for cash, etc., when the bull market began and the stock market went into full surge. They had little time or need to improve things, as the market was willing to take their story on faith. So they popped the IPO into the market and pocketed their return in record time. But it was the market that did it; Simon and Chambers were blessed by their sense of timing, not by their management skill. But what made them so rich was the leverage in the deal. It wasn't long before the LBO market took off. From about $2 billion per year in transactions in 1980, the market exploded. In 1984 the volume had risen to seventy-six deals totaling $11.8 billion. And in 1988, the peak year when RJR Nabisco was done, 239 LBOs worth $81 billion were completed, approximately 40 percent of all mergers-and-acquisitions business (by value) during the year.

The LBO business quickly captured the attention of the major investment and commercial banks, eager to participate in this highly profitable new business sector. But the business also inspired a number of financial entrepreneurs who saw bright possibilities in carving out different niches for themselves, niches that they could occupy before the big battalions did. Indeed these niches created a new form of arranger in the mergers-and-acquisitions process, the takeover and LBO money manager.

The Buyout Kings

LBOs were originally called bootstrap acquisitions and are thought to have been pioneered in the 1960s by Jerome Kohlberg, Jr., then at Bear Stearns. The essential bootstrap deal was one in which the owner of a privately held business, who wanted to sell out but couldn't find a cash buyer, would contract with some smart Wall Street guys instead. The owner could sell most of his business and take the cash out. But he would still keep his job and a small continuing interest in the company. Leverage could make that interest a lot more valuable. The owner and the Wall Street guys would put their heads together and come up with a way to maximize the cash flow generated by the business. Then they would go to a bank and borrow as much as the bank would lend against the cash flow. The amount of the bank loan, and a bit more to reflect a small amount of equity that the Wall Street guys would put up, would become the purchase price. The deals worked well because the banks were fairly cautious about how much they would lend, while the owners were friendly to the deal and wanted to do all they could to increase the cash flow. The businesses themselves were not seasonal or subject to sharp cyclical fluctuations, in fact stable if mundane businesses were preferred. Kohlberg figured out some important refinements—management could be given incentives to stay involved with the business until the debt was paid off, and a *mezzanine* level of subordinated financing was created for higher risk finance companies which were looking for higher returns. Mezzanine financing was so named because it fit in between the first floor of senior bank debt, and the bottom floor, the equity.

Kohlberg's ideas paid off and Bear Stearns' deal flow increased considerably. In the 1970s Kohlberg recruited Henry Kravis and George Roberts, two first cousins who were young associates with the firm, and in 1976 the three left to form their own firm, Kohlberg Kravis & Roberts, with capital of $120,000. In April 1977, using mostly borrowed money, KKR bought a maker of small truck suspensions, A. J. Industries, for $25.6 million. Eight years later they sold the company for $75 million. KKR was now in the investment business, not the investment banking business. They were no longer in the business of providing financial services to clients but of managing a portfolio of investments for them. They were now money managers operating in a new high-risk, high-return sector of the market that operated like a hedge fund. The managers would be paid not only a generous management fee of 1.5 percent but also approximately 20 percent of the overall profits made by the investors. They also charged investment banking fees for deals done for the companies their investors owned, and, as general partners, they owned 1 percent or so of the equity invested in each of the deals.

In 1978 KKR went to the market to get more money to manage and offered its first $30 million LBO fund to institutional investors seeking alternative, off-market investments. The offering papers suggested returns in the 30 percent to 40 percent area. Selling the funds was Henry Kravis's job, and he developed a number of loyal supporters, especially in the Northwest, where the state pension funds of Washington and Oregon were early investors. In

1979 the firm surprised Wall Street with a $355 million buyout of Houdaille Industries, the largest LBO deal ever and the first of a publicly traded company. LBOs would not be just for little people anymore. In 1984 KKR sold its fourth LBO fund, this one for $1 billion. Assuming that LBOs could be done with equity constituting only about 10 percent of the cost of the acquisition, this meant that KKR had acquired purchasing power in the market of more than $14 billion. This made KKR the big gorilla of the LBO business, which was proving to be highly lucrative.

KKR's total return on its 1984 acquisition of Amstar, a sugar refiner, shows how it worked. The acquisition price was $465 million, of which only $52 million was to be in equity—of this only $830,000 (1.6 percent of the equity) was put up by KKR itself. The rest of the equity was provided by the KKR funds. Three years later Amstar was sold to a Merrill Lynch LBO partnership for a profit of $232 million, a compounded rate of return (before KKR's 20 percent carried interest) of over 80 percent. KKR received its 20 percent override, $46 million, plus a capital gain of 1.6 percent of the profit, another $3.7 million. The investment banking fees for the acquisition were about 1 percent ($4.65 million) on the acquisition and another 1 percent on the sale ($6.97 million). Finally there was the 1.5 percent management fee for managing the $52 million of equity invested in the Amstar equity. Together these fees provided a combined return for KKR of about $62 million on an investment of less than $1 million in a three-year period. And this deal was only one-fiftieth the size of the RJR Nabisco colossus four years later.[12]

LBO's were all-cash and debt securities deals. They usually involved a premium over the last sale price of the target company, and to get the needed cooperation of management this premium had to be generous. This process presented irresistible opportunities to a number of ambitious CEOs. Many would have liked to sell their companies to KKR at a big price, then go to work for KKR as CEO of a new leveraged management team that would divide up 20 percent or 30 percent of the new stock of the company. The restructured company would be run for cash for six or seven years and its debt paid down. Then, with little debt and high earnings plus a streamlined, efficient, highly motivated management team, the company would go public again and management's stock, for which it had paid little if anything, could be valued at many millions, maybe many hundreds of millions of dollars. About 18 percent of all LBOs done in the 1983–1988 period were going-private transactions. Another 16 percent involved the restructuring of family owned companies or other privately owned corporations doing their second or third LBO. The majority of deals, however, involved the sale of divisions of companies that no longer fit into the companies' revised business strategies, such as at Gibson Greetings. But it didn't matter what the source of the deal was, the returns the LBOs were making were terrific and attracted even more money and interest to them. KKR's first four funds each produced total annualized returns of between 30 percent and 44 percent, after carry.

In 1986 the business changed again when KKR and a tough Chicago operator named Donald Kelly acquired Beatrice Foods for $6.7 billion in a deal opposed by management. The transaction was partly financed by the public sale of $2.5 billion of junk bonds, a huge offering by market practices of the times. This was the first time the explosive combination of LBOs and junk bonds had been linked. But the deal violated several of Jerry Kohlberg's basic principles of LBOs—Kohlberg insisted on friendly deals to gain the cooperation of management, which would be needed to squeeze costs out of the business to increase cash flow. This deal was hostile and resisted by management. Kohlberg did not like paying high prices for the businesses to be acquired; this one involved an exceptionally high price as a result of a competitive bid from management. Kohlberg didn't like his deals to be overleveraged; this one was. Milken's junk bond market seemed to have no limit, so they took on a huge amount of high cost long-term public debt. The debt was so extensive that the company would have to sell off parts of the core foods business to pay it down, which meant that the sponsors had to assume the additional risk that these businesses could be sold for high prices in the future. Kohlberg dreaded such deals, but he had left this one to his two partners and had to live with it.

Kohlberg, in fact, had been away dealing with a brain tumor for a year or so before the Beatrice transaction, and when he returned he found his two proteges to be fully grown into the shoes he had left behind. They were no longer happy playing second fiddle to their former mentor. They were bringing in most of the business themselves now and felt that their approach to LBOs was more in keeping with the changing times and opportunities. Access to junk bonds would make a big difference in the ways deals got done, and to get the better properties you had to go hostile every now and then. They talked about it, failed to resolve matters, and agreed to separate. Kohlberg withdrew to start up a new firm of his own, Kohlberg & Co., and the partners became increasingly estranged, even bitter in their dealings with each other in subsequent years.

But Kohlberg had a point. Foregoing management participation, going hostile, paying too much to start with, and using the easily addictive junk bond market to push leverage up and over reasonable limits was not going to be good for long-term returns. The Beatrice deal came when the market was peaking and starting to become more difficult. In the end all eleven of the separate subsidiaries of Beatrice were sold off, the debt retired, and the company liquidated, with very little return going to KKR's limited partners, its investors. KKR and Drexel Burnham made their fees, but it was not a very successful LBO by the standards the market had come to expect.

But these factors didn't stop the LBO market from roaring along. From 1986 through 1988 more than 300 LBOs over $100 million in size (with a market value of $250 billion) were attempted, as compared to ninety-two deals of this size which were completed between 1980 and 1985. Now KKR was joined by numerous other firms that specialized in LBOs and by major Wall Street firms seeking to act as principles in these transactions. There seemed to be no limit to the availability of funds for deals, from either the banks or the junk bond market. The market crash of October 1987 made little difference—LBOs were considered alternative asset classes that were not dependent on stock market measures for success, though, of course, they were. No matter what happened, of course, KKR made money from its fees and profit sharing arrangements and had little of its own money at risk.

The RJR Nabisco deal was the monster deal of the era, in more ways than one. It, too, violated most of Jerry Kohlberg's principles, especially the one about paying too much. KKR's initial bid was $90 per share, in response to a $75-per-share bid from Ross Johnson, RJR Nabisco's CEO, working together with Lehman Brothers and Salomon Brothers. At somewhere around $112 per share, with both bids valued by the investment bankers at about $109 per share, the two contenders were tied and virtually exhausted. Both had proposed, as part of their financial package, some variable-rate notes. To break the tie the company's banker asked each side if it would agree to a formula for resetting the interest rates at the end of a year if the bonds were not trading then at par. This was an opened-ended commitment to increase the interest rate in the future if market conditions or other factors changed. The Johnson/Lehman/Salomon group declined to do so, but the KKR guys said okay. With that decision the KKR team won the battle for the company, and all the considerable publicity that it attracted, but it also promptly lost the war.

A year later the reset provisions came into effect, and a cash-stressed RJR Nabisco had to meet them. To do so it offered a refinancing package, in which most of the bonds would be bought out from cash supplied directly from the KKR funds, which of course significantly diluted their equity and reduced their leverage. The deal never got any better. Despite brilliant financial restructuring and debt reduction efforts on the part of management, whatever gains were made were offset by continuing losses in the increasingly intense tobacco wars. (Tobacco was not the sort of business that Jerry Kohlberg would have thought of as safe.) In the end KKR finally sold off its position and realized a return over about six to seven years of about 5 percent for investors, well below their expectations.

Actually it could have been worse, and some of KKR's LBOs, such as Seamans Furniture and Jim Walter, Inc., were. LBOs, though having the potential to create gazelle-like returns, were also very fragile creatures. The extreme leverage meant that the company could be fighting for its life just because of a few bad quarters, in which the market slumped or a mistake was made. Every entrepreneur knows that it is easy to make mistakes in business, however hard you try to avoid them. A market turn, a sudden raising of interest rates, a failure to deliver goods, a big lawsuit, things that more solidly capitalized companies can withstand, LBOs often cannot. During the 1984–1988 period, when most of the larger deals were done, those that were successful came earlier in the period (while the bull market was still going and interest rates were declining), and they were the ones that followed the Kohlberg rules to the greatest extent. Some, which got caught at the end of the period and were more aggressive in borrowing bridge financing, were disasters. The bridge deals were supposed to be taken out by the sale of junk bonds, but when the junk market collapsed in 1990, the bridge-loan providers were stuck. The value of their deals kept going down, and they couldn't get out of them.

But the basic principles of LBOs have stuck. Borrow as much debt as the cash flow can service, using riskier, subordinated mezzanine financing to supplement bank loans. Motivate management with options or other incentives to run the company flat out for cash, and only cash, for at least three or four years to repay as much of the debt as possible (at least a third of it), as quickly as possible. Sell assets not essential to the business, minimize taxes, manage working capital as aggressively as possible, rethink every little operating procedure that might increase cash flow, and think about partial refinancings along the way to ease the debt-service burden, and therefore the risks of bankruptcy. Then look for an exit opportunity.

Since the RJR Nabisco deal, KKR has maintained a much lower profile. It has worked hard to keep its funds funded and to persuade its investors that other opportunities abound. It has taken positions in financial service companies (First Interstate) that were later bought out in merger deals, has moved into other types of deals, and most recently has been building up its portfolio of leveraged deals in Europe.

Returns have recovered somewhat since the early 1990s, though many of the investments undertaken by the big LBO firms of the 1980s are no longer classic leveraged buyouts. They now represent a mix of different private equity investments, though most of their investments are still in buyouts. During the 1990s, the average large LBO fund earned 22.4 percent returns, versus 18.9 percent for the S&P 500. LBO investments, of course, are illiquid and usually require three to seven years for returns to be earned.[13] They are also risky, as they involve a great deal more financial leverage than ordinary investments. One observer of the LBO scene in the 1980s, Leon Cooperman, head of the Omega funds group (then head of research at Goldman Sachs), noted in 1987 that by leveraging purchases of the S&P 400 stocks at the same ten-to-one ratio used by LBO operators, an investor could have earned an annualized rate of return of 75 percent from June 1982 to September

1987 (from the market low to just before the crash). This was nearly 20 percent more than KKR had earned for its investors over its best ten-year period. Doing it for yourself would have meant not paying performance fees or sacrificing liquidity, but not many of Cooperman's clients undertook to do it for themselves.[14]

But the run was great while it lasted. *Forbes* listed Kravis and Roberts as princes of the LBO fund managers at about $1 billion each in 1999. The former king has done well too: Jerry Kohlberg, now seventy-three, is still in the game with his own firm, Kohlberg & Co. He registered a 1999 net worth of $850 million. And there are hundreds of others who made big money, and lesser forms of it, too, investing in, arranging, or financing LBO investments.

The Midas Touch

The markets of the 1980s gave rise to several major innovations that permanently changed the way financial markets operated, and each of these had its own special beneficiaries, especially among those who were there earliest and were the most forceful in getting the new idea to be accepted. LBOs were one of these innovations, though they had existed long before the 1980s. Mortgage backed bonds were another, and these, too, had existed in a different form before, but Louis Ranieri at Salomon Brothers put *Collateralized Mortgage Obligations* together in time for them to help bail out the S&L crisis. Another innovation, also one that was not totally new in the 1980s, was the sale of risky corporate debt securities called high yield, or junk, bonds. In the case of the other innovations, one or two names stood out as leaders of the movement, but there were many firms and individuals participating in it. In the case of junk bonds there was only one leader, while he was active, and that was Michael Milken.

Milken discovered risky bonds when he was in college at Berkeley in the sixties. When everyone else was running around smoking pot, burning bras, and shouting foul language at everyone over thirty, Milken was absorbed in a study by W. Braddock Hickman of bond performance and default rates from 1900 to 1943. Milken was struck by the fact that throughout that long period, during which two wars and a depression had occurred, the prices of lower-grade bonds reflected a lot more defaulting than actually happened. Later he found a study by T. R. Atkinson, covering bonds from 1944 to 1965, that reached the same conclusion. The bond market obviously had a risk aversion that was so significant that whenever a low-quality bond had to be valued, it was priced much lower than it should be. If this was in fact so, Milken realized, there was a fortune to be made by buying the bonds and holding them. That fortune could be enhanced, he also realized, if one were especially careful in selecting the better of the bonds from the market (where the actual default rate would be even less than for the market as a whole). Further, if Milken could convince others of the wisdom of investing in such risky securities, then the prices of the bonds he owned would rise and he could sell some of them to the new market converts at a profit. This is starting to sound pretty good, he thought, but it can be even better. What if Milken were to be the only person who knew where all these obscure bonds were, the only person who could make a market in them for all the new customers that he would create over the years? The spreads that a market-maker could get under those circumstances, all perfectly legal, could be enormous. And having developed the market to such an extent, who else could arrange for new issues of such low-grade paper? There had to be hundreds of entrepreneurial companies who would love to have access to the corporate bond market, even at high rates.

Milken went on to Wharton, where he was a straight-A student (though he did not graduate). He took his interest in low-grade bonds with him, and a professor recommended him for a job at Drexel Firestone. This was an old line investment bank, once the Philadelphia partner of J. P. Morgan, that had fallen on hard times and was being bailed out by the wealthy Firestone family. Milken was made head of fixed income research but migrated into trading. He began to look for the low-rated bonds that he had identified, most of which were *fallen angels*, once-investment-grade securities that had suffered reversals and seen their paper downgraded by the rating agencies.

In 1973 Drexel Firestone was acquired by Burnham & Co., a small, scrappy New York City brokerage firm with a great thirst for a great name. The firm was renamed Drexel Burnham, and Milken was encouraged to trade more and to develop the junk business if he could. Milken never looked back.

Milken's contribution to the world of finance was that he spent ten years developing the market for high-yield securities from no more than a trickle. And he did it not by persuading traditional and conservative insurance company bond investors to buy stuff that would horrify their trustees and regulators but by completely rethinking what a high-yield market could do for those not now in it. He began by asking what investors had problems that high-yield securities could help solve?

The 1970s were very rough years for those who depended on investment results. Mutual funds were in this category, of course, and property and casualty insurance companies, but also throughout the S&L sector there were distressed banks desperately looking for higher-yielding investments to keep them afloat. Milken located the most aggressive, entrepreneurial investors in each of these communities. He found aggressive mutual fund managers like Mass Mutual, Keystone, and Lord Abbott, and the number-one performing bond fund in the U.S., First Investor's Fund. He also found a group of financial entrepreneurs who had bought property and casualty insurance companies to finance their investment operations. These included Larry Tisch, Saul Steinberg (a 1960s raider and 1980s greenmailer), Meshulam Riklis (a flamboyant and controversial figure from the 1960s), and Fred Carr (a celebrated money manager of the 1960s who was running a small insurance company in Beverly Hills). Milken also convinced Columbia Savings and Loan Co., also of Beverly Hills, to make a significant commitment to junk bonds, one which grew to about $5 billion, or 35 percent of all the bank's assets. These were not your ordinary bond investors. They understood that junk bonds could provide equity-like returns in the form of interest payments and capital gains. But they also understood that if their portfolio mirrored the market, and the market only experienced modest default rates of 2 percent to 3 percent, then the market prices of the bonds probably reflected a substantial risk-adjusted profit for them. And when defaults did occur, some of what was defaulted on could be recovered in bankruptcy proceedings, so the actual default losses realized would be less. For example, if the risk-free interest rate (a U.S. Treasury long-term bond) was 10 percent, and the actual default loss on all similarly rated junk bonds was 2 percent, then anything offering more than 12 percent was providing a return greater than the risk inherent in the security required. So if you could get the bonds at a yield to maturity of 15 percent, then you had an annual risk-adjusted profit of 3 percent. And if you were careful to select your own portfolio from amongst companies with credit ratings in the upper half of the market, well, you might even make more.

Things of course could go wrong. Last year's default rate may not be the right one to use in making the calculation. Your ability to assess junk-grade credits may be less than it should be, and some of the companies may be in worse shape than they publicly disclose.

But the investors still liked what they heard, and before long, Milken had more money to invest than he had bonds to fill the orders. He had to find some companies that needed money badly enough to pay outrageous rates for it. These were not your ordinary New York Stock Exchange sorts of companies.

Actually, at the time when Milken was looking for more borrowers, Lehman Brothers was trying to assist some of its distressed clients (Pan American Airways, Zapata Oil, and LTV Corp.) by selling bonds with below-investment-grade ratings (the official definition of what constitutes junk). They managed to pull the deals off but ended up selling most of the bonds to Milken, who fed them to his clients. If he could sell them and the other guys couldn't, Milken wondered, shouldn't Drexel (not Lehman) be getting the mandates to do these deals? Milken began to look for companies who wanted to issue junk bonds, and he soon found some. In April 1977 Drexel led its first deal, and six more followed before the end of the year. By 1978 it had led 14 junk bond issues, valued at $440 million, nearly three times its nearest competitor. In 1983 Drexel underwrote $4.3 billion of junk bonds, with an average underwriting commission of 3 percent. This was $129 million of new underwriting revenue.

By this time Milken, to whom Drexel had given a 35 percent share of the profits from junk bond trading, was already getting rich. In 1976 he and a close colleague split $5 million in earnings at a time when senior partners of the best Wall Street firms made nowhere near that amount. In 1978 he stunned his colleagues by announcing that he was moving Drexel's junk business to an unmarked office in Beverly Hills. By now Milken was already the firm's biggest producer, and no one could refuse him. He owned 6 percent of the firm, more than any other individual, but he provided most of the income. In 1982 his share of the firm's income reached $45 million; by 1983 it would total $120 million. The rest of Drexel was becoming hostage to Milken.

Soon after arriving in California, Milken began to cultivate the budding corporate raiders of the 1980s, who only needed a stake to get started. Milken offered it. He issued "highly confident" letters to them when they wanted to demonstrate that they had credible financing to support a takeover bid or greenmail operation. Milken said he was highly confident that the money could be raised, and that was enough for a market that regarded such statements as money in the bank. Later he issued the bonds needed to fund the takeovers, and before he knew it, he was the champion of the small, unknown financial entrepreneur out to make a name for himself by taking someone else over. These entrepreneurs soon became known as the predators of their age, and Milken's annual junk bond conference in Beverly Hills was known as the "Predators' Ball." This is where the issuers and the investors met, under Milken's governing eye. They met to meet each other and exchange views, but also to begin discussions of financing large, public deals with junk bonds.

One of the things they talked about was how Milken could make all this possible. He would pick the favored few that would have access to the money to finance takeovers. Without Milken these new men would be nobodies. Those who got money, of course, were grateful and willing to agree to almost any terms. Among the terms Milken insisted on was that he receive stock purchase warrants for 15 percent to 25 percent of the company to be acquired or restructured, which Milken would distribute to investors and others as he saw fit. That was a steep price to pay, some thought, for in the future the warrants could become extremely valuable. Few of the entrepreneurs would be able to hold on to as much as 15 percent to 25 percent of these companies themselves, after sharing with their partners and covering financing costs. But they had no choice because Milken could deny them the funding they needed to go for the really big deals. Milken, however, kept most of the warrants for himself and a few chosen colleagues. The warrants were highly volatile, and some would never be worth anything. But they were, after all, a form of double leverage—an option on the equity of a company already financed 90 percent with debt—and could be enormously valuable when the deals were successful.

In the Beatrice deal with KKR, Drexel agreed to underwrite $2.5 billion of junk bonds to provide the mezzanine financing for the deal, without which the KKR group would not have been able to meet the selling price required by the Beatrice board. Milken insisted on being allowed to buy warrants for 24 percent of the company, with an exercise price of $5 per share. Milken's price was twenty-five cents per share. Two years after the deal, an SEC filing revealed that Drexel still held warrants for 22.5 percent of the company—they had not been given to investors, nor were they owned by Drexel; they had been placed in a special account for Milken and some of his close associates. Beatrice stock was then estimated to be worth $26 per share, valuing the warrant position at about $650 million. Not all the large takeover and LBO deals of the 1980s would work out so well, but Milken financed most of them and took warrants in virtually all of those he financed. No one complained.

In 1985 Milken's earnings from Drexel were $135 million; in 1986 $295 million, and in 1987 an incredible $550 million. These amounts probably do not include many of his secretive warrant deals or income from other investments. Milken was earning more than the entire firm and certainly more than any other person on Wall Street. He completely dominated, Rockefellerlike, his sector of the financial services industry.

But it was not to last. A chance event set off a chain of other events that resulted in charges being brought against Denis Levine, Ivan Boesky, Martin Siegel, and Robert Freeman that ultimately resulted in Drexel's bankruptcy (after being fined $650 million for criminal violations of securities laws). In March 1989 Milken was indicted on ninety-eight felony counts of violations of securities and mail-fraud laws, engaging in insider trading, racketeering, and making false statements to the government. Milken, then forty-two, put up a ferocious defense that he maintained for several years.

The economic value of the transactions in question was surprisingly low—Milken's great fortune did not come from these transactions. Almost all of what he made was earned honestly, but in order to preserve his dominance of the market, or to answer other demons haunting him, Milken engaged in practices that he later admitted were illegal. In the end he was forced to pay fines, penalties, and expenses of $1.1 billion in connection with the charges. He was sentenced to ten years in jail but served less than two years before being released in 1993.

After Milken's indictment the junk bond market went into a nosedive, with new-issue volume dropping nearly to zero and secondary market prices crashing. It took a few years for the market to come back. By then junk had become more respectable as an alternative asset class, and most well-regarded firms on Wall Street were dealing in it. By 1995 the new-issue volume had shattered old records, Record levels of mergers and acquisitions were again announced, but this was a different era, and junk bonds were rarely used for such deals. This, in the mid-1990s, was the age of the growth stock and the strategic investment, in which companies did their deals for stock, and large LBOs of public companies were a forgotten species. Still, lots of people manned the junk bond desks of trading firms, many making a very respectable income. But the "good old days," just a few years back, when one man dominated the entire market and could completely command his terms, had passed into history. Milken, however, together with his brother and former colleague Lowell, after all their fines, penalties, and legal expenses, and the Milken family's many large contributions to charities, were still listed in 1999 as being worth about $1 billion.

THE BRICKS-AND-MORTAR GANG

The 1999 *Forbes* list of the four hundred richest Americans contains thirty-one individuals who list their source of wealth as being from real estate. Fortunes in real estate have come from office buildings, homes and apartments, hotels and casinos, shopping centers and malls, country clubs, storage systems, golf courses, and land development. Most of the real estate rich are self-employed entrepreneurs and, like Donald Bren of Newport Beach, California, one of the richest of the group ($3.2 billion), are not well known outside their own business communities. There are thirteen billionaires among the twenty-seven in the group, including Eli Broad, sixty-five, who made his fortune in building homes for baby boomers (Kaufman & Broad), then later sold the business and bought SunAmerica, an insurance company specializing in annuities. In 1998 he merged this business in a $15 billion transaction with American International Group. In 1999 Broad was worth $4 billion.

Among the other real estate billionaires was Sam Zell from Chicago, who built his fortune from mobile home parks, real estate vulture funds, and publicly owned real estate investment trusts. Zell was estimated to be worth

$1.8 billion in 1999. Another was Robert Henry Dedman from Dallas, the nation's country club king ($1.2 billion). Two others were from California—John Arrigalla and John Sobrato, with aggregate worth of $2.3 billion—and four were from New York with combined wealth of $7.2 billion.

Among the New Yorkers were Leona Helmsley, who was seventy-eight in 1998 when she inherited $1.8 billion from her husband, Harry. Leona, once featured in advertisements as the "queen" of the Helmsley Palace Hotel, which she ran with an iron fist, was jailed for eighteen months for tax evasion. Her personal behavior ("she has the mouth of a stevedore and the compassion of a cluster bomb") associated with the trial and events leading up to it, caused the New York papers to label her the Queen of Mean.[15] There were also legendary apartment builder Sam LeFrak, eighty, and Leonard Stern, sixty, who developed the New Jersey Meadowlands from cash thrown off by his Hartz Mountain pet supply company. There were also Mortimer Zuckerman, sixty, who had diversified into the media world, and Donald J. Trump, fifty-two, the real estate industry's most flamboyant and notorious character.

The Art of the Deal, the Comeback, and More

Few Americans are indifferent to Donald Trump (whose New York nickname is "The Donald"). To many Trump is as much the poster child of greed in the 1990s as Michael Milken ever was. Unlike Milken, however, Trump (author of three different autobiographies so far) flaunts absolutely everything about himself in the most public ways imaginable. He has outdone even Ted Turner as big mouth and champion of the outrageous. He is the reigning rogue of the (never shy) bricks-and-mortar crowd. To others, his many admirers, he is a symbol of how a guy with chutzpah and big balls can get ahead in the world, overcoming all the obstacles the already established people constantly put in his way. He is obnoxious but effective. New Yorkers either love him or hate him, and that seems to be just fine with him.

Born into a wealthy real estate family in Queens, Trump was able to parlay a modest inheritance into a great fortune by the time he was forty. Building on his father's political contacts, Trump ventured into property development in Manhattan, believing that the sun would never set on rising real estate prices. He bought office buildings, apartments, and New York's landmark Plaza Hotel. He ventured into a shuttle airline and into Atlantic City casinos, and named many of his projects after himself. He bought a huge yacht and the elegant 118-room Palm Beach estate of Marjorie Merriweather Post, one of America's richest women in the 1920s, and turned it into an exclusive country club with a $100,000 member initiation fee, then tried to get the City of Palm Beach to move its airport because the noise bothered the members.

Trump, however, was typical of many of the real estate tycoons of the 1980s and 1990s. He was an extremely confident, fully-leveraged high roller, and when prices collapsed in the early 1990s, he nearly went under. Two of the giants of North American real estate, the Reichmann Brothers and Robert Campeau, both lost most of their money in the sharp downturn that occurred then. In the black days of 1991, Trump is said to have remarked, when seeing a panhandler on the street, "That bum isn't worth a dime, but at least he's at zero. That puts him $900 million ahead of me." Trump had personally guaranteed $960 million of bank loans to support his aggressive expansions in Manhattan and Atlantic City, and default could mean losing it all.

But The Donald pulled it off. He fobbed off the yacht, his shuttle airline, the Plaza, and the Grand Hyatt, and decided to work for the banks for a while rather than declare bankruptcy. He worked out deals to exchange real estate holdings and cash for the bankers releasing their liens on the casinos, which he believed were the key to his recovery. After all, the casinos there were a powerful draw for gamblers, and Atlantic City is only an afternoon's drive away for 100 million people. After the State of New Jersey allowed twenty-four-hour daily operations of the casinos in 1993, Atlantic City surpassed Las Vegas in total revenues collected. Trump persuaded everyone that his bankruptcy would not be good for business, and little by little things began to recover, allowing him to repay the banks and recoup completely his ownership of the golden-egg-laying geese. In 1995 he decided to take the hotels and casinos public, raising $300 million in cash and selling $1.2 billion in junk bonds, using the money to further repay bank debt. Then he used the public company to buy out another of his hotels for $485 million, including the assumption of $385 million of Trump's debt and the payment of a dividend to Trump of $130 million. He was "baaaack."[16]

The Donald is now into beauty pageants, condos, and the world's biggest ship-casino. He is exploring gambling-deal possibilities with his counterparts in Moscow, which is his kind of town. In 1999 he passed up an opportunity to run for president of the United States on the Reform Party ticket, after giving it serious consideration. Deals go on, and the comeback artist is back on the *Forbes* list, though Trump has complained that his true net worth is much greater than the $1.6 billion reported by *Forbes* in 1999.[17]

Real estate operators seem often to be on the edge of bankruptcy. They have to arrange financing for their projects (office or apartment buildings, shopping centers, hotels) long before they are completed and can begin to attract business at going rates. Long-term forecasts, crucial to understanding the essential economics of the projects, are often unreliable. And even when all is going well, things can change quickly. A sharp increase in interest rates brings down the value of the property, which is determined by capitalizing the current rental and revenue streams by an appropriate interest rate. If the economy turns into recession, or if a competitor builds next door, vacancies can occur. Lenders rely on the resale value of the buildings as collateral, but that, too, can change quickly.

Those who succeed in this tricky business certainly have to be willing to take the risks. The real payoff comes from using the leverage potential that is inherent in any real estate deal. If you can borrow 75 percent of the cost of a building, bring the project in on cost, and rent it out so that the capitalized rentals are worth 150 percent of your investment in three years, you will have made a three-fold return before interest and other costs. The ones who succeed in this business over the years are the ones who know the true value of the properties better than others do. These people can buy good properties cheaply when the properties are distressed (as good properties often are). They also know how to create value by changing the purpose or use of a building (making a hotel into a hotel/casino), or they know how to finance it more cheaply (by using low-cost funds from publicly sold real estate investment trusts). Real estate development is a business filled with special techniques and dangers not dissimilar to the LBO and junk bond businesses. Over the years, since the time of John Jacob Astor, it has been the source of many great American fortunes.

CHAPTER 3

The Investors

On December 31, 1999, the market capitalization of all publicly traded common stocks in the United States was $16.7 trillion, up from $1.3 trillion in 1981. The gain over that period, $15.4 trillion, reflects an eighteen-year compounded annual growth of 15 percent in the value of stocks. This is twice the nominal (i.e., not adjusted for inflation) rate of growth of the U.S. GDP of 7 percent, indicating the extent to which this nearly fourteen-fold increase in stock market capitalization has created wealth in excess of underlying economic growth.[1] You know you are in a serious bull market when financial wealth is being created twice as fast as the growth rate of the whole economy.

Peter Lynch, the famous former manager of the Magellan Fund at Fidelity, frequently reminds us in his television ads for the mutual funds group that "earnings drive the stock market." Well, they do, but not all the way. Corporate earnings (measured by analysts' forward-looking estimates), in fact, have increased only about three-fold since

1981. Interest rate changes are also important. The future earnings of companies are capitalized by the stock market at rates which are determined in part by government interest rates; the lower the rates, the better the stock prices. This has been very good for our market because interest rates have gone down significantly since December 1981, when two-year government bonds traded at a yield to maturity of 14.5 percent. On December 31, 1998, two-year treasuries traded at a yield to maturity of 5.1 percent. (A year later interest rates rose and the two-year treasuries traded at 6.3 percent.) The overall decline in rates was almost two-thirds by the end of 1998 and almost 60 percent by the end of 1999.

The increased earnings, together with the lower interest rates, should explain all, or most all, of the large increase in stock market values during the eighteen-year period. But they don't quite. According to a July 1998 study by financial market historian Barrie A. Wigmore, these two variables only explained 70 percent to 80 percent of the growth in the S&P 500 index between 1981 and 1998. Wigmore attributes the leftover 20 percent to 30 percent of market value increase to "overvaluation." However, by this he meant to include all the many other things that can affect the market but had not been directly measured in the study—such things as the dramatic decline in inflation and generally strong performance across all sectors in the economy as a whole, structural imbalances in the supply and demand for equities that can affect pricing, and changing attitudes and behavior on the part of investors. The overvaluation might be explained, for example, by a reduction in the amount of risk that equity market investors perceived when they bought stocks. Current investors in stocks seemed to treat the market as being less risky than in earlier periods, and therefore they paid higher prices and bought more. This change in attitude toward risk (academics call it the risk premium) may be reflected in the considerably lowered difference in volatility (a standard measure of risk) between debt and equity securities.[2] The Wigmore study was very catholic—if price increases were not directly tied to earnings or interest rate improvements, they were not explained and were thus assigned to over-valuation. Wigmore also concluded that the party was nearly over because as much as 60 percent of the stock market's gains to date, he claimed, were the result of one-time events (tax cuts, corporate mergers and restructuring, low inflation, etc.) that probably would not be repeated in the future. This study, and a variety of others like it, clearly left you with the impression that the market had leapt into unreality and that a strong correction was due.

Indeed a sharp correction in stock prices did occur in the summer and fall of 1998, right after Wigmore's paper was finished. The market shuddered with concerns about future corporate earnings and worrying conditions in Russia, Japan, and Brazil. Stock market indices dropped almost 20 percent but recovered by year's end to mid-year levels, at which the S&P 500 was presumably overvalued again, but somewhat less so because, in the meantime, more earnings had been realized and interest rates had dropped a bit more.

But even if stocks were still overvalued at the end of 1998, and due for a further correction, they didn't get much of one in 1999, a year in which the S&P 500 increased by

21 percent, while the yields on two-year treasuries actually increased. In the first quarter of 2000 some further correcting took place, but it was still clear that an extraordinary amount of personal wealth had been created (and sustained) by rising stock prices during the previous two decades. Of the $16.7 trillion of market value in American stocks at year's end 1999, nearly $10 trillion, or 60 percent, was owned by American individuals and their families in the form of direct investments in stocks and mutual funds. Additional equities were held by their pension funds and as reserves to support their life insurance policies. In addition to benefiting individuals, the rising markets also benefited nonprofit institutions such as colleges and other charitable endowments, and enabled a greater flow of appreciated securities as gifts to charities.

With the rising market came also many stories about the new alchemists of the times. These were the new masters of the financial marketplace who excelled at managing investments, at creating and distributing mutual fund companies, and at bringing all the parts and pieces of the financial world together for their own benefit, and for others, less skilled, to invest alongside of.

THE SAGE OF OMAHA

Warren Buffett was the first self-made Richest Man in America (1994) to get there just by investing in stocks, which anybody can do. The others all had to make or sell something, developing an important business from scratch. Buffett, who was listed on the *Forbes* 1999 list at $36 billion, hasn't exactly done that. He started out with a nearly defunct textile company, Berkshire Hathaway, which he bought in 1965. Two years later he merged the company with two Omaha-based insurance companies to gain leverage and the use of the float, and invested most of the money in a few good stocks that he intended to hold for a long time.

On December 31, 1998, the Class A stock of Berkshire Hathaway closed at $71,500 per share (Buffett doesn't like splits but he did create a Class B stock that trades at one-thirtieth of the Class A). The company's market capitalization was $106 billion, more than that of all but a handful of large American companies. It ranked sixty-fourth in operating revenue among *Fortune*'s top 500 American companies. Berkshire Hathaway employed 45,000 people and was named by *Fortune* as one of the ten most admired companies in the U.S. and the world. Its estimated cash operating earnings, excluding investment gains, were $2 billion, thus making the company's forward looking P/E ratio a robust fifty-three. Dividends were nil; Buffett doesn't believe in paying dividends. But cash earnings and dividends were not what mattered to his investors, even though earnings per share had compounded at 27.2 percent for the past thirty years. Stock price returns were what they cared about and had received in abundance.

Through 1998 the stock performance of Berkshire Hathaway was extraordinary. It underperformed the S&P 500 in only four of the thirty-three years from 1965 through 1998. A $10,000 investment in Berkshire stock in 1965 would have been worth $51 million in December 1998, as compared to $132,990 for an investment in the S&P index. Most investors associate Berkshire Hathaway's success to the long-term investment philosophy, stock-picking ability, and general market savvy of Warren Buffett, the company's founder, CEO, and all-around lifetime stock market genius. Indeed Buffett's investors seemed not to care what he did; they were in the stock because they believed that whatever he did would be good for the stock. They invested to get a piece of him, and according to *Grant's Review* and *Barron's*, they paid a premium to do so (over the market value of all of the company's holdings) of about 7 percent during 1998. Those who considered Berkshire's eclectic collection of investments (insurance, large holdings of large capitalization companies, and a diverse group of smaller, sometimes quirky, privately held businesses) a conglomerate, or closed-end investment company, know that very few such companies ever trade at a premium. Most (including Larry Tisch's Loews Corp., see Chapter 2) trade at significant discounts to the sum of the market values of all of their separate holdings.

In December 1997 *Money* magazine published a comparison between the investment records of Buffett and Larry Tisch. Loews traded at a low of $0.75 and a high of $115.50 in the 1971–1997 period, after which Larry began his expensive bear market hedging strategies (which drove the stock below $60 by year-end 1999). Tisch had put together a 154-fold increase over twenty-six years. But the market value of Loews Corp., *Money* estimated, was 22 percent less than the market value of its various parts. If Loews had traded at Buffett's premium over its net asset value, instead of at a discount, the compounded growth rate of Tisch's funds would have been 23 percent, good, but still not quite enough to close the gap with Buffett.

In October 1997 *Grant's Interest Rate Observer* estimated that 57 percent of Berkshire Hathaway's market value was represented by seven core holdings in public companies. A further 19 percent was represented by its insurance businesses, 14 percent by the privately held noninsurance businesses that Buffett loves and has collected over the years, and 10 percent by miscellaneous investments in other public companies.[3] This has been the unique Buffett template for nearly twenty years. He has bet his ranch on a small number of large consumer-products companies with huge intrinsic value, and held the positions for substantial periods of time, making him appear to be a sensible, long-viewed, philosophic sort of investor, one most Americans can readily approve of. His privately held investments, about which he writes extensively in his colorful and informative annual reports, are simple, homey businesses that most folks can understand easily (candy makers, furniture stores, the *Buffalo News*, et al.). He believes in fully informing stockholders about the company's activities but rarely mentions his active role as a stock trader, arbitrageur, and commodities speculator.

Beginning in 1996, however, things began to change. He acquired the portion of GEICO (an auto insurance company) that he did not already own, and began a variety of sometimes-hard-to-follow, but important, adjustments to his investment strategy. Essentially Buffett was bothered by the thought that market prices had driven too many stocks to levels that exceeded their basic long-term business value. He couldn't find much to buy in the market, so he had to start looking in other places. He took some profits in his portfolio and reinvested in commodities (huge quantities of silver, crude oil, and zero-coupon U.S. Treasury securities). He also made several acquisitions of additional private businesses, though in much larger amounts. FlightSafety International, Inc., a pilot training company, was acquired for $1.5 billion in 1996; International Dairy Queen, for $585 million in 1997; Executive Jet for $785 million in 1998; and in 2000 a 76-percent interest in Mid-American Energy Corp., a public utility, for about $2 billion.

The main move, however, came in 1998 with his $23.5 billion acquisition of General Re Corp., a very large reinsurance business, which he paid for by issuing new shares of Berkshire Hathaway stock, something he had never done before. Afterward he said, "I like the insurance business and to some extent I understand it . . . I see us making large acquisitions outside the insurance field, but insurance will be our main business." The General Re transaction would mean that on December 31, 1998, the insurance portion of the market value of the whole of Berkshire Hathaway would increase from 19 percent to 73 percent.[4] This was a very big change for the company, and it came at a time when the property- and casualty-insurance business was about to go into one of its painful, profit-squeezing cycles.

Alice Schroeder and Gregory Lapin, two insurance analysts at Paine Webber, argued in a report in January 1999 that Berkshire indeed had been transformed from an investment company into an "extremely profitable insurance business that traded at a market price well less than its long-term intrinsic value." They pointed out that of Berkshire's 1998 year-end market capitalization of $106 billion, only $29 billion was attributable to its much-discussed major equity investments and another $10–$15 billion to its low-visibility portfolio of private businesses. So that left about $65 billion as the derived market valuation of Berkshire Hathaway's major business, its insurance operations. Then you look at Berkshire's combined book value— $59.2 billion on December 31, 1998—and subtract the book value (cost) of the noninsurance and intangible insurance assets, and you arrive at a tangible book value of about $27 billion for the insurance business. The ratio of market value to tangible book value is commonly used in the insurance industry to compare different firms, and this ratio was then 2.4 for Berkshire Hathaway. The average ratio for the publicly traded property-casualty insurance industry in late 1998 was 2.6. At American International Group, the premier company in the industry to which Buffett's insurance operations were often compared, the market-to-book ratio is 3.9. Thus, the analysts said, there should be some potential, when the insurance part of the Berkshire stock is better understood, for a big rise in its price. At 3.0 times tangible book value, Berkshire Hathaway stock would be worth $95,000 per share. It was then trading at $72,000. However, by the end of 1999, Buffett's first full year as primarily an insurance executive, the Berkshire Hathaway stock was trading at $57,000 per share. The year had been Buffett's worst ever, his stock was down 21 percent in a year in which the S&P index was up 21 percent. Buffett, however, commented in his annual report of 1999 that the year had been his worst because the company's *book value* had hardly increased at all, which was well below its average annual increase during his tenure of 24 percent. Not everyone agrees that book value is what really counts, but even so, going back over the past twenty years, only a handful of investment managers could claim to have done better for their shareholders, and none did better for himself than Buffett, whose own money has been fully tied up in the business from the beginning.

The Legend and the Method

What amazes many on Wall Street is how easy Buffett and his longtime partner Charlie Munger made it all look. They have no complex holding company structure, no pyramiding or financing from junk bonds, no brilliant trading strategies involving global markets, derivatives, or foreign exchange. They don't do takeovers or LBOs, nor do they invest in start-ups, complicated technology, or unseemly or controversial industries like gambling, tobacco, or alcohol. They don't get ahead by obfuscation, bamboozlement, or too-cute deals. They are not confrontational. They don't have a fancy office or a large staff. They just buy into a few good businesses and hold on to them. Indeed most of their investment success has come from a carefully chosen cadre of (noninsurance) core stocks, including Coca-Cola (through 1998 the star performer of the portfolio, first acquired in 1988), American Express, Freddy-Mac (the Federal Home Loan Mortgage Asso.), Wells Fargo & Co., Gillette, and the *Washington Post*. These core stocks represented about $30 billion of market value at the end of 1999, about 80 percent of all noninsurance equities by market value held, as in most years. These core holdings also used to include GEICO insurance, one that Buffett had owned and increased since his earliest days as an investor. But he became so infatuated with the business, in 1996 he acquired for $2.3 billion the 49 percent of the shares he did not already own, starting his major transformation into insurance as the new core.

Buffett, the son of a right-wing Nebraska congressman, has been fascinated by investments from the beginning. A certifiable financial prodigy, he bought his first stock at age eleven, and hoarded paper-route earnings to buy more. In 1950 he enrolled in Columbia's school of business just, he says, to study under investment guru Benjamin Graham, the much revered father of value investing and coauthor, with David Dodd, of the classic *Securities Analysis*. Graham believed that if you studied companies hard enough you would inevitably uncover some that traded at prices that were very low priced relative to their future business worth, or intrinsic value. He liked to pour over the S&P guide looking for companies trading for less than the value of their cash in the bank, which certainly you could do when Graham published the book in 1934. Graham had never had a disciple like Buffett, and he took him under his wing. Buffett, too, became a compulsive reader of annual reports and seemed to retain everything he ever learned. He, too, went out in search of undervalued companies to invest his small amount of capital in. He worked briefly as a broker in Omaha, then for a while for Graham's investment company, but he was soon out on his own.

As an independent investor in the 1960s, Buffett did well, forming an investment partnership which specialized in small companies with Grahamlike characteristics. During this period he discovered Berkshire Hathaway, a struggling New Bedford, Massachusetts, maker of linings for men's suits, which had not made a profit for ten years (and thus had significant tax-loss carry-forwards). He invested in the company, later taking control and installing another manager. Buffett was following the moves of

Royal Little, founder of Textron, who had forged a successful conglomerate out of a similar old textile company. Most of the assets were sold off, and the company was managed on its cash flow and tax credits until the business could be converted into a financial holding company. Buffett thus engineered Berkshire's conversion from textiles to investments, and then sweetened the mix by acquiring insurance companies.

Insurance offered Buffett the opportunity to leverage his capital substantially. He could invest the money that the insurance company held on behalf of its claimants, its ultimate liability for all the insurance policies on its books. This includes the assets set aside for insurance claims and the annual cash flow from new policy sales. Insurance people call this amount the float. It is a large sum, and if you can acquire the use of it inexpensively and reinvest it profitably, you have made money on the money. And the larger the float, the larger the profit. But this all depends on your being able to obtain the use of the float cheaply (writing insurance policies that do not involve high underwriting losses) and investing the money at a rate higher than its cost. This process is something Buffett has become especially good at, but until the acquisition of the rest of GEICO and General Re, it was not crucial to his business. Now it is, and the amount of float involved is enormous. At the end of 1999 Berkshire Hathaway's float was $25.3 billion, on which its underwriting business imposed a cost of 5.8 percent, a rate much lower than the cost of borrowing funds.[5] The Paine Webber study estimated that this amount of float would produce net income (after tax and after the cost of underwriting the insurance policies) of at least $1 billion a year. Using conservative assumptions about Buffett's investment returns, the study predicted Berkshire's float will have grown to nearly $53 billion by 2008, and the after-tax income on it will have increased to $2.4 billion. In Buffett's hands insurance float can be a gold mine.

Other financial entrepreneurs, such as Harold Geneen (ITT), James Ling (LTV), Saul Steinberg (Reliance), and Larry Tisch, also bought insurance companies in the 1960s to leverage their investment results. Most of these investors used their insurance arm as a way of magnifying their power in the takeover market. Buffett, however, was content to just wait for good companies managed by other people to come along, and then to invest as much of his float as he could in them. He made a few bad stock selections and other mistakes in his career, but these never included buying control of a large company at a big premium price.[6]

Buffett eschewed such acquisitions, which he would have had to justify by managing the company better or more strategically, because he did not believe that many of them worked. Buffett believed most large-acquisition deals squandered stockholders' capital unnecessarily. He believed in buying companies cheaply, not dearly, which he believed almost always happened in acquisitions. He was, after all, a bona fide Graham-and-Dodd value investor. And value investors don't pay too much in acquisitions.

The merger boom of the 1960s and the high market prices at the end of the decade worried Buffett. He didn't understand that market, he said, so he got out of it. He liquidated the partnership, taking most of his own capital in Berkshire Hathaway shares, which was to be retained.

It was a publicly traded company then as now, but Buffett turned it into his personal investment vehicle. After the market break in the early 1970s, Buffett was back in the market buying up cheap stocks. He kept doing so until 1987, when he sold everything but the core stocks and the private businesses before the market crash in October. After that he came back in again in a fury, picking up his initial position in Coca-Cola. Much of his success has come since the crash—his annual investment returns have beaten the S&P 500 in every year since then, by an average of nearly 10 percent, and his investors have been made very happy. Until 1999 when, again confronted by a market he didn't understand, he headed off in a different direction.

Despite being so rich, Buffett has great press. If ever there was an American Capitalist Hero from among stock market investors, it is he. There have been other famous investment men, such as Bernard Baruch, J. P. Morgan, Jay Gould, Edward Harriman, Joe Kennedy, and Larry Tisch, but none of these ever made it with the public. There was also Fidelity's Peter Lynch, who managed the imminently successful Magellan Fund from 1977 through 1990. He is very popular but much less well known. Besides, he worked for somebody else, never amassed the fortune that Buffett did, and retired early. There was not much heroism in this. Buffett's long success with the press is partly because of his cultivated nerdlike ways; he seems to be a simple, plainspoken, unpresumptuous man from Omaha who still is married to the same woman and lives in his first house. He votes Democratic, drinks Cherry Cokes, does his owns taxes, is genuinely nice to everybody, and has stood by his basic investment principles since he was in his twenties. He stands for "clean" investing, uncorrupted by the sleazy Wall Street crowd. Indeed Buffett became the embodiment of the stock market's most positive public image. He made money doing what anyone could do, studying the market and picking stocks. He is also seen as self-effacing, moral, and responsible. When Salomon Brothers got into trouble for falsifying its bids in government bond auctions while he was its largest stockholder, he did the right thing. He became chairman, took responsibility for the firm's actions, fired those involved, apologized, and helped the firm work its way out of its problems. Mainly because of Buffett, the government decided not to indict Salomon for its actions, which probably would have finished the firm off then and there.

Widely known as The Oracle of Omaha, he exudes financial wisdom and common sense. Many people buy a single share of Berkshire stock just to get the annual report, a priceless document full of business philosophy, humor, and clear and simple explanations of just about anything that happens to interest Buffett at the time. His image enhances his record, his style, and apparently his ability to attract investors.

Naturally such elegant images are meant to pretty up the real thing. Even Buffett is not quite what he is made out to be, though he is close. True, he works on the image—and seems to have a gift for projecting it. He is extremely articulate and careful and has made very few public relations mistakes. Nonetheless, this simple Nebraskan has a global, jet set side to him. He flies around in his own plane to meetings with the richest, most powerful, and most fa-

mous people in the land. He likes showy media and political people as much as he is supposed to like the simple
folks back home. He does a lot of public speaking and TV
interviews. Still he can be dreadfully dull, even by Mid-
western standards—his idea of a good time is to read annual reports all night. He is amicably separated (but not
divorced) from his free-spirited wife of many years, Susan,
who has become a late-in-life nightclub singer. Thanks to
him, she has her own little nest egg of about $2.5 billion.
He has a mistress, however, a former waitress in an Omaha
cafe that his wife thoughtfully arranged for him. Buffett is
also cheap. He has given very little money to his children,
whom he tells not to expect anything much in his will as
he has left almost all of his fortune to the Buffett Foundation, which currently doesn't have much in it. He figures
there will be problems in the world when he has left it,
and his successors can figure out what to do with the
money. In the meantime his contribution to mankind is to
do what he does best, i.e., to make more money for the
foundation to have in the future. He has these kinds of
faults, but still it is almost impossible to find someone
who really dislikes the man or thinks he is phony.

Buffett's business dealings can sometimes be puzzling,
though, given his strong positions against in-and-out trading and raiderlike takeover activities. Over the years,
Berkshire Hathaway has made a lot of money doing
merger arbitrage and investing in junk bonds—just a side-
line for the excess cash, no doubt, but he did make over
$600 million on a couple of takeovers and $200 million
more from RJR Nabisco junk bonds. He apparently spec-
ulated Soroslike with a $4.6 billion bet on zero-coupon
treasuries, from which he made several hundred millions.

Another bet of $1 billion on the future price of silver appeared to backfire, recalling the disastrous efforts by the Hunt Brothers to corner the silver market in 1980. And for a guy who painstakingly avoids industries he doesn't understand, what was he doing in crude oil and public utilities? He claims that good companies should be held forever, but he has sold more stocks than he has held over the years and was quick to advise Cap Cities to sell out to Disney. He has long criticized expensive mergers, especially hostile ones, and for years was said to have prevented the *Washington Post* from succumbing to merger fever. But as the largest shareholder of Wells Fargo, he was deeply involved in its decision to make an unfriendly, overpriced bid for First Interstate Bank at 3.1 times book value. He was similarly involved in Gillette's $7 billion acquisition of Duracell. The Wells Fargo deal, especially, was not a success for its shareholders, and within two years it resulted in a forced change of management and the sale of the bank to Norwest. The jury is still out on General Re, for which Buffett paid a full price and about which he said, "The deal's main attraction is 'synergy,' a word that has never been used in listing the reasons for a Berkshire acquisition."[7]

Buffett claims that the only way to pick good stocks is through careful analysis, but he promises answers to offers of companies for Berkshire to buy "in five minutes." Some of the analysis seems shallow, and sometimes there seems to be no analysis at all, as in the case of his investment in Salomon Brothers to support his good friend John Gutfreund. There seems to be no explanation for a disastrous investment in US Air, which he admitted was a big mistake. Perhaps he is more intuitive, and less theoretical, than he lets on. Perhaps he is just more human than we allow for.

Graham and Dodd Revisited

When Buffett studied under Graham, the stock market was made up of households, a few investing institutions and a handful of "gamblers," such as mutual funds. Individual investors owned 85 percent or so of all stocks listed on the New York Stock Exchange. There was very little in the way of stock market research in circulation. Graham's contribution to investment theory was that by good analysis of publicly available data, backed up by resourceful detective work, an investor could assess the intrinsic value of a company. By comparing this to the traded market price, the investor could encounter bargains of potentially high value, if held over the long term, that is, long enough for the intrinsic value to be appreciated by the market. Of course in the thirties you didn't need Graham to tell you there were bargains around, and even superficial research might have revealed a lot of great investments. Nevertheless Graham's work developed an analytical methodology, which when thoroughly applied by open-minded, industrious, and smart people, could produce investment success. By diligently applying the methodology for many years, Buffett became perhaps the world's most proficient expert in the mathematics and microeconomics of corporate finance.

Nor was he stuck on Graham's techniques, which were quantitative and tangible. Buffett pushed the envelope to embrace at least some intangibles, such as the enduring value of a trade name or business franchise, market share leadership, and even the special qualities of business leadership found in rare individuals. As prices rose, Graham's ideas on their own would have faded into irrelevance— Buffett renewed their license, but, of course, the intangibles were not always easy to evaluate. That took faith.

During the late 1990s Graham and Dodd were out of style, much to Buffett's displeasure. The field of corporate finance has developed additional techniques to help determine intrinsic values, and valuation methodologies have changed to focus more on discounted cash flow and future expected growth rates. But most important, investment management has shifted its basic thinking. It now follows the Efficient Market Theory, which was developed during the 1950s and 1960s and claims that in an efficient market, all information that might affect a stock's price already has, so predicting a future price by analysis of what is already known is impossible. The markets have become efficient, the adherents claim, because of the huge increase in volume of traded stocks, which created an environment of constant trading and price setting, much like the foreign exchange markets or the markets for U.S. government securities. Because of this, analysis of stocks according to the methods of Graham and Dodd would produce no better results than random selection, or by throwing darts at the stock pages in the newspaper. Over time great investment managers would simply be luckier than those to whom they were compared. As no one could tell who would be luckier than others, sensible investors were better off with a well diversified portfolio that would balance out the risks.

The Efficient Market Theory produced offspring called the Capital Asset Pricing Model and the Modern Portfolio

Theory. These first determined that what produced value for an investment portfolio as a whole was how individual stocks performed relative to the market. Though we could not predict the future based on present prices, we could determine how volatile individual stocks were, relative to the market, and, holding that volatility constant for a while, estimate the value to the portfolio as a whole of having stocks with such volatility characteristics in it. Volatility of 1.0 meant the stock's price rose and fell exactly as did the whole market; a volatility of 2.0 meant a sensitivity twice that of the market. By assembling a large portfolio of many stocks, the investor could diversify away the risk of anything special happening to any single stock, so what the companies that one invested in actually did didn't matter. The only thing that did matter was how volatile they were. Therefore if you knew the volatility of a stock, and other data such as interest rates and dividends, you could predict the price that the stock should trade at. Because you could weigh out the volatility of the whole portfolio and see if it was likely to outperform the market or not, managers began to manage their funds differently. They searched for stocks with higher or lower volatility, which they called beta, after the Greek letter used to represent volatility in the equation for pricing capital assets. The basic idea was that you had to have higher volatility than the market to beat it, but you could also justify market-returns if your volatility was lower than the market's. This was the stuff of Nobel prizes—something poor old Graham never was able to collect for his efforts.

Individual stock analysis didn't matter? He was just lucky, after all, not a genius? These were certainly not welcome thoughts to Buffett, who once asked an academic who was explaining the new theories, "Well, if you're so smart, how come I'm so rich?" If all this volatility theory has really replaced Graham and Dodd, how come Buffett has been able to beat the stuffing out of the market, not just a few times but (until he became an insurance company) consistently for more than 30 years? Is he really good at this, or just a lucky survivor of a long-term investment management contest in which only the big winners advance.

Maybe the jury is still out on this question. Even academics specializing in modern portfolio theory, such as Professor Martin Gruber of NYU, believe that there is plenty of evidence to suggest that some fund managers are consistently better than others. Even while expounding efficient market theory, leading economic scholars like Nobel laureate Paul Samuelson, Arnan Alchian (a noted UCLA theorist), and *Wall Street Journal* investment columnist Roger Lowenstein were investing in Berkshire Hathaway stock. There seems to be room enough on the planet for both schools of thought, their actions suggest, even if one of them is only a hedge against the other being wrong.

Even so, one must not lose sight of the fact that Buffett's approach is *decidedly not* that of a passive investor, such as is reflected in the S&P 500 index. He is extremely active, using leverage, arbitrage, and insurance float to augment results, and eschewing many of the risk-reducing benefits of broad portfolio diversification. He picks stocks he thinks will outperform others and concentrates very heavily on them. He takes positions big enough to become very influential with management and helps shape what the companies do. He avoids trading to minimize taxes and commissions, but he dumps stocks that disappoint him.[8]

Academics have been puzzled by Buffett's record for years. They have tried to study it to determine whether the outstanding performance of the man, even after stripping away all the benefits of leverage, concentration, arbitrage, and float, is because of something permanent that others could learn. Or, they ask, does the record simply reflect an incredible talent for the business, which others cannot learn. Or, indeed, is this just a guy who had successfully flipped heads twenty-nine times out of thirty-three? And then maybe flipped out entirely by pulling out of the investment management business at its peak to concentrate on one of the toughest of all the old economy businesses, property-and-casualty insurance. Some of his critics say his reluctance to invest in technology stocks (which he says he does not understand) signals the end of his time in the limelight as an investment manager, and making up the ground he has lost may be impossible. Others, especially others of his generation, are not so sure. The man is still a genius, they say. He knows what he is doing. What happens to all these other people when the market comes to its senses? Buffett has a plan. Insurance is cheap and he's buying when no one else is. Technology is seriously overpriced, and if Buffett is not selling it, he's not buying it either. The overheated, overexcited stock market of the 1999–2000 era is not going to be followed by more of the same, a point Buffett hammered home in his 1999 annual report. It's going to be followed by something more reasonable, like the collapse of tech-stock prices and the rise of sound, well-managed companies of the sort that Graham and Dodd would have approved. Buffett, who was sixty-nine in 2000, says he plans to work for as long as he lives and to live for a long time. So he'll be around to see how it all turns out. We'll have to wait and see.

TRADERS

From its earliest days Wall Street has been peopled by traders. Traders are the ones who buy financial instruments for the purpose of selling them a short time later to capture the movement in prices. Sometimes they do it backward, selling first, then buying to cover their short position. But they are in and out of the market almost every day, living on the market's momentum, their hunches, and their reputations, which determine their ability to get financing for their trades. Jesse Livermore was a famous trader in the early part of the twentieth century. Bernard Baruch was another one.[9] They were called speculators. Livermore traded in anything that caught his fancy, making and losing several fortunes during his career. Baruch made a million when he was in his twenties, buying and selling railroad securities. In the 1920s there were a variety of traders, including Joe Kennedy and Ben ("Sell 'em Ben") Smith, who operated bull and bear pools in order to manipulate the prices of stocks. After the markets were cleaned up in the thirties and returned to normal following the forties, new faces emerged including Gustave Levy of Goldman Sachs and Salim Lewis of Bear Stearns, who specialized in arbitrage trading and market-making in large blocks of securities for institutional investors.

Traders essentially are of two types. The first is the market-maker, who has the job of serving clients who wish to purchase or sell a particular security, say, the ten-year U.S. Treasury bond, in the over-the-counter markets. Every day the market-maker stands ready to buy or sell these bonds to accommodate clients. Often the trader will have to utilize some of the firm's capital to do this, so there is almost always a small trading position going at every market-maker's desk. Most firms hope to manage these positions sensibly (not let any of them get too big, and keep them under control by covering long and short exposures frequently). Market-makers are not in this business to make money from market movements. They want to make a routine bid-asked spread on trades that accommodate their customers. The market-makers try to minimize their exposures to market price changes while maximizing the throughput of customer orders. They are not speculators.

The other kind of trader is the proprietary trader, who trades only for the firm's own account, does not service customers, and rarely tells anyone what he or she is doing. These are the speculators of today, and they have all the qualities you would expect: they are quick-thinking, fast-acting, cold-blooded individuals who can spot an opportunity, analyze it quickly, and then boldly plunge into it entirely for the sake of the market exposure. They have to be able to manage several positions at once, to keep track of hundreds of prices in their heads, and to change their minds quickly when necessary. When the proprietary trader is right, large sums are earned; when wrong, losses follow, though it is usually better to be wrong in a rising market than a falling one. We have had a lot of rising markets since 1982. These have helped a lot of traders, though the volatility in the markets has killed off more than a few of them when they were caught off base.

Bruce Kovner has succeeded admirably in sailing these seas and weathering the storms. He is a prototype of the modern proprietary trader, with all the qualities needed to master this demanding business. He also has $900 million, according to *Forbes*. Kovner, fifty-four in 2000, is a Harvard graduate who spent his early years drifting. He was a cab driver and a student of the harpsichord at Juilliard. He learned the commodities business by speculating on a $3,000 MasterCard line of credit. He lost most of his profits and decided to join a real firm, Commodities Corp., in the later-1970s. He went out on his own in 1983 and quickly built up his funds under management. In 1996, after a flat year, he returned $1.25 billion of $2 billion under management, and formed Caxton Corp. for a fresh start. He is mainly a commodities trader, though, like most of the masters, he has been comfortable moving in and out of securities and foreign-exchange positions when the opportunities struck him.[10] Marc Rich and Pincus Green are two more successful commodities traders, worth nearly $2 billion between them; however both are fugitives from justice, living in Europe to avoid arrest in the United States for tax evasion and other charges.

Kovner, like a number of successful traders in the 1960s, attracted investors who wanted him to manage some of their money. These were sophisticated, wealthy investors who could afford to take losses or have their positions be underwater for significant periods. They were looking for exceptional returns that they believed only someone of exceptional talent and professionalism could deliver. The investors were willing to allow such a person to set the rules—to invest in whatever he wanted, in long or short positions, and to use borrowed money to leverage exposures. He could also take for himself 15 percent or 20 percent of any profits made, in addition to a more modest annual management fee. One of the first of these investment vehicles, called a hedge fund, was set up in 1949 by the legendary A. W. Jones, who mainly invested in the stock market.

Originally a method for protecting an investor against unexpected market reversals by having a side bet on the downside of a position, hedge funds came to utilize a variety of skills and investment strategies to make money, regardless of which way the market was going. Mainly, though, it was a way for really smart investors to raise other people's money to invest with. And for really ordinary, but rich, people to invest alongside the really smart investors of the times, to share in the extraordinary returns that these investors always seemed to come up with. It was like flying the Concorde—the ticket was expensive but you got there way before everyone else. It didn't always work out that way, of course, but that was the basic idea in the beginning. Later the funds became more numerous and more sophisticated, and they focused on their risk-reward ratios and their particular investment focus.

The risk-reward ratio (actually the Sharpe ratio, which measures return per unit of risk) reflects the degree of hedging in hedge funds, or the extent to which their returns are insulated from market volatility. A 1998 Goldman Sachs study demonstrated that from 1993 through 1997, all of four different types of hedge funds studied produced *less*-risky returns than the market as a whole. The four different types of funds were designated by investment strategies: market neutral, event-driven, long/short, and tactical trading. The first is a strategy that does not depend on the market per se but on forms of financial arbitrage in which particular price aberrations are isolated. Event-driven strategies depend on concrete events like a bankruptcy reorganization or the completion of a merger that has been announced. Long/short strategies are those in which a bold long position is offset by a cautious short position (through short sales, futures, or options contracts) to hedge the exposure against an unexpected market shift. Tactical trading is a polite term for placing bets on future price movements of currencies, commodities, equities, and/or bonds in the futures and cash markets. The Goldman Sachs study concluded that the average returns of the hedge funds had been the same or better than the returns of the S&P 500 and other indices of investment performance over the five-year period. But, unbelievable as it sounds, the hedge funds also showed less volatility and more consistency of returns than the market indices. The study thus suggested that conservative pension funds and other institutional investors should invest in a portfolio of diversified hedge funds to improve investment performance and *stability*. This was certainly not a conclusion previously associated with hedge fund investing.

In 1998 there were over 1,300 hedge fund management groups, offering over 3,500 different investment vehicles with about $400 billion of assets under management.[11] Some of the best-known, successful hedge fund managers of the 1990s were Julian Robertson (Tiger Management), and Michael Steinhardt (Steinhardt Partners), who made a great pile of money in the early 1990s and then retired. There have also been some spectacularly unsuccessful hedge fund managers. These include David Askin, who lost all of his Granite Partners money ($600 million) in the collapse of his mortgage-backed securities hedge fund in 1994, and Victor Niederhoffer, who lost all of his investors' money (about $130 million) in 1997 by misjudging the S&P 500 futures market. Niederhoffer had just published an autobiography, *The Education of a Speculator*.[12]

By far the most spectacular hedge fund failure, however, was the $3.5 billion collapse in 1998 of Long Term Capital Management, the prince of all such vehicles. This was a fund formed and managed by ex–Salomon partner John Merriweather, the gutsy trader who supposedly offered to play liar's poker with John Gutfreund for $10 million in Michael Thomas's book by that name. LTCM was staffed by the best and brightest of Merriweather's former colleagues and two eminent, Nobel prize–winning academic economists, Myron Scholes and Robert Merton. The firm was only a few years old in 1998, but it was very prestigious. Merriweather had a reputation as a sure-fire moneymaker from his days when heading Salomon's peerless bond arbitrage department. Money flocked to the fund—more, probably, than he could successfully invest. In its first year the fund returned over 40 percent, then less. In its third year the investors' return was down to 14 percent (far less than the S&P 500 index), and the fund returned a substantial part of its capital to its investors. In 1998 its plan was to make more money by undertaking more leverage by running a larger portfolio of as much as $100 billion of investments on investors' capital, now reduced to about $4.8 billion. The fund loaded up with all sorts of different investment positions, though few if any of these were much different from what similar traders all over the world were putting on at the time. There was no technical genius involved; they mainly just bet on the chances that the markets would price risky assets in the future more generously, relative to less-risky ones than they currently did. But the market, already showing some strain, panicked in August 1998 (after Russia defaulted and Japan and Brazil looked bad, too), after which everything risky looked even worse and their prices dropped even further. LTCM owned a lot of this risky paper, and its dropping value meant margin calls and a downward spiral of still worsening prices, more margin calls and a rapid depletion of the firm's capital. It was impossible to raise more money under these circumstances. By September it was all over. LTCM, on the verge of collapse, had to beg assistance from its creditors and induce the Federal Reserve Bank of New York to intervene in the situation by calling for a meeting of LTCM's creditors. After an opportunistic offer from (of all people) Warren Buffett to buy the whole fund was rebuffed, fifteen of the creditors (including seven reluctant foreign banks) dug deeply into their pockets and came up with a $3.5 billion rescue fund. The effort would save LTCM from insolvency and collapse, and presumably (though this is still much debated) would also save the world from a powerful shock to its suddenly vulnerable financial system. By the early days of 1999, the rescuers' investment (still managed by Merriweather, who retained a small economic stake in the fund) was beginning to show a small profit. The creditors planned to liquidate all of LTCM's positions during the year and expected to make quite a bit of money from doing so. LTCM, its founders claimed, had been hit by a lightening bolt on a clear, sunny day. They were well positioned to take ordinary market risk, they said, but not as much as eventuated. Certainly the LTCM experience did not make readers of the Goldman Sachs report on hedge funds feel any safer.

It is stories like LTCM that understandably attract so much attention to hedge funds. They are seen as the stuff of bold and exciting events, good or bad. Many of the group's most prominent players have become celebrities, widely known in all financial circles, some even beyond those. But as well known as some of these players are, the best known of all the hedge fund players is George Soros.

The World's Greatest Investor

In 1981 *Institutional Investor* magazine labeled George Soros the world's greatest investor, based on what it understood of the record of the Quantum Fund, a secretive offshore investment company that he managed. Quantum was a hedge fund for non-American investors that could operate outside the investment restrictions of the SEC or the tax constraints of the IRS. Soros' wealthy clients, brave enough to allow him to take great risks with their money and clever enough to keep the profits beyond the reach of their national tax authorities, had truly discovered a goose that laid golden eggs. Established in 1969 Quantum had produced a compounded return for its investors of 35 percent through mid-year 1994, after which Soros began to withdraw from its management. This was an investment return significantly higher than that produced by any of the leading investment gurus of the time, including Warren Buffett and Peter Lynch. Quantum, however, was a different kind of investor. It traded, and it traded actively and aggressively. Soro's investment style was to find opportunities anywhere in the world, in any form, and take huge positions. If the idea was really any good, he would say, it was probably worth a bigger bet. When others playing the same strategy reached the limits they thought were prudent, George was doubling up. He invested all over the world, and in 1994 an average trading day involved buying and selling $750 million in securities.

George Soros was born Dzjchdzhe Shorask (pronounced "Shorosh") in Budapest in 1930. His father was a lawyer who had served in the Austro-Hungarian army during World War I, been captured, and spent three years in Russia, from the revolution to the beginning of the civil war. During World War II the Soros family, being Jewish, constantly employed survival tactics learned by the father. The family did survive, and when George was seventeen, he went to England to finish his engineering studies. He arrived lonely and broke but managed to support himself and attend the London School of Economics two years later in 1949. Afterward he landed a job as a trainee in a small London brokerage, where he was greatly frustrated by the firm's unwillingness to entrust him with responsibilities and opportunities. In 1956 he encamped to New York where he joined a small firm offering advice to American investors about European stocks. Mostly this firm supported itself by arbitraging U.S.-dollar-denominated American Depositary Receipts against their underlying European securities, a fairly dull if steady business in which traders made a few pennies per share on a lot of little trades involving virtually no risk. In 1959 Soros moved up market to Wertheim & Co., where he continued to devote himself to foreign-securities arbitrage and the occasional client interested in European stocks. In 1963 he moved again, to Arnold & Bleichroeder, once a famous European house, that was then a small niche player in the securities market. In 1967 he was made head of investment research. His job was to find interesting investment opportunities in undervalued European stocks, in which U.S. interest was virtually nonexistent but which European expatriates, wealthy families investing through private banks in Switzerland, and London money managers were always looking for. Soros, when he had a good idea, would find out were the stock was and offer to buy it before explaining the idea to his clients. In this way, like Milken with his exotic little market in junk securities, Soros could make a good trading spread on his deals and profit by positions taken in advance. In 1969 he founded an offshore hedge fund with a personal investment of $250,000, and approached his former European, South American, and Middle Eastern clients and other investors he knew to let him manage some of their money. They came up with about $6 million. Not long afterward Soros split from Arnold & Bleichroeder and, taking his fund with him, set up Soros Fund Management. By 1972 the fund was worth $20 million. By 1980, during nearly a decade when the U.S. stock market had appreciated hardly at all, though inflation had averaged about 8 percent per year and the dollar was devalued, Soros' fund (in dollar terms) had appreciated nearly twenty-fold.[13]

In the 1970s Soros's investments covered a lot of ground. In the U.S. he looked for industries undergoing special changes. He bought into real estate investment trusts (REITs) expecting that they would rise when the market recognized the aggressive investment styles of the sector. Afterward, however, Soros believed prices would be over-hyped and begin to decline. Viewing the opportunity this way, he made money going both ways, first by buying the REITs and promoting his ideas, then by switching to a net short position in time for what he called the "third act" of the drama, when the prices would start to drop. He was gifted at spotting undervalued sectors in the U.S. markets and overseas. When U.S. stocks were getting creamed in the middle 1970s, he bought Japanese, Canadian, French, and Dutch stocks, with the Japanese representing about a quarter of the entire portfolio. He bought out-of-favor stocks and sold high flyers short. He noticed the rapid increase in the U.S. imports of foreign oil and bought oilfield services and drilling stocks before the Arab oil embargo in 1973. He bought a billion dollars of British Treasury bonds at historical lows and shorted the pound. Everything he did seemed to be contrarian, but he made money. He told the *Wall Street Journal* in a 1975 interview, "The stock market is always wrong, so if you copy what everybody else on Wall Street is doing, you are doomed to do poorly."[14]

Soros professed his own "theories" about investing. These were not heavyweight ideas but a kind of practical, marketplace common sense, easy to prescribe but difficult to apply to particular situations. He believed that reality was different from perception, and therefore the market (reflecting perception) constantly misvalued securities, leading to investment opportunities for those capable of finding them. He believed, too, that markets developed momentum but could change from overvaluation to undervaluation with a sudden shift in confidence. Like Buffett and Tisch and other value investors, he looked for buried treasures, where perfect-market theory, then spreading in academic circles, did not apply. Sometimes the treasure would take two to three years to be dug up, but Soros seemed to be able to see and to invest that far out. In 1973 and 1974, the two worst years of the decade for the Dow, Soros reported gains of 8.4 percent and 17.5 percent, respectively. From January 1969 to December 1974 the fund's shares tripled in value. During this time the Dow fell 3.4 percent. In 1978 and 1979 the Soros Fund increased by more than 50 percent in each year. In 1979 he changed the name of his fund to the Quantum Fund, in honor of Heisenberg's uncertainly principle in quantum mechanics. In 1980 his new fund reported a stunning 102.6 percent return, and its assets under management rose to $380 million. Soon afterward *Institutional Investor* put him on its cover[15] as the world's greatest investor. He was described as mysterious, remote, aloof, tricky but not dishonest, and very hard to follow, in the markets or in his explanation of his theories of the markets. He was certainly the world's first *global* investing superstar.

The following year, 1981, after all that publicity, was Soros's worst. The fund lost 23 percent, and about a third of his European investors, who had made so much investing with Soros over the past twelve years, withdrew their funds. Soros was shocked and hurt. The investors thought that Soros had run out his lucky streak, and no manager is any better than his last year. So they withdrew, just as the Reagan bull market was beginning.

The fund was up 56 percent in 1982, and another 25 percent in 1983. In 1984, however, the increase was only 9.4 percent. At this point Soros, who had withdrawn somewhat from active management of the fund, reinserted himself. He saw a "hundred-year storm coming." This was the dark downside of the deficit-loaded, but happy, early Reagan years. He looked to foreign markets again, in particular to Britain, which was privatizing its state-owned industries. An associate wanted to take a position in Jaguar, which was then being sold through an IPO. Soros crossed-examined the associate, and, satisfied that he had made a good choice, told him to increase his order by another quarter of a million shares. If you are going to bet, Soros believed, you must bet big.

This belief he put into practice in September 1985, just before the famous Plaza Hotel Agreement. That was when the finance ministers of the G-7 countries met in New York to do something about the soaring dollar, bolstered by Reaganomics, that had pushed the yen-dollar rate to 239. Soros was convinced that the dollar had run its course, that its high valuation relative to the yen and the mark could not be justified on economic grounds. He also felt that the exchange rates were causing a lot of grief in the world economy and might have to be adjusted by strong government interventions, though these did not usually work well. So in early September he accumulated an $800 million position in the yen and the mark—$200 million more than the entire fund's value, a big bet—and settled in to wait for things to happen. On September 22 an agreement was announced by Treasury Secretary James Baker in which all the major countries would participate in an effort to create an "orderly appreciation of non-dollar currencies by cooperating closely." This produced a disorderly rout of the dollar and sharp recovery of the yen and the mark in the foreign exchange markets, just as Soros had foreseen. He made $40 million overnight and, by October, when the yen was at 205, a total of about $150 million. He had also invested in foreign stocks and long-term treasuries.[16] The fund was up 122 percent in 1985.

Soros was now very rich himself. He owned a significant percent of the shares in his fund, and he benefited from the management fees and manager's 20 percent share of the profits too. In 1985 *Financial World* estimated his personal income at just short of $100 million. He began to give more interviews and chat with the press about his market views. In September 1987 he predicted that the U.S. market would not experience a setback but the Japanese market would. The U.S. market crash, when it came on October 19, 1987, was especially rough on Soros, whose positions reflected his optimistic predictions about the American market. The Dow Jones index was off 508 points, or 22.6 percent, on that single day. Soros's fund had been up more than 60 percent on the year but gave it all back. *Barron's* claimed that Soros lost $840 million in just two weeks. Soros pointed out that at the end of October his fund was up 2.5 percent for the year. It would end the year up 14.1 percent.

In 1988 Soros began to look for someone to whom he could hand over the daily operations of the fund. He found a kindred spirit in Stanley Druckenmiller. George was beginning to shift his interests to philanthropy, especially in Eastern Europe, which was just then in the process of becoming free. Druckenmiller performed very well with long and short positions in various markets and currencies. In 1991 and 1992 Soros and Druckenmiller spun off some of the Quantum Fund into different, smaller units. The Quasar Fund had been established in 1991, and the Quantum Emerging Markets Growth Fund and the Quota Funds, a fund-of-funds managed by others, were set up in 1992.

In September 1992 Soros made the killing that fixed him in the public eye once and for all. He had placed a huge bet that the British government would devalue the pound, which the government firmly denied. But Soros knew that the pound was in deep trouble—it was then a part of the European Exchange Rate Mechanism (ERM), in which the participating Common Market countries were obligated to maintain the value of their currencies within a narrow range of the others. If this became difficult to do, then the struggling country would be expected to raise interest rates if the currency was weak, or lower them otherwise. This ERM system worked fairly well until the fall of the Berlin Wall and the reunification of East and West Germany. As popular as reunification was, it was hard on economic agreements. The Germans immediately were faced with a gigantic bill for "acquiring" East Germany. This bill was for new investments, subsidies, and welfare payments needed to bring the East German economy up to the standards of the West. Spending all this money meant that Germany had to issue more government bonds, which pushed DM interest rates up. The higher these rates went, the stronger the DM currency became, and the weaker the other currencies in the ERM became in turn. The ERM, however, required that countries like Britain raise interest rates to protect the pound-DM exchange rate, even though Britain at the time had a recession and very high unemployment. The ERM, therefore, was passing some of the cost of German reunification on to Germany's partners in the European Economic Community, and there was no telling how long this would last. Soros and a number of other currency traders assumed that the British would rather pull out of the ERM than strangle their own economy. So he went long (bought) DMs and shorted (sold) sterling. He could do this easily by borrowing British government securities, then selling them and reinvesting the cash in German governments. The cost of carrying the position would be the interest rate difference between the cost of borrowing the sterling and receiving interest on the DMs. If the strategy worked, and the British did drop out of the ERM, in order to lower its interest rates, the sterling-DM rate would drop sharply and the positions could be liquidated by reversing them (buying the cheaper sterling to cover the sterling borrowed and selling appreciated DMs). A number of other traders had similar positions, but what made Soros unique was the enormous size of his positions, reportedly around $10 billion in each currency. (Positions of this size are more easily taken in the futures markets than in the cash market, in which you have to deal in physical securities.)

As the traders started to set up their positions, they began to put pressure on both currencies, and their respective governments began to intervene in the foreign-exchange markets to ease the pressure. This is the ideal situation for a foreign speculator—when a big government is on one side of the market, and you are on the other. You keep borrowing sterling and selling it back to the Bank of England for Deutsche marks. If you and your fellow speculators do this all day, every day, it may start a run, or loss of confidence in sterling, which causes further intervention. This time, however, the intervention could require drawing down Britain's foreign exchange reserves, adding further to the potential for panic. As the news gets out, the velocity of the traders' activities increases. At some point the Bank of England might have to say enough is enough, and decide not to buy any more of the sterling being offered to it. At this point an announcement would have to be made that Britain will temporarily drop out of the ERM, and sterling, no longer supported by the Bank of England, would go into free fall for a while. That's when most of the speculators, having won, cover their shorts and begin to exit the strategy.

What makes this so dangerous for the countries involved is the enormous volume of foreign-exchange-market trading that occurs, about $1 *trillion* a day in 1992 (it was close to twice that in 1999). In 1992 the British and German governments reported intervention in the foreign exchange markets to the extent of about $20 billion to keep Britain inside the ERM, but this amount, as large as it was, was still only a tiny fraction of the foreign exchange traded daily. Altogether Soros, who was back in charge of trading these positions again, made a profit of about $1 billion on the sterling-DM bet and another $1 billion on a variety of other European currency positions. All of this was earned within just a week.[17]

After the size of Soros's positions became known he was branded as "the man who broke the Bank of England" by the *Economist*. The reputation stayed with him well into the late 1990s, when angry prime ministers, lashing out at international "speculators," often referred to Soros by name, even when he had no position at all. After 1992 Soros left most of the trading to Druckenmiller and went on to a variety of extremely high-profile activities, including (in addition to his extensive charitable work) giving advice to public figures, writing articles critical of economic policy, and appearing on TV talk shows. But he wasn't entirely out of the business. In the summer of 1998 Druckenmiller reported that the Quantum Fund had lost approximately $2 billion on investments in the Russian market, despite an overall performance of the fund, which was expected to be up about 19 percent for the full year. The losses were reported about two weeks after the *Financial Times* of London published a letter from Soros in which he expressed concern for the rapidly deteriorating economic conditions in Russia and urged the IMF and the G-7 countries that "immediate action" be taken. Such actions, which were not forthcoming in the limited time before the market collapsed, would have helped to bail out Soros's positions.[18] Quantum survived however, whereas LTCM failed, and struggled to find the next bit of buried treasure. After a poor start in 1999, Druckenmiller jumped on the "new economy" bandwagon and bought heavily into technology stocks. For 1999, a year that saw Soros's rival Julian Robertson gasping for breath, the fund's return was 35 percent. By the end of 1999 *Forbes* had Soros, sixty-nine, down for a net worth of $4 billion, after more than a decade of very active philanthropy in Eastern Europe and elsewhere. Druckenmiller, forty-six, weighed in at $850 million. In April 2000, Soros announced his and Druckenmiller's withdrawal from large-scale and aggressive hedge fund investing and said anyone continuing to invest in the group's funds should expect lower returns in the future. "Our large macro bet days are over," he said, adding "We are bringing an epoch to an end."[19]

MUTUAL FUNDS

In the 1990s the mutual fund industry exploded. The general public was determined to participate in the growth in equity values and in the higher interest rates available to them in commingled money market funds. The public, however, was apprehensive about the complexities of the market, and feared that simple folks on the bottom, like themselves, would be the last to know things and the first to be taken advantage of by the exploitative salesmen of Wall Street. So they decided to hire their own managers, sophisticated investors who would put their money to work for them in exchange for some modest fees. The way they did this, of course, was to buy mutual funds that invested in stocks, or shares in closed-end investment companies that did the same. In 1982 there were approximately 860 mutual funds in the United States, representing assets under management of $287 billion, of which only $47 billion was invested in equity securities. By December 31, 1998, there were more than 7,000 mutual funds, managing $5.5 trillion of assets, of which approximately $3 trillion were invested in equities. This amount was only a bit less than all pension fund investments in equities and about the same as the total amount of money that American individuals had invested in bank deposits and CDs.

Mutual fund investments in equities on December 31, 1998, were 26 percent greater than the year before (though this was the smallest annual increase since 1994). The increase was the result of net new investments in the funds, and investment performance. Net new money flows into mutual funds amounted to $159 billion (down from $227 billion in 1997, the peak year). Investment performance, however, increased equity mutual fund assets under management during the year by 18 percent (during a year when the S&P 500 increased 27 percent).

In 1998 there were more mutual funds and closed-end investment companies than there were publicly traded stocks. The performance of these individual funds varied all across the lot, depending on the specialty of the funds, and there were a great many specialties to choose from. There were money market funds, tax-free municipal bond funds, taxable bond funds, junk bond funds, balanced funds, global funds, country stock funds, growth funds, income funds, growth-and-income funds, sector funds, hedge funds, tax-efficient funds, currency funds, and so on, indefinitely. Clearly performance of these funds could not be measured against a single benchmark.

However, competition for funds under management is among the most intense in any industry. And it is heightened by analytical services such as Lipper and Morningstar, which publish the performance records of funds in terms of risk and return over different holding periods. *The Wall Street Journal, Business Week,* and *Fortune* also publish regular scoreboards among publicly available mutual funds. Indeed, mutual fund scoreboards are among the hottest items on the magazine racks. Accordingly, the jobs of fund managers are among the most challenging in the financial services industry. Despite clear warnings that past performance is no assurance of future results, a rise in the rankings often brings in a flood of new investments, with the manager being handsomely compensated and promoted to bigger and better things in the fund management game. At the same time, serious performance slippage can cause investors to withdraw funds. If too many withdrawals occur, the manager's bonus and job may be in jeopardy.

Despite their popularity, and the tough competition for

the investor's dollar, the performance of most stock mutual funds has been unimpressive. Between 1986 and 1996 Morningstar reported that no more than 26 percent of stock mutual funds beat the S&P 500 index during four different time periods. Performance in other sectors hasn't been much better. In all, 197 funds underperformed the indices, but only forty-nine outperformed them during the eleven-year period covered, though we must remember that the S&P 500 index is not the most appropriate benchmark for many stock mutual funds. The index, of course, is not reduced by the funds' fees and expenses, and when most managers try to beat the index they commit themselves to strategies not that different from the whole market. The largest funds, of course, can have great difficulty in changing their positions without affecting the prices in the market. Unless the retail investor knows something special about a given fund manager, or wants to bet on a particular investment strategy that differs from the market as a whole, it may be that a low-fee, passively managed index fund would produce more satisfactory results than investing in an average fund.

Still, the fund management companies do well from their fees, expenses, front-end loads, digressive back-loads, and other charges, which make theirs one of the most lucrative businesses in the securities industry, despite its highly competitive character. The management, administrative, and marketing expenses of the funds, which in combination average about 2 percent of assets under management annually, must be paid for by the funds' investors. But it is not a simple business. It is highly regulated; requires a number of independently constituted funds, which hire a fund management company to manage their assets; and consumes considerable invest-ment in research and portfolio management capability, and in administration. The funds also require an extensive dis-tribution system that enables them to be sold to investors. Over recent years, the major retail brokerages have per-formed this service, for appropriate compensation, for the fund management companies.

The fund management company is at the center of the business. It assembles the talent, and comes up with the plan for, say, a growth stock fund. It also organizes the fund and arranges for its "independent" directors. These direc-tors, not very independently, in turn hire the management company to manage the assets of the fund for a fee and the reimbursement of a variety of administrative expenses. In the case of a front-end-load mutual fund, the investor also pays for the cost of distributing the fund by agreeing to a discount in the value of the fund, which he receives at the time of investment. An 8 percent load, for example, would result in receipt of $92 of fund stock in payment for $100. Many funds have avoided front-end loads, which are un-popular with investors, by adding the cost of distribution to management fees or reimbursed expenses. Don't worry, the load is in there somewhere.

The management fee charged usually varies, sometimes considerably, with the type of assets, with equity funds receiving the highest fees. For a typical growth stock fund, the management fee would be about 0.75 percent per year on the market value of the funds under management. This is the all-important number to fund managers, the number on which everything depends. It is increased by sales to new investors and by market price (performance) appre-ciation, and it is decreased by investor withdrawals and price declines. Fund manager companies must spend as much time thinking about how to generate fund sales as they do in managing the money. The way to get more sales is by having a great record, yes, but also by continuing expansion in the number and specialty of funds offered and by catching the latest trends. They can also increase sales by increasing sales commissions paid to brokers, or by finding ways to distribute funds directly by using alternative distribution channels (e.g., the telephone or electronic means). They can also keep customers from withdrawing their funds by encouraging them to transfer from one of their funds to another to keep them on board even when markets start to sink. The biggest danger in the business is the sudden and substantial withdrawal of funds by investors experiencing a generalized panic or a loss of confidence in their particular funds. The former is caused by economic shocks of various kinds, and the latter by a scandal, a suddenly demonstrated history of underperformance, or the inability to provide a superior technology that a competitor may have introduced that improves customer satisfaction. Managing a large mutual fund company is much more than just picking good stocks.

The first American mutual funds were formed in Boston, a city in which there was much wealth under management by trustees. In 1830 a legal opinion issued by a Massachusetts judge, Samuel Pitman, dealt with the fiduciary duties of trustees and established what became the "prudent man" rule. This rule simply stated is that a person managing money for others had only to "conduct himself faithfully and exercise sound discretion," and to do that he should "observe how men of prudence, discretion, and intelligence manage their own affairs," and in essence, do the same. Other states at the time took a different view, that the trustees were required to preserve the value of the original capital at all costs. Judge Pitman allowed that trustees could look beyond just this and consider investment strategies that were aimed at growing the principal, as well as preserving it. "Prudent speculation," in other words, became the thing to do in Massachusetts, and just in time.

In the late 1800s, the investment trust (or a pooling of investor funds to acquire securities) was introduced in Scotland, and cloned many times in British financial markets. In the early 1920s investment trusts began to appear in the United States, as closed-end investment companies (you bought the stock of a company that acquired shares, then liquidated your position by selling the stock, not the underlying assets). Among the states, however, only Massachusetts had a legal doctrine of trusteeship that suited the type of investing that the trustees intended; namely, prudent speculation. It also had a substantial number of trustees needing to invest funds entrusted to them. In 1924 the State Street Investment Corp. (a closed-end fund) was incorporated, and later that year so was the Massachusetts Investors Trust, the first of the modern mutual funds. In 1925 the last of three pioneering Boston funds, Incorporated Investors, was formed.

Mr. Johnson's Company

In 1999 FMR (Fidelity Management and Research Co., the management company of the Fidelity Group of mutual funds) was America's largest single money manager, with over $1 trillion of assets under management. It is a family owned and managed business, acquired in 1946 by Edward C. Johnson II, a legendary figure in modern American finance, known in his time simply as "Mr. Johnson." A Boston lawyer who specialized in the investment business and had served as general counsel and vice president of Incorporated Investors, Johnson had been involved with mutual funds for almost twenty years. He had seen everything that had happened to this spectacular Boston-based industry, from its origins through the stock market mania of the 1927–1929 period (when mutual fund shareholders grew from 55,000 to 525,000), through the Crash in 1929 and the hollowing out of equity markets over the next four years. In 1932 the Dow Jones average, at its low point, had dropped 80 percent from its 1929 high, and many of the leveraged investment trusts had performed much worse. In 1933 the federal government began the introduction of a series of laws and tougher regulations that aimed at substantially greater investor protection against fraud, market rigging, and other abuses that were common in the 1920s. The equity market gradually improved after this, but only gradually, and fund managers had a very tough time of it.

In 1946, when Johnson took over the tiny Fidelity Fund (and owned all of FMR), it had assets of only $13 million. By 1949 he was able to increase these to $20 million, but the following year sales of new fund shares exploded. In 1958 the Fidelity funds group managed $416 million in four separate funds.

In 1940 more than half of the industry's assets was managed out of Boston, but by 1958 Boston's share had decreased to about a third. Funds operated out of New York accounted for 27 percent of the industry, and the rest were scattered all around the country. The leading mutual fund in 1958 was Investor's Diversified Services in Minneapolis, which marketed funds aggressively door-to-door. IDS, with $1.5 billion of assets under management, had just displaced Massachusetts Investors Trust from the top position. The Wellington Fund, from Philadelphia, was in third place, and in fourth was the Investors Management Company of Elizabeth, New Jersey Fidelity was in fifth place. But Fidelity was about to overtake the others.[20]

Johnson was not a portfolio manager himself. He hired others to do that work and supervised them carefully. He liked young people and gave them as much responsibility as he thought they could handle. He hired, and was a powerful mentor for, several of the leading money managers of his day, one of whom, Gerald Tsai, especially stands out. Tsai, an eager Chinese-American, joined Fidelity in 1952 in his early twenties. By 1957 he was managing a growth fund of his own, which by 1964 had over $200 million. Tsai was the prototype of the bold, aggressive young gunslinger portfolio manager of the go-go years of the 1960s. He concentrated on growth stocks, especially the hottest, most trendy of them. He traded in blocks of stock, encouraging Goldman Sachs and Bear Stearns to become specialists in the block-trading business. He churned his portfolio more than any of the old-style managers of the 1950s, turning over as much as 35 percent in a year. He traded noisily, so everyone could see what he was doing, and (he hoped) jump in to ride up the stocks he had selected. He squeezed corporations for information about their affairs, and used Fidelity's investment clout in powerful and aggressive ways to outperform his rivals. In the first five years of the 1960s his fund returned in the area of 60 percent per year, and Tsai was a VP and stockholder in FMR. But by 1966 he had resigned.

As good as he was, Tsai lacked something important to Johnson in a family business. Tsai was not Johnson's son, and Edward C. Johnson III, called Ned, was. Ned joined the firm in 1957 and in time became a portfolio manager, also heading a trendy growth fund. He did well; if not as spectacularly well as Tsai, well enough for his father to select him officially as his heir. Surely Tsai must have expected as much, but he waited to be sure, then he left to start his own fund, the Manhattan Fund, which was vastly oversubscribed when it was offered to the public, raising $247 million. The Manhattan Fund, surprisingly, was never much of a success, and Tsai faded from the scene.

Johnson spent the rest of the 1960s straightening out regulatory and legal problems that mainly were caused by the rapid pace of growth in the industry. In 1972 he began to gradually hand over the reins of the firm to Ned, who assumed full control in 1977. Mr. Johnson picked a good time to leave. In December 1972 the firm had $3.9 billion of assets under management, and a year later $2.9 billion. The 1970s were tough years for stock market investments, and the mutual fund industry was first to feel it. What helped at Fidelity was that it had hired Peter Lynch in 1969, and he was about ready to become one of the most famous fund managers ever.

Lynch became head of Fidelity's research department in 1974, and three years later took over a small, nonpublic fund called the Magellan Fund, with $22 million of assets. While he was running it, the Magellan Fund became the largest mutual fund in history, with $12 billion under management and over a million shareholders in 1989. A

$10,000 investment in 1977 was worth over $200,000 in 1988, a 31 percent annual compounded return over eleven years. A workaholic who was committed to researching everything and investing in the 2 or 3 percent that was better than the rest, Lynch gave up managing the fund himself in 1990.[21] He always seemed to make investing seem easier than it was, but he probably knew that it would be extremely difficult to equal the performance record he had already compiled. So he stepped down, wrote three books, served on some boards and as a senior advisor at Fidelity, and took long vacations. The company recently brought him back from retirement as Vice Chairman, resident sage, spokesperson, and advertising pitchman, all things he is very good at. Others, however, suggest he has become a dinosaur in a dynamic industry, and not managing money himself any longer detracts from his credibility. Maybe so, but Lynch is reported to own about 6 percent of FMR, a stake that was thought to be worth about $1 billion in early 1999.[22]

Ned Johnson, however, had the really difficult job at Fidelity during the twenty years he was CEO. During this time Fidelity had to be rebuilt to become everyman's mutual fund company, with a broad selection of funds for every interest and systems that permitted seamless transfer of funds and accurate record keeping for millions of accounts. It worked out distribution arrangements with brokers and banks all over the country, so its funds could be sold aggressively. He battled regulatory and publicity problems and handled an endless number of basic management problems of the sort that glamorous portfolio managers would scorn. But Fidelity came to be known as an especially customer-friendly company that could be accessed efficiently by phone at any time. These systemwide improvements in capacity, product-quality, and service were as important as its reputation for funds management in propelling Fidelity to the number-one slot in American mutual funds. "Fidelity is the premier brand, not just in the U.S.," said Milton Berlinski, a Goldman Sachs executive specializing in the funds management business, "but in the world." At the end of the 1999, it actively managed more assets than any other financial services firm in the world and was 60 percent larger than its closest rival, Vanguard Funds. In 1998 nearly one in five dollars invested in American mutual funds were in Fidelity's hands; one of four dollars of stock fund purchases that year were of Fidelity funds. Fidelity's funds owned 5 percent or more of 700 public companies. FMR is a privately owned company that does not disclose its financial results, but Berlinski put its market value in early 1999 in the area of $20 billion.[23]

But now Ned, too, has shed some of his responsibilities, in favor of his daughter Abigail, called "Abby." Ned has chosen Abby, thirty-seven in 1999, to be his successor, and transferred most of his FMR stock to her. She joined FMR in 1988 and has risen through the ranks, managing portfolios and dealing with the increasing array of managerial issues related to the rest of the business. *Forbes* estimated her wealth in 1999 to be $7.4 billion, and her father's to be about half that. Altogether Mr. Johnson's family has done well by his efforts.

THE BEST AND THE BRIGHTEST

Few businesses have ever benefited to the degree the U.S. securities industry has from the almost continuous eighteen-year economic and financial tailwind from 1981 through 1999. At a time when world and United States GDP increased at a compound (nominal) rate of 7 percent, U.S. and world equity market capitalization and trading volume all increased at twice that rate. Worldwide pension assets increased at a compounded rate of 15 percent, and U.S. mutual fund assets at 20 percent. The worldwide volume of new issues of equity securities increased at 19 percent and debt at 25 percent. Worldwide mergers and acquisitions also increased at more than 25 percent per annum during the period.

It would seem that with such buoyant market conditions, it would be difficult for investment banks, which provide services related to all of these activities, to do poorly. In fact, however, the burden of managing such rapid growth effectively was a great one, and not all firms fared well. Indeed for several once great firms, the opposite was true. Drexel Burnham went bankrupt and Kidder Peabody was subject to a distress sale. So was First Boston, a casualty of bridge loans in the late 1980s, which had to be reclaimed by its principal stockholder, Credit Suisse. Lehman Brothers and Smith Barney were also sold, then sold again (in Lehman's case, back to the public). Salomon Brothers, wounded from its scandalous behavior in the treasury auction market in 1990 and never fully recovered, was sold to Smith Barney, a division of the Travelers Group, which in turn merged with Citicorp. Salomon

Brothers, now shorn of its virile proprietary trading business, occupies but a tiny spot in the massive new Citigroup. Prudential Securities would have died a number of times had it not been for its deep-pocketed parent. Such experiences were not confined to the U.S. In Britain, Baring Brothers, a firm nearly 250 years old, was sold to avoid bankruptcy, and the market leader, S. G. Warburg, was forced into a merger with a new Swiss-owned banking conglomerate, which later merged with its largest Swiss competitor, Union Bank of Switzerland. In Japan, Yamaichi Securities, the country's fourth largest investment banker, failed. Bankers Trust, damaged by derivatives scandals, was acquired by Deutsche Bank. And a number of other firms that were unable to keep up with competition found merger with a stronger partner their best alternative. Not all was quiet contentment resulting from the gloriously favorable market conditions during these years.

With all the financial market expansion, globalization, and new technology, there was also an avalanche of competition. For those who could make the most of the new environment and compete effectively, opportunities for growth and enrichment appeared limitless. For all others in the financial services industry, the times were those of as much turmoil, confusion, and distress as in any period of nearly two decades that the modern world had ever presented.

Some firms, such as Lazard Freres, Donaldson Lufkin & Jenrette, and Bear Stearns, benefited from sticking to their original knitting and not altering their special roles in the markets very much during the period. They grew, but their gain from the markets' explosive burst was only moderate in relation to the big winners: Merrill Lynch, Morgan

Stanley Dean Witter, and Goldman Sachs. Merrill, the world's largest securities firm before the merger of Citicorp and Travelers, dominates the market in most investment banking products—brokerage, trading, and underwriting—but Morgan Stanley and Goldman were the industry's most profitable firms, with the highest reputations for financial skills, talent, and service among the industry's clients. The three firms were not only good, but they had become global and were able to do what they were good at in a new, much larger marketplace that was increasingly recognizing the value of their products and services relative to those offered by indigenous banks and securities firms.

Morgan Stanley had been a wholesale finance firm since its beginning as a spin off from J. P. Morgan in 1933. It inherited all of the famous Morgan clients, and had been the bluest of blue chip firms since its fortuitous birth. In the 1980s Morgan Stanley changed itself into more of a full-service, international firm and began to add investment management businesses aggressively in the 1990s. It was disappointed in its market valuation, however, and decided that its future would best be made by merging with a retail brokerage, Dean Witter, that had once been owned by Sears Roebuck and still retained its valuable *Discover* credit card business. Merrill Lynch continued during the 1990s to expand internally and externally—acquiring a British trading house, a leading asset manager, and the remains of the bankrupt Japanese brokerage Yamaichi Securities. Its aim was to become the world's only firm that could excel at all retail and wholesale financial services in both its home market and in all important markets abroad.

Goldman Sachs was left as the most unchanged firm among the majors of Wall Street. The last of the large investment banks to remain a partnership, Goldman Sachs was organized in 1869 as a commercial paper house. Over the next 130 years its main effort was to grow organically and to increase its market share and profitability. I joined the firm in 1966, becoming a general partner in 1976 and a limited partner in 1988. I remained in that capacity until the firm dissolved the partnership in 1999 to effect its initial public offering. This event meant a great deal of change to an old organization with many traditions and legacies, including one of preferring to do its business out of the public eye. The IPO would end Goldman's unique partnership structure, it would require including several hundred of its more senior employees into its coveted ownership status, and force it to govern itself in the future by the quarterly rise or fall of its share price.

An Industry Blossoms

When I joined Goldman Sachs I was one of only two graduates of the Harvard Business School that year to do so. Altogether probably fewer than a dozen or so of my classmates joined major Wall Street firms at that time (one, Michael Bloomberg, joined Salomon Brothers). It wasn't a hot industry then—most of the hot jobs seemed to be in consulting or at the more glamorous *Fortune* 500 companies—but we liked finance so we went. I was paid a salary of $9,500, with no guaranteed bonus or signing fee or anything like that. Only those who were very successful, who became partners of their firms or the equivalent, could expect to make much money. To become a partner took a long time, ten or fifteen years, but it was reasonably assured that Harvard MBAs ought to be able to make it if they kept their noses clean and did what they were told. Investment banking then was not a well-known industry outside of the business schools. No one in my family had ever heard of my new firm, though they thought it must have something to do with Saks Fifth Avenue.

In the 1960s, however, a bull market and a merger boom increased the importance and visibility of investment banks and the opportunities for young employees. We evolved into skilled and talented deal-doers, eager to generate transactions. Competition between firms, once very light ("gentlemen did not call on the clients of others"), increased rapidly as the stakes went up. There was now a lot of money involved in the increasing flow of deals, and firms began successfully to woo clients away from their traditional bankers. Things were going well for Goldman Sachs, in part because we had been awakened by the opportunities that increased competition meant to us. But two volcanic changes that would irreversibly change the business awaited us.

The first of these was deregulation. Ours was an industry regulated by the Glass-Steagall Act, which kept banks out of our business, and by traditional self-governing practices such as the rules of the New York Stock Exchange, which set minimum commissions and limited membership in the Exchange to broker-dealers who were U.S. nationals. All of this has since changed in the U.S. and all significant overseas markets. Securities markets now are, in general, open to any competitor who is able to meet the regulatory requirements.

The other volcano was the technology developments

that created the computer and telecommunications revolution that has made it possible to send enormous amounts of information anywhere in the world at the speed of light at virtually no cost. After these volcanoes erupted, business expanded exponentially, and, the business being easy to enter, there was no limit on competition seeking to grab some of the profits. Soon the markets we covered comprised the whole world. In 1970 Goldman Sachs had no international offices. In 1999 it had twenty-three, employing five thousand people, 36 percent of the firm's entire headcount.

Trading and Risk

In the value-investor, hostile-takeover, and LBO-dominated markets of the 1980s, investment bankers became extremely visible for the first time since the days of J. P. Morgan. Their star performers (the ones the press could learn about from the deal activity) became, briefly, a media phenomenon. But the real change was in the increase in securities trading. In the 1980s all the major firms shifted from being advice givers and deal facilitators to becoming principal investors, making markets for clients in government securities, collateralized mortgages, junk bonds, and stocks of companies from all over the world. Trading required capital and huge credit lines. It was a highly leveraged business—the big firms often operated with capital of less than 5 percent of total assets. If you got the trade right, you could make a bundle. To get it right, you had to be willing to pay extraordinary amounts of incentive compensation to find out which individuals really traded effectively. If you got it wrong, you could lose the bundle and more, and then your own capital was highly exposed—large pieces of it could disappear instantly if you didn't act quickly to cut your losses. The only part of the firm's expense burden that you could cut, however, was the payroll. So when things went badly, there was no choice but to cut people, quickly and ruthlessly. This was a big change. It passed the volatility of the market directly onto the people who worked in the firm.

During the 1980s the firms made a lot of money, more than ever before, and the money was being paid out to the big hitters and the not-so-big hitters alike. Wall Street reveled in money on a scale perhaps not seen since the 1920s. Although the biggest money was being made by innovative people not employed in the old-line firms, such as Michael Milken and the KKR team, it was the first time when the top thirty or so people in all the major investment banks each expected million-dollar annual compensation packages. This was a privilege available only to a very few during most of the 1970s. The compensation of investment bankers far exceeded the compensation paid to their contemporaries at law firms or commercial banks, or to any other form of professional-services firm. It also vastly exceeded the compensation of their clients. The banks paid it because they had it to pay and because they had to pay it to keep the folks that made it. If your firm lacked some of the necessary talent to make the big money, why not hire some of the talent away from your rivals. Sure, you would probably pay too much, but if the revenues looked worth it, then you went ahead. Few persons who were offered such deals would refuse them. Everyone assumed they were worth more somewhere else. Such vicarious pay increases both fuelled and disrupted Wall Street for years.

The eighties, however, ended with a dull thud as profits died, and firms found themselves overcommitted to proprietary bridging deals done to accommodate aggressive, big-fee-paying clients. Many firms decided to invest their own capital in these deals, in which they offered to lend money to clients who were attempting a takeover or reorganization, with the understanding that the loans would be refinanced as soon as possible. But when the merger and junk bond markets suddenly collapsed in 1990, they were stuck holding the bag—the refinancings couldn't be done, and without the refinancings the cost of the transactions became prohibitive. That year in particular, the first in which Wall Street firms as a whole lost money since the 1930s, was very difficult for investment bankers. Many had to face the hard reality that their firms only pay for profits that are earned, and without profits there are no bonuses or, perhaps worse, no jobs. Hundreds were let go, especially those with long service in the industry (and relatively high levels of compensation) who were not thought to be essential. Indeed the business was changing so fast, the more experienced players were often thought to be in the way. They were not well attuned to the newest developments in using computers or proficient in the latest financial techniques. But younger people were dropped, too, especially if they were not seen to be at the top of their peer groups. What many learned was that a few years of exceptionally high pay were accompanied by a huge, if unseen, increase in career risk. Some firms, like Drexel, got into trouble, and senior people there, like one of my

Harvard classmates, then a partner, found that most of what he had earned during his entire working life had been lost in the bankruptcy of his firm.

The firms had to pay for performance, either to reward those who had been with the firm for a long time but might be lured away by higher pay promises elsewhere, or by buying in talent the firm didn't have but needed. And the players wanted cash. It was hard to expect much satisfaction in rewarding employees with company stock if the market didn't value the stock very highly. It was a rare investment bank that traded at more than ten times earnings or twice book value before 1996, and plenty of firms saw the value of their stock holdings sink disturbingly during the weak years. After a weakened Lehman Brothers was acquired by Shearson American Express in 1984, the consolidated effect on the stock price of American Express was seen to be negative—the Shearson Lehman unit was pulling it down. So American Express sold stock in Lehman to the public and to its employees in 1987 at a price of $34 per share, and much of subsequent year-end bonuses were paid in stock. Lehman, however, did not fare well at the end of the 1980s, so American Express had to buy the stock back in 1990, for which it paid $12.50 per share. This was not a great deal for Lehman's talented pool of investment bankers, who were encouraged to buy at $34, and sell at $12.50.

Whenever anyone working in a firm as troubled as Lehman was at the time could get another job; he or she took it and hoped for the best. Also, with layoffs in times of adversity an unavoidable necessity, firms were losing most of what was left of their ability to retain the loyalty of their employees. Increasingly individuals working in the investment banking business were in it for the short run. Make the money when and as you can, they thought, and look out for yourself (some, however, cut corners and found themselves in trouble on insider trading and other securities law violations). They began to feel that they had to strike while the iron was hot or otherwise risk ending up like my Drexel classmate. Indeed it wasn't all fat paychecks for ordinary folks just lucky enough to be there. The ones who got it tended to earn it, and earn it repeatedly. The true story of Wall Street riches has to be told with those who did not survive being taken into account too. If you took *all* the people who started careers on Wall Street in the 1980s and 1990s, and determined their annualized increase in net worth over their entire careers, I doubt that the Wall Street numbers would be much higher than for any other profession.

But those who worked at the firms did consume most of what cash their firm made, leaving comparatively little on the table for outside investors. In 1998 the average ratio of total compensation expenses to net revenues (total revenue minus interest expense) of all the major Wall Street firms was over 50 percent.

The Goldman Story

In May 1999 Goldman Sachs ended 130 years as a private partnership to "better match our capital structure to our mission of becoming the preeminent global investment banking and securities firm." The firm had considered going public on at least six previous occasions and always had pulled back. There was something unique, something special about being Wall Street's last surviving partnership (among major firms). There was something to be said, the partners of those times would say, about preserving that which makes us different from the rest of the industry, especially if the difference is one of the reasons for our success. All agreed the Goldman partnership was unique— it enabled a special sort of culture to develop and be preserved, a culture of cooperation, mutual dependence, and shared values. It was the Goldman culture that helped the firm keep its head when so many others on Wall Street seemed to be losing theirs. Anyway, based on Goldman's results, it was clear that it had worked. Goldman Sachs was among the industry's most profitable and successful firms.

The prospectus for the 1999 IPO revealed much of this story. In 1998 its net revenues (after netting out interest income and expense) were nearly $8.5 billion, on which the firm had pre-tax earnings of almost $3 billion, averaging over the past three years a 50 percent return on partners' capital, which in 1998 was $6.3 billion. The financial results for 1998 were actually disappointing. The firm had considerable trading losses in late 1998, and its fourth quarter results were 80 percent less than for the previous year's fourth quarter. Still, its compounded annual growth rate of pre-tax earnings from 1995–1997 was 48 percent. It held the leading market share in many of the competitive sectors of investment banking and was acknowledged as a preeminently successful wholesale finance firm, offering services in investment banking, trading, and asset management. Because it was a partnership (which did not pay taxes directly; the individual partners paid their own shares), the profitability numbers had to be restated for the IPO. Pro-forma net income after tax in 1998 was $1.3 billion.

So why did the firm decide it ought to go public after operating successfully for more than a century as a private partnership? If it was just a matter of capturing a good market, why hadn't the firm gone public in other good markets, as virtually all of its rivals had done? Why had the previous general partners resisted the temptation to cash in on a large premium when they had the chance? Had greed finally caught up with the current bunch? These were the questions that surrounded the IPO from the very beginning, capturing the attention of all of the country's financial media as well as all of the serving general and limited partners of the firm.

The firm's officially stated reasons for the IPO were to secure permanent capital to grow, to share ownership more broadly, and to permit the use of an acquisition currency should a suitable opportunity present itself. The first of these three was the principal reason. It was becoming hard to imagine how Goldman Sachs could continue to grow in all its areas of business, especially in trading securities, without its equity capital becoming permanent, not, as it was, subject to a two-year partnership agreement. After all, the firm had over $200 billion in total assets on its balance sheet, for which its capital coverage was only 3 percent. The nightmare that all the firm's leaders for many years envisioned was a bad year made worse by large trading exposures that went wrong and partners clamoring for their capital back. The limited partners just had to ask for it, and the general partners had to resign and become limited partners to get theirs back, but if the process was begun in earnest this could happen. Indeed this did occur in a lesser form in 1994, when there was a rush to the exits on the part of general partners fearing a sharp decline in the firm's earnings. All capital redemptions had to come out of the firm's retained earnings. Even though changes in the partnership agreement had stretched out the time period over which capital could be withdrawn, knowledge that lots of partners wanted out would be devastating to the firm. The rating agencies might be shocked into a sudden downgrade; banks and other lenders might stop lending money and ask for what was already loaned to be repaid. Cut off from credit, the firm would be unable to function and would begin hemorrhaging. This would all be bad enough, but worse, it could panic other partners into pulling their own plugs. Soon a capital redemption death spiral could result, which in bad market conditions could be extremely harmful to the firm, even if otherwise it was strong enough to weather the storm. And what if the drought lasted a couple of years—as it did in the early 1970s? Some partners thought this picture was too extreme, and that the firm had power to control withdrawals and to find other sources of finance. Others thought that sooner or later such an event could occur, and indeed probably would occur. After all those years of accumulating capital in the firm, no partner wanted to risk seeing it vanish because of such a sudden, unexpected chain of events. And if the firm wanted to grow in parallel with its peer group, it would probably need more capital to invest in new product lines or marketplaces or client services. Permanent capital was the real reason. The question was when to do it.

The firm had taken up an IPO several times before without reaching a consensus on doing it. Partly this was because of the windfall effect that would favor those who were senior partners at the time, and disfavor junior partners (not yet senior) and non-partner employees who would have been the partners of the future. In order for it to work, there would have to be a market price available that was sufficiently higher that the firm's book value (at which price partners had always done business with the firm) to provide a generous premium that could be shared with those otherwise disfavored by the decision.

In February 1999, when the partners voted to approve the plan to go public (an earlier effort had been withdrawn in late 1998 due to poor operating results and adverse market conditions), they were expecting a valuation of the firm in the area of three and a half times book value, or about $22 billion. But $22 billion was a lot of money to be shared by approximately 220 general, 100 limited, and two special limited partners, the Sumitomo Bank from Japan and Kamehameha Activities Association, an associate of the Bishop Estate, Hawaii's largest landowner. Altogether the limited and special limited partners accounted for approximately $3 billion of the firm's capital. This capital was mainly entitled only to a fixed income return and, beyond that, did not share in the firm's annual profits. With the exception of the special limited partners, the rest of the limited partners were not entitled to anything more than to receive their contracted income for differing maturity periods selected by them, and/or to be redeemed at 100 percent of book value.

The general partners, then, were the ones entitled to receive whatever premium the market decided to put on the book value of the firm when it went ahead with the issue.

At a valuation of $22 billion, for example, you could subtract $3 billion for the limited partners, and that would leave $19 billion for the 220 general partners to divide among themselves according to their partnership agreement, which allocated to each partner a certain percentage of the firm's net income. That would be a lot of money, approximately $85 million for the average general partner in payment for his or her capital retained in the firm over the years and his or her share of future profits.

But the firm believed that such a distribution of the premium would be ruinous. First there was the need to retain key employees who were not general partners, and those general partners who had just become such and were then entitled to but a small share of the firm's income. These people could never become general partners (or in the case of those who just had, senior general partners), which was part of the incentive that had kept them at the firm and justified turning down offers to work elsewhere at greater pay. Then, too, there were legions of valuable employees ranking behind this group—those with three to five years experience but who were just reaching their full strides. And if the firm was going to be able to withstand future market pressures and possible takeover threats, it would be wise for it to continue to have its officers and employees own more than 50 percent of the firm's stock. These considerations militated toward having a substantial number of shares in the new corporation be set aside for future grants to key employees.

And there was the question of whether the limited partners should share in the premium. When some of the other firms had gone public, the limited partners were not included in it. But most of the general partners knew that the decision to go public could have been made, but was not, by the previous generation of partners, and they knew that the value of the Goldman Sachs franchise, built up over so many years, was, in fact, attributable as much to others as to them. The general partners, in other words, were getting very rich because they had Goldman Sachs to sell when the market really wanted to pay a lot for it.

In the end the general partners, led by their executive committee, adopted a plan that reserved about 10 percent of the firm for future compensation and pension awards, and 10 percent for the limited partners (who were offered a choice of fixed income notes, cash, or stock for their interests). The special limited partners (after selling some stock in the IPO) ended up with about 10 percent of the firm between them, leaving 57 percent for the general partners, no small windfall at that.

The stock offering was brought on May 3, 1999, at $53 per share, and immediately rose to $77. The firm's largest individual shareholder was Jon Corzine, who owned 4.4 million shares. His shares were worth $340 million by the end of the day. Jon had fought hard to see the IPO through, but along the way he had some serious disagreements with his executive committee partners, and he resigned after the offering and was replaced by his co-CEO, Hank Paulson. By the end of the year, the stock was at $92 per share and Jon Corzine was an announced candidate for the U.S. Senate from New Jersey.

The nonpartner pool of recipients of the stock grants and options included some 300 to 400 senior employees, which made all of them millionaires, though some of them already were. The limited partners had been millionaires for many years, and many, by investing the money they had withdrawn from the firm, were very well off. The offering, however, produced an average of about $25 million in wealth per managing director, though the money would be locked in for years and subject to future market risk. Nevertheless, in May 1999 the Goldman Sachs money machine was responsible for having created at least 1,000 living millionaires. And that was before the stock doubled within the year.

CHAPTER 4

The Tycoons

I n a period in which the stock market has risen so much, it is no surprise that the pay of corporate executives has too. In America, but not in most other countries, chief executives make a great deal of money because a large part of their compensation is tied to the stock prices of the companies they head. So if the market increases fourteen-fold over a twenty-year period, these professional managers, and the thousands of corporate executives who work for them under similar stock-tied compensation arrangements, are going to get very rich. Very rich but, of course, not so rich as the founders of the companies. The managers do not take anything like the risk of failure that the founders do.

Professional managers are different from the entrepreneurs described earlier. They are usually formally trained and have spent lengthy periods learning how to operate in a competitive corporate environment. Part of what they have to learn is how to make money for the company, and part is how to operate in its unique political environment. Such managers learn that making money in a large company when commanding a team of people and large resources is a special skill of its own, a blend of organizational management and control and power-politics. It has little in common with life in a start-up company where business success or failure is a day-to-day thing, highly dependent on the leader's personal skills and abilities. A corporate general doesn't have to have any particularly well-developed skills of his or her own but he or she has to have a knack for generalship.

Wealth creation for corporate executives is a process of moving up the ladder into compensation packages of increasingly greater value and complexity. When great companies were smaller than they are now, a manager-CEO like Alfred Sloan (General Motors, 1923–1946) could gain access to a significant amount of stock in the company, which increased greatly in value during his tenure, permitting him to retire quite rich. It is more difficult in companies that have already grown to huge size for any CEO to get a comparable stake, or indeed to be CEO for quite such a long time. But in the 1980s and 1990s most CEOs saw their stock prices rise considerably, and their share holdings made them rich. No one wanted to remember the depressing 1930s or the dismal 1970s, when almost no one got rich just from the company stock. But in the past two decades, in which everything has gone so well for so many, executive compensation finally became a major source of wealth for the country as a whole.

PATTERNS OF EXECUTIVE COMPENSATION

CEO compensation increased substantially, especially during the 1990s. Median CEO total compensation (in constant dollars) for the companies included in the S&P 500 index increased 55 percent from 1992 to 1996, according to one of several such studies, to $3.2 million. Over this period financial service executives did even better—their median pay was $4.6 million. About half of the typical pay package was from salary and bonus, and two thirds of the rest was from stock option that the executives had exercised. The remaining 17 percent was from a variety of insurance programs, pension benefits, and other perquisites.[1] A stock option provides the right, but not the obligation, for the recipient to purchase shares of the company in the future at a purchase price that usually equals the market price at the time the option was granted. Executive compensation options usually have a life of ten years, which gives them plenty of time to ripen. The recipient does not have to exercise the options before they expire (though he may do so) or put up any money until the options are exercised. When that happens, some of the shares to be purchased under the option can be sold to pay the cost of exercising the options. If the stock price exceeds the exercise price during the option period, the options are considered to be "in the money," as they would produce positive value if exercised. If they would not, then the options are "out of the money," and the market price of the stock is below the exercise price. If an executive's stock goes down while he holds options, he may simply leave them on the shelf until the stock price recovers. Of course if they are out of the money when they expire, all those years after having been granted, then the executive has been unlucky.

Most companies give options to management as a wealth-creating incentive and to encourage their interests to be aligned more exactly with those of ordinary shareholders. At least that's what they think they are doing, but over the years the mechanisms of executive compensation have become very complex, and not everyone involved with it fully understands all the ramifications that are involved. Most companies want to be neutral about compensation practices; that is, they are willing to be generous to their executives but not to be taken advantage of. However, because the CEO is held in high esteem, and perhaps arranged for many of the individual directors to be appointed to the company's board, the boards tend to err on the side of supporting their CEOs rather more generously than they have to. They also want to follow what other companies do and frequently copy other companies' initiatives without much question. The boards are also often quite unsophisticated about the value of the options granted to their executives, and strongly resist disclosing these values as part of the companies' actual expenses for management compensation. Perhaps they think it makes their management team look overcompensated, but if so, maybe they are!

The convoluted methods of reporting executive compensation can add to the confusion that surrounds these other issues. It is clear that an executive's salary and bonus, and other forms of cash compensation, are appropriately disclosed as compensation. So should be the *value* of any new stock option grants, valued according to various generally accepted formulas and programs for determining the value of particular options to the holder at any given time. Current shareholder proxy statements, however, do not require that more than the *number* of shares being granted under option programs be disclosed, and the companies' accountants do not require that the value of the options issued be considered an expense. If options are not worth anything, then why grant them? If they are worth something, then why not account for them as a business expense?

Executives actually can make more (often much more) from the appreciation in the value of the company's stock than they can from their total annual cash compensation from all its various sources; that is, assuming they own a fair amount of stock and/or unexercised options in the company's stock. If they do, then the odds are that the stock or options they own were received as a result of some prior year's compensation award. But it is the appreciation in the value of the stock, not performance-related bonuses, that has made these executives rich over the past twenty years. Some executives also get to sock away generous retirement and post-employment consulting programs, and are the beneficiaries of golden parachutes, or special severance compensation provisions in the event of a merger or change of control of the company. These items, though potentially significant, are still small change relative to the potential for executive enrichment that flows from a series of generous options awards in a continually rising market. Obviously, getting a lot of options under these conditions helps a lot.

The annual increase in the value of shares already owned by the executives is not counted in the annual compensation numbers, nor should it be. The number of options actually exercised during the current year (another required disclosure for the proxy statement) also does not affect either compensation or wealth. The options were granted before, and whether exercised or not they represent the same value. Exercising options does not create wealth, though it may realize it. The SEC also requires disclosure of the number of shares underlying unexercised options that the executive may own (but the value of these options need not be disclosed) and the *value* of *in-the-money* options held as of the end of the fiscal year. This value is calculated by subtracting the exercise price of the option from the year-end market price, not by any effort to apply the valuation programs of Messrs. Black and Scholes to either these options or the out-of-the-money options. The required disclosure of information about an executive's options, therefore, can be pretty misleading. Consequently it is very difficult to estimate the wealth of an executive from the information furnished by the company's annual proxy statement. This is the information that appears in all the widely published annual executive compensation tables.

Further, we have the convention of reporting a company's earnings per share on a fully diluted basis, as required by the SEC. Here, however, only in-the-money options are counted, and it is assumed that money paid in the exercise of the options is used to repurchase outstanding stock. In many companies a large portion of all the options that have been granted to employees is out-of-the-money options.

American companies lead the world in tying compensation to stock price appreciation. Elsewhere there seems to be a greater value put on prudent stewardship and meeting obligations to all of the company's "stakeholders." If admirers or critics of our system want to know why things happen the way they do in American business— that is, why companies take the constantly proactive actions they do, in merging or investing or restructuring— they should follow the money, or check the compensation programs. Managers understand they are supposed to contribute to shareholder value while they are in charge, and if they do they will be paid enormous sums for it. The idea, however, is not to let the fox into the hen house, and to have all compensation arrangements approved by the company's independent outside directors and all details fully disclosed. Even so, the bias is to overpay for results.

How It Works

Most public companies have special committees of the board of directors, made up exclusively of nonexecutive directors, which recommend executive compensation programs. The committees often take advice from outside professional compensation consultants. These consultants are not owned by the companies involved, but neither are they any more independent than any other enterprise would be when wanting to please an important paying client.

Most American executive compensation plans are aimed at providing the incentives for executives to create value for shareholders. Shareholder value, however, is only realized from stock appreciation. If the stock price goes up, the stockholders don't mind being generous, and conversely, if it goes down, they want the CEO and the management team to share in the suffering. That's the idea, anyway, but there are a great many important details in executive compensation, and the devil is always in them.

A typical executive receives a base salary based on what other CEOs of comparable companies receive, plus an annual bonus that is tied to the company's accounting results, stock options, and other long-term incentive compensation, and a range of retirement benefits and perquisites. The bonus, paid in cash or stock or both, is usually determined by a formula based on the company's earnings, return on investment, or stock price. Some programs distinguish between designated "long-term" and "short-term" results. Stock ownership is encouraged and sometimes funds are loaned to permit the executive to purchase shares. Stock compensation arrangements can be in the form of grants (of stock subject to sale restrictions) or options to purchase stock in the future. The typical corporate stock option is exercisable at the market price at the time of issuance.

How the managers make out often depends as much (or more) on the deals they negotiate, and on how the market moves over the time they are in office, as on anything the executive actually does. Still, the logic is that the CEO and the top executive team should be rewarded for doing things that make the stock go up, even if it might go up anyway all on its own. Some companies, after all, just expand or contract more or less with the economic growth rate of the country, and stock prices (as we have seen during the past two decades) can go up simply because interest rates go down. No one doubts that Jack Welch of General Electric is a great CEO, but equally no one ever thought he caused the sharp decline in interest rates that occurred during his watch and helped GE's stock price rise.

As an example of how an executive's compensation is arranged and how wealth is created in the process, let's take the case of David Komansky, chairman and CEO of Merrill Lynch, in 1998. This was not a typical year for Merrill Lynch by any means. Its stock was about $72 at the beginning of the year, rose to $109 in mid-July, and then plummeted to $35.75 in early October, before returning to $66.75 on December 31, 1998. Merrill's net earnings in 1998 were $1.3 billion, down from $1.9 billion, and its return on average shareholder's equity decreased to 13.4 percent from 26.5 percent. Several of Merrill's peer group firms had similar results, and it was a hard year for many financial stocks. Certainly Komansky's performance as CEO was nowhere near as volatile as the market, but still it was difficult to evaluate. The compensation committee applied a predetermined formula that reduced Komansky's pay because of the decline in earnings, without punishing him for stock price movements that were assumed to be beyond his or anyone's power to control. Because the market acted as it did, and because he already owned a lot of stock in the company, he was less well off at the end of the year than at the beginning by an amount greater than what he received in total compensation.

His total reported compensation for 1998 was $9.9 million. This was made up of $700,000 in salary, a cash bonus of $4.5 million, and a stock bonus of $4.7 million, $3.6 million of which was in the form of ten-year options with an exercise price of $72.34. The bonus was determined by formula, which applied a 36 percent decrease to the prior year's bonus to reflect Merrill's decreased earnings and return on investment during the year. In addition the firm's Management Development and Compensation Committee, comprised of five outside directors and chaired by a former chairman and CEO of a major pharmaceutical company, recommended an adjustment to Komansky's 1997 compensation. In an earlier mid-year compensation review, the committee found that "the compensation of Merrill's CEO had fallen meaningfully behind the median amount provided to CEOs at Merrill's public competitors." The catch-up amount was paid in additional stock options. Needless to say, adjusting Komansky's 1997 compensation will increase the median amount that other firms in the peer group must consider in compensating their executives.

Komansky also received a total of $35,700 in miscellaneous company savings and retirement benefits, so his grand total rounded up to about $10 million for 1998. This amount, however, does not include (it was not compensation) an additional $14.2 million in profits on exercising options on 220,000 shares that Komansky realized during the year. Nor does it include the change in value during the year ($72 to $66.75 per share) on Komansky's 2.1 million shares and unexercised options. Komansky has been an employee of Merrill for thirty years and CEO since 1996, so his $150 million equity stake (less than 1 percent of all Merrill shares) had been built up over many years, but mostly in the last few. He is also entitled to pension plan annuities totaling $1.7 million on retirement. And, should he be terminated after a change of control of the firm (i.e., through a merger), then he is entitled to a severance payment of 2.99 times his average annual salary and bonus for the preceding five years, plus a variety of other payments that would total about $30 million.[2]

Though Merrill's CEO's compensation was much higher than the median for the S&P 500 companies in 1998, the method by which it was determined is representative. Though Merrill is a large American company, it is not by any means among the largest. Komansky is likely to retire, after less than 10 years as CEO, with wealth derived exclusively from the firm in the area of $250 million. That's surely big money, but not as big as some CEOs who have created huge amounts of shareholder value over longer periods of time, or as big as those coming from smaller companies, who have appropriated more of the companies' market value for themselves.

THE DOMINATORS

Almost all of America's billionaire corporate leaders head companies they founded. They are principally successful entrepreneurs who have lasted a long time as CEOs. Founders of successful public companies are different from ordinary people. They have been through a lot that has rewarded their judgement and energy at crucial moments, and they tend to be extremely self-confident individuals. Quite a few are eccentric, and most probably don't much give a damn what other people think about them. They run their companies as they choose, and certainly, while they are around, are the dominant persons in them. Often they are around for quite a long time, as Warren Buffett and Larry Tisch and a few others have demonstrated. Most CEOs who were appointed to the position by a board of directors when it became vacant, however powerful they may get to be, do not manage to dominate their companies to the same extent as the founders. The second or later generations of executives, who follow the founders, are different. Usually these executives accumulate some reasonable amount of wealth but nothing at all like what the founders got for their efforts.

Sometimes there is a niche between the first and the second generations, of founder-successors or founder-substitutes, that leaves room for those who move in after the founder to take on many of the original, dominating qualities. The line is thin between some of these people and others whom we might classify as founders in the first instance. But two American tycoons of the late twentieth century stand out as executives who have become masters of the companies they head but did not found. They are Maurice ("Hank") Greenberg, seventy-five in 2000, CEO of American International Group since 1968, and Sanford ("Sandy") Weill, sixty-six, chairman and CEO of Citigroup. Both have been CEOs for more than thirty years, both are stubborn, hard-driving workaholic New Yorkers whose hands are never far from the controls. Both chose the insurance industry in which to build their careers and fortunes. Neither intends to retire anytime soon, despite having reached retirement age. Both have had up to two of their children working in the business for them in senior positions. Both have a long history of being the most important reason that their companies have done so well. They are winning jockeys you bet on rather than the horse. Both have made their money as a result of accumulating stock in their respective companies over a great number of years, and of course, watching the stock price rise. Both are billionaires as a result only of their own efforts.

The Great Greenberg

Of the two, Greenberg is the richest (*Forbes* scored him in 1999 at $3.7 billion, and Weill at $1.1 billion) and one of the longest-serving CEOs among all publicly traded American companies. Greenberg is the son of a Catskills, New York, dairy farmer, who ran away from home in search of better opportunities, joined the Army in World War II, and let the G.I. bill put him through college at the University of Miami and New York University Law School. In 1960 he joined AIG, a smallish, privately owned, multi-line insurance company founded in Shanghai in 1919 by a twenty-seven-year-old American, Cornelius van der Starr, who ran the company himself for forty-nine years before turning it over to Greenberg eight years after he had been hired. Greenberg took the company public the next year at a market capitalization of $300 million. There followed a long, grinding period in which AIG developed its property-and-casualty and life businesses in markets all over the world and exploited its prewar Asian heritage, especially in Japan, Taiwan, and the People's Republic of China. In 1999 the company operated in 130 countries, through more than 300 insurance subsidiaries in some of the insurance industry's toughest businesses and in many of its toughest markets. But the company had built a rock-solid franchise for its businesses, managed costs superbly, and used its increasing amount of insurance float to fund new products and activities and the purchase of new businesses. Earnings per share increased in every year but one in the thirty-two years that Greenberg has been in charge, growing at a compounded rate of 19 percent. In 1999 it ranked twenty-second on the *Fortune* 500 list with 40,000 employees and revenues of over $30 billion. In early 2000 its market capitalization of more than $170 billion was the largest market valuation of any financial services company in the world after Citigroup ($210 billion).[3]

In 1998, having refused to pay too much to acquire American Bankers Insurance, a Miami credit insurance firm in competition with Cendant Corp., Greenberg turned his attention to a much bigger opportunity. In August he announced the acquisition of SunAmerica, Inc., a pioneer in selling variable annuities and other investments for retirement, for $18 billion in AIG stock. SunAmerica was the creation of Eli Broad, a successful homebuilder (cofounder of Kaufman & Broad) who shifted into insurance in 1971 when he bought Sun Life Insurance. In 1989 Broad spun off his homebuilding business and transformed the life insurance business into a financial services company specializing in retirement savings and investment products and services, which he renamed SunAmerica. This company went public in 1989, with Broad owning 42 percent. The stock was one of the best performers on the New York Stock Exchange, increasing in value by more than 40 percent per year for a decade.[4] As a result, and because of the premium of 25 percent paid in the acquisition (that enabled him to exchange his stock for about 23 million shares of AIG), Broad, sixty-five in 1999, became richer even than Greenberg, with his total wealth being valued at about $4 billion.

The two men are old friends and share a number of personal characteristics. Both claim to be type-A personalities and are very competitive. Both are quintessential hands-on owner-operators. They see a large potential to create new value together through the merger by selling each others' products to each others' customers. SunAmerica's nearly 10,000 independent brokers have begun to sell AIG's life insurance and other "mortality" products that SunAmerica has lacked. The companies will also launch a variety of SunAmerica products internationally, using AIG's distribution system in Asia and Western Europe. SunAmerica's global expansion is aimed first at Japan, where foreign-managed, dollar-denominated investment products are in great demand. Greenberg called the combined firms' retirement products a growth business for the future, and predicted that by the end of 1999, AIG's combined earnings per share would be greater than if the acquisition had not occurred.[5] A year after the announcement of the merger (which closed on January 1, 1999), AIG stock had risen a further 50 percent, and the deal looked like a natural success. Broad would continue to run his part of the business, and Greenberg his, though in Greenberg's case his part would consist of every part of every division of the whole company.

Greenberg is a control freak who expends all the energy it takes to make AIG all it can be. And a battalion of 100 powerful internal auditors insures that it doesn't become what it does not want to be. But Greenberg also is a man of vision, looking far ahead to plan the company's future. More than one third of the company's profits (prior to SunAmerica) still comes from Asia, which has had serious problems in recent years, though the company has been able to hold on to its earnings. Nevertheless Greenberg believes that the potential for AIG's business in Asia, played off its great market position in the area, is enormous. In 1998, for example, AIG started a credit card business in the Philippines and hired the former head of Citicorp's consumer business, Pei Chia, as a consultant, putting him on the board of directors. Greenberg also saw the company's heavy exposure to the volatile property-and-casualty insurance business, which had hurt so many of its competitors over the years, to have the potential to wreck earnings, and thus to worry shareholders. So Greenberg began to paw over the insurance businesses he was in—to exit the weakest and to fortify the rest. Also, at least a decade ago he decided to diversify into a variety of special investments and financial services. In 1999 these financial services, consisting of leasing, project financing, and trading activities, comprised 11 percent of the company's revenues and over $250 million of pre-tax profits.[6]

Greenberg also has an unusually paternalistic management style in which strong incentives are offered to those whose services he values and who stay with the firm until retirement (which for everyone else is at sixty-five). On December 31, 1998, 20.8 percent of AIG stock was owned by its management and directors, including Eli Broad. Greenberg himself owned (directly and indirectly) about 27 million shares of AIG, which were worth $2.7 billion. His salary, bonus, and stock options are very modest by comparison to virtually all other financial service executives except Warren Buffett. At Citigroup, by contrast, and at Merrill Lynch, less than 3.5 percent of each company's shares are owned by management.

Reloading Sandy

The other great dominating presence among CEOs of successful American companies in 1998 was Sanford Weill, after April 2000 the sole surviving chairman and CEO of Citigroup, the country's largest financial services organization. Citigroup was created in 1998 by the merger-of-equals of Citicorp, the bank, and Travelers Group, the insurance, finance, and securities company. Travelers was headed by Sandy Weill at the time of the Citigroup merger, and Citicorp was headed by John Reed; the two became cochairmen and co-CEOs until Reed, dissatisfied with the power sharing arrangements, announced his retirement in early 2000. "Sandy needs to run Citigroup," said a long-time colleague, "like you and I need to breathe."[7]

Weill is the personification of the scrappy, ambitious, and limitlessly determined middle-class Brooklyn kid (son of a Polish dressmaker) who goes out to make his name in the financial world with little more to guide him than his brains and his energy. Though Sandy graduated from Cornell in the 1950s, he worked as a $150-a-month clerk for Bear Stearns to learn the securities business. A few years later, he and three friends set up their own firm: Carter, Berlin, Potoma and Weill (later Potoma dropped out and was replaced by Arthur Levitt, who became chairman of the Securities and Exchange Commission in the 1990s).[8]

The little firm was Sandy's forge of experience. Here he learned how to manage a small retail brokerage, then larger ones. He developed a pattern all his own—first master all the details of the operational side, which most Wall Street executives eschewed, minimizing the costs of the back office and increasing its capacity while reducing headcount to the minimum. Then look around for another firm to acquire to expand the business, preferably a weak firm that had seen better days and could be acquired for little if any premium over its net asset value. Then move quickly to integrate the new firm into the old one, sucking its entire business into the expanded operations capacity and laying off all redundant operations personnel and the weaker members of the sales force. In the end what he did was take over the firm's customers (and some of its star brokers) at virtually no cost, then scrap the rest of its business. A few customers may have been unhappy with all this and left, but most stayed and were well serviced by the new firm. Then the process was repeated, again and again, until finally Sandy's little firm, a veteran of a dozen or so mergers of once prominent firms in about twenty years, had become one of the largest American brokerages, then called Shearson Loeb Rhodes, Inc.

During this time Sandy developed great reliance on a small number of bright, hard-working young associates, favored protégés who received much of Sandy's attention and guidance. The protégés were given great responsibilities, opportunities to develop their abilities, and exceptionally generous compensation. In return they were expected to adapt to Sandy's work habits and patriarchal characteristics and to spend hours in his presence, night and day listening to his views and desires. Sandy, as far as anyone knows, is always working. If he is awake, he is working, and when he works, he likes to have his confederates close to hand. The protégés have included Frank Zarb, now CEO of the NASDAQ/American Stock Exchange; Peter Cohen, the former CEO of Lehman Brothers during its American Express days; and Jeffrey Lane, former chief operations officer of Shearson Lehman, vice chairman of both Travelers and Citigroup, and, in 2000, CEO of investment manager Neuberger Berman. The last to join Sandy was Jamie Dimon, who served for fifteen years in many posts, ranging from Sandy's personal assistant to president of Citigroup, before he left in a surprise management shakeup in late 1998, only to resurface a year and a half later as CEO of the troubled Bank One Corp.

In 1981 Sandy sold Shearson Loeb Rhodes to American Express for $930 million in stock and became American Express's largest stockholder. The firm became Shearson American Express, and in 1984 it acquired the blue-chip investment banking firm Lehman Brothers, which was then on the ropes, for the bargain price of $380 million. The firm then became Shearson Lehman Brothers, and Sandy, leaving it behind, became president of American Express. But he chafed badly in the role of what he called "deputy dog"; that is, as a subordinate to Jim Robinson, American Express' longtime CEO. In 1985 he quit. He ranged around looking for a new opportunity (including proposing himself to head a weakened Bank of America) and finally settled on Commercial Credit Corp., a broken-down finance company, which he bought and immediately restructured in 1986. In 1988, continuing his well-polished practice, Commercial Credit bought Primerica, a financial holding company that owned Smith Barney Harris Upham, a fading old-line investment bank that had combined with a third-tier retail brokerage which was also weak at the time. Primerica, in a major move in 1993, then bought the retail arm of Shearson Lehman Brothers, which American Express was trying to get rid of before its poor results dragged down the stock price of the parent. Under Peter Cohen's management, Shearson Lehman had acquired the seriously troubled retail brokerage E. F. Hutton in 1987 for $1 billion, approximately its net asset value, in order to create the country's second largest retail firm after Merrill Lynch. But the deal, though substantially increasing Shearson's market share, had been difficult to manage and was losing money. Cohen was fired, and so was Jim Robinson, who was replaced by Harvey Golub. American Express then decided to get rid of its entire investment in the securities business. It split the security business into two parts—the Shearson Lehman Hutton brokerage arm, which was offered to the highest bidder, and a made-over Lehman Brothers, which was reoffered to the public in 1994.

In 1992 Weill bought a 27-percent interest in Travelers, and four years later acquired the rest of the life, and property-and-casualty, insurance business for $4.3 billion. Travelers was then combined with all the other companies Weill had accumulated, Commercial Credit, Primerica, and Smith Barney. Then, after an unsuccessful effort to build up Smith Barney by putting a former Morgan Stanley M&A star in charge, Travelers acquired Salomon Inc., the investment bank and trading house, for $9 billion. Salomon was merged into the Smith Barney/Shearson/Lehman/Hutton brokerage subsidiary, which was renamed Salomon Smith Barney. The parent holding company, the Travelers Group, had by now become a large-scale player in the financial markets. Its shareholders (now including the shareholders of several predecessor companies) were happy as could be as the Travelers stock roared upward in the bull market for financial services stocks in the late 1990s. Sandy had continued to apply his method successfully, and had returned to Wall Street in triumph after only a few years away. His trademark style had fully developed: buy something bigger that is weaker, fix it by cutting operating costs ruthlessly and invigorating the good parts of the business, then use the resulting enterprise to buy something else that is bigger yet, and repeat the process.

At the end of 1997 Weill was $400 million richer than he had been at the beginning of the year, due to the improvement in the market price of his stock. A year later, after the merger with Citicorp, his wealth had increased by at least another $400 million, due to still further rising stock prices. (Weill owns 15.4 million shares of Citigroup.) In 1998 he exercised stock options that realized $156 million. He also had compensation during 1998 in salary and bonus and other payments totaling $12.5 million, and he still held unexercised options valued at $41 million at the time of grant. The company's retirement plan will also pay him at least $620,000 for the rest of his life (once he retires, if he ever does). Altogether, slamming all these companies together has worked very well for Sandy Weill, whose wealth first exceeded $1 billion at the end of 1998.

Weill's wealth, by the way, is considerably greater than that of John Reed, Citicorp's former chairman and co-CEO. Reed owned 2.4 million shares of stock on December 31, 1998, worth about $125 million; stock options with an in-the-money value of $88 million; and received 1998 compensation of about $10 million. His annual retirement payments are to be approximately $6 million. Altogether Reed was probably worth something around $250 million.

One reason for the disparity is that Sandy owned much more of Travelers (the direct successor of Commercial Credit) than Reed did of Citicorp. In 1984, when Reed became CEO of Citicorp at forty-five, Sandy Weill was president of American Express, having already sold his substantial interest in the assemblage of various brokerages to the firm. His stake was subsequently invested in Commercial Credit, and the stake grew with subsequent acquisitions. Sandy, however, also relied on something else to increase his stockholdings, and hence his wealth. This something else is called reload options, an executive compensation device first introduced in 1988 by compensation consultant Fredrick W. Cook & Co. for Norwest Corp. (now Wells Fargo & Co.) and used a decade later by 17 percent of new stock option plans in American companies.

A reload plan, in essence, automatically issues new options to replace shares that were sold by the recipient to exercise options already granted. The replacement options are not tied to the executive's current performance and indeed are issued automatically when the recipient sells shares to exercise options. They have no cost to the recipient, although all options, whatever their exercise price, are worth something, usually something like 25 percent to 30 percent of the exercise price. The reason that boards of directors adopt the reloads is to get executives to accelerate their exercising of options into shares so they can become significant shareholders earlier than they might otherwise. This is something that many shareholder activists like to see. As shareholders, management's interests are more exactly aligned with those who acquire shares in the market, and the value of this alignment is seen to be equal to the cost of issuing the options. But reloads are complicated, and it is doubtful that many boards actually understand what they are giving away.

An executive with ordinary shares granted to him or bought will gain or lose as market prices change, just as will ordinary shareholders. The executive's and the shareholders' interests are thus fully aligned. But it may take years for the executive to accumulate enough shares to become wealthy, and so the board decides, as an incentive and reward for past performance, to grant the executive options to acquire shares in the future. If the stock price declines below the exercise price the options will not be exercised; if the stock price rises they may be exercised because the executive can use the gain in the stock price to fund his requirement to buy the shares from the company at the exercise price. Either way, the executive wants to see the stock price go up, not down, and if it does he gets some of the benefit of owning shares without putting up any money at all.

For example, to make your CEO feel well rewarded for performance, you grant him options on 200,000 shares at an exercise price of $20. Assuming an option value of $5 per share, the award has an economic value of $1 million, which was not reported as compensation. Three years later the stock is $40. The executive profits by exercising the option into $8 million of stock, for which he must pay $4 million. This he does by selling 100,000 shares, retaining 100,000 shares worth $4 million. To make a $4 million profit, an ordinary shareholder would have had to invest $2 million. Options permit you to make money in the market without investing any, and they don't appear to cost the company anything when they are granted because they do not have to be accounted for as a compensation expense. But they were definitely issued as part of a pay-for-performance compensation incentive scheme. The economic effect of the scheme was to leverage the executive's ownership position in the company (by allowing him to acquire the shares without investing any money of his own).

Leveraging the ownership interest effectively means that the executive wants the stock to go up, and not to go down, more than the ordinary shareholder does. Shareholder activists don't have to worry.

But reloads are different and can change the alignment of management incentives significantly. In the case of reloads, after the exercise of his original options, the executive now has 100,000 shares, owned outright, and no options. He continues to perform well, so you grant him 200,000 options at $40, perhaps worth $2 million, valued at $10 per option. Say three years later the stock price is $60 and the executive exercises the options for $8 million and receives $12 million for his stock, a $4 million gain. But if the executive instead sells his first 100,000 shares in order to exercise the options, the reload program will *automatically replace those shares with free options,* in this case 100,000 new options exercisable at $60. This occurs regardless of the executive's performance. In effect the reload provides the executive with a free put option on his initial 100,000 shares. The executive is guaranteed that he can sell his stock to the company (to exercise options) when he wants to, and thus it can be seen as a way of hedging the executive's exposure against a downslide in the company's stock price. Such a hedge has actual value—you would have to pay to buy a put—but the company gave it away for free. But further, ordinary shareholders do not have a hedge against the stock price falling so the interests of shareholders and management can be seen to have diverged. Maybe management would like to venture on a particularly risky proposition, knowing it has some downside protection against a fall in share price if the plan fails. This is a situation that economists call moral hazard, in which owners end up with more risk than managers; not something shareholder activists like to see.[9]

The reload process can continue for quite some time, with new options being issued periodically, for which all the executive has to do is to exercise old options. This has nothing to do with performance, but it does rapidly increase the number of shares an executive can accumulate in a bull market. The board approving reloads seems to be acting as if it only wanted the CEO to get rich as quickly as possible, regardless of performance. Sandy says he "loves reloads." Who wouldn't?[10]

Thus under the Travelers reload provisions, which Citicorp did not have, Sandy Weill in 1998 exercised options on 7.1 million shares, for which he was required to pay the exercise price of $156.5 million to the company. He raised this sum, however, by selling 5.9 million of the shares he already owned. Under the reload provisions, these 5.9 million shares were automatically reissued to him in the form of new options with an exercise price equal to the then-prevailing market price. So he exercised options on 7.1 million shares, using 5.9 million shares he already owned to do so, which shares were reloaded. On balance, he came away with a net addition of 1.2 million shares and 5.9 million options to the Weill stash. Over the years this practice has allowed Sandy to accumulate much of his 15.4 million share holdings. In 1999 Citigroup changed its option plan to incorporate reload options for everyone in the plan.

In 1998 Citigroup had 205 million shares set aside for options. This was 8.5% of the group's total outstanding shares of 2.4 billion, though the 1999 plan would increase the shares reserved for options closer to 10 percent. At

Merrill Lynch, which does not have reload options, the percentage of total restricted shares outstanding and those reserved for options was 21.2 percent. Rather than reload, Merrill's board just grants more options to more of the key employees. If they can't make the CEO rich one way, the board has a variety of other ways to do so.[11]

FOUR CAPTAINS

The *Forbes* 400 list published in 1999 included only a few of America's best known captains of industry. True, you had to have more than $600 million to make it, but that sum didn't seem so large in a world of so many large companies with soaring stock prices. Among those who headed public corporations they or their families did not found were only Hank Greenberg; Sandy Weill; Michael Eisner of Disney; and Cuban-born Roberto Goizueta, former CEO of Coca Cola (a billionaire on the 1997 list), who died in 1997. Among those prominent, longtime CEOs who have never made the list are Jack Welch, the legendary CEO of General Electric, one of America's perennially most valuable companies; and colorful Irish Anthony O'Reilly, now chairman of the H. J. Heinz Corp. Four of these—Goizueta, Eisner, Welch and O'Reilly—had much in common. They all became CEOs of run-down, tired-out, large nonfinancial American corporations in the early 1980s (O'Reilly in 1979) and revived them. The compounded average growth rate of the stocks of these four companies averaged 20 percent over the eighteen-year period 1981 to 1998, as compared to about 14 percent for the S&P 500. Coke had done the best (through 1997, when Goizueta died), increasing forty-six times in value during this period but selling off significantly since then. Heinz did the worst, increasing only sixteen times, and its stock was fairly lackluster during many of the middle years of the period. Disney, too, dropped in price in the late 1990s as its basic business weakened. But these four captains were perhaps the best known of all American CEOs during the 1980s and 1990s. They were famed for their dramatic examples of leadership after the dreary, low-performance 1970s: dynamic leaders who reshaped the companies they managed and created large amounts of shareholder value over a sustained period. Surely such leaders would be worth much more than their weight in gold (approximately $1 million for a 200-pound man at late 1998 prices) to their grateful shareholders. In fact many would take the attitude that if the CEO could make the stock price rise significantly, there would be no objection to sharing the gains with management. Make us rich, they said, and you can have a healthy percentage of the gains. The four captains delivered, and in turn they got rich. So did thousands of other CEOs and senior executives throughout the country—but all not equally so.

The Coca-Cola Kid

Of the four most prominent captains of industry, Roberto Goizueta was the richest, when he died of lung cancer in 1997 at sixty-five, and probably the most unlikely to have become rich. He was born in Cuba in 1932, attended Yale, became an engineer, and joined the Coca-Cola Company in Cuba before Castro as a local employee, having answered a want ad. He found himself on the fast track rather by accident, helped by fortuitous heart attacks and sudden vacancies. Once there he quickly adapted to the fustian, old-Atlanta managerial style of the company's real boss, ninety-year-old Robert W. Woodruff, the one-time management genius behind the company, who had retired but not given up much of his power. Goizueta shamelessly courted and flattered Woodruff and was successful in gaining his sponsorship. In March of 1981, after twenty-six years with the company, he took over as CEO at the age of forty-eight. His record as chief executive seems, in retrospect, to be marked as much by mistakes as by great achievements. He was behind the strategy that led to the purchase of Columbia Pictures in 1986, but recognized the failings in the concept soon enough to offload it to Sony in 1989 for a profit. He was also the guy behind the disastrous switch to New Coke, which the marketplace rejected at once. What he did do, however, was to simplify the company, by deconglomerating it and concentrating on the thing it did best—sell soft drinks that cost next to nothing to make, especially to foreigners. He tightened cost controls, sold off the company's bottling subsidiaries to free up capital and improve returns, and watched earnings grow. He also attracted Warren Buffett as a major shareholder, and a slew of institutional investors who swooned over Coke's inestimable, intangible franchise value. When he started, the company's stock was especially depressed, but in 1991, a decade after his appointment as CEO, it had a market capitalization nine times greater and a 35 percent compound rate of return. But his 1991 compensation package was to put Goizueta in the headlines as America's highest paid CEO, for that year the Coca-Cola board approved an outright gift of 1 million shares of restricted stock to him, as a bonus. Though he was prohibited from selling the stock until he retired, he was entitled to dividends and voting rights. The grant also provided that Coke would pay any taxes that might be due on the sale of the shares in the future. The original million shares were subsequently split and rose further in value, and further grants were made. By the time Goizueta died in 1997, 11.2 million shares had been granted to him, and the company was due more than $1 billion in deferred tax credits due to his compensation. After Goizueta died, however, the company's performance slid backward, and his successors have struggled to restore the company's record of earnings and stock price growth. But by then, maybe the streak had been played out, and the strategy of concentrating on earnings in a major bull market had produced all the benefits it could.[12]

"Mickey" Eisner

Michael Eisner, Walt Disney CEO, has been a prominent member of the *Forbes* club since 1993. He became CEO in 1984, at age forty-two, and, like GE's Welch, continues to serve as chief executive. During his time in office, Eisner also transformed a poorly managed, troubled company into the most dynamic corporation in its industry. During the fourteen years that Eisner was CEO (through 1998), Disney stock increased at an annual compound rate of 25 percent, as compared to 17.7 percent for a four-company composite of entertainment industry companies. Eisner, in his years as CEO, probably made more changes to the company and backed more innovations than even Walt Disney himself.

Walt Disney died in 1966 at sixty-five, with his first

theme park, Disneyland, in operation and Walt Disney World in preparation. However, he had failed to prepare a successor, and his seventy-one-year-old brother Roy, the CFO, ran the company for a while before he died in 1971. The Disney family stock passed to Roy's son, also called Roy, who was rightfully unhappy with the way the company was being run. For several years Disney floundered, being the subject of greenmail raids and continuous rumors of LBO attempts. The Disney board finally settled on Michael Eisner, then president of Paramount Pictures, to lead it out of its troubles. Eisner is widely given credit for rebuilding the Magic Kingdom into a highly successful, multimedia entertainment conglomerate. He reorganized the businesses and attracted extraordinarily talented people to work for him. He introduced new concepts for commercializing Disney's existing entertainment assets and real estate, added several new theme parks, including major ones in Tokyo and Paris, and pursued independent movie and TV show production. He also acquired one of the most admired companies in the media and entertainment industry, Cap Cities/ABC, for $19 billion in 1995. The record was not entirely flawless, of course. His closest associate, Disney president Frank Wells, died suddenly in 1994, after which Eisner became embroiled in a couple of ugly, and extremely expensive, senior executive personnel problems, and left his shareholders wondering about succession after a quadruple bypass operation. But nonetheless the stock price continued to rise, nearly doubling from the beginning of 1997 until the early part of 1998. Then, suddenly, Disney, like Coke, seemed to have used up all of the market's confidence in it, and the stock sold off sharply. It recovered somewhat afterward, but some of the magic was lost.

As of the end of 1998, Eisner owned nearly 11 million shares of Disney stock (worth $387 million) and had been given options on another 26 million shares, which Disney valued at $107 million. The majority of the options, however, were issued with exercise prices that increased over a fifteen-year period, expiring in 2011. These options would not come into the money unless Disney's stock price increased at an annual rate of at least 4.7 percent from 1996. This was a relatively new idea in the options field in the late 1990s, intended to prevent companies from giving away too many shares for just ordinary performance. During 1998 Eisner exercised options on 22 million shares (selling most to finance the cost of exercising them) and realized $570 million in profits in doing so. He was worth over $700 million at the end of 1998, a little less a year later, according to *Forbes*.

Neutron Jack

On December 31, 1999, General Electric stock was trading at around 35 times earnings and had a market capitalization of more than $500 billion, the largest market capitalization of any company in the world, including Microsoft, which had just given up the position. The company has been headed for eighteen years by John F. Welch, sixty-three in 1999, who joined the company in 1960 and took over as CEO in 1981. Jack Welch has certainly made more difference to GE than any previous CEO since Thomas Edison, and indeed may have made more difference to the company he led than any other CEO in history. The old General Electric was a sleepy, bureaucratic conglomerate of industrial companies that was in danger of falling behind its many rivals for market share and profits. Jack shook everything up, sold off underperforming businesses, and made several major acquisitions. He preferred higher technology and growing markets. He wanted his organization to be lean and mean. He was perceived as being ruthless and uncompromising, qualities he felt were necessary if the go-slow inertia of General Electric was to be changed. He developed the nickname "Neutron Jack," which he hated, from the so-called neutron bomb that killed all the people but left the buildings standing. He understood that to change an aging dinosaur like GE as much as he wanted to, almost as much energy would be required as in a nuclear detonation. Few CEOs would have even attempted such a task.[13]

The new company's objectives, Welch said, were to be only in businesses in which it could be a major player, ranking among at least the top three firms by market share. GE owns businesses in thirteen distinct sectors, including NBC; the world's largest nonbank financial services company; and the leading maker of aircraft engines, power generating equipment, and medical imaging machines. Welch has focused on enhancing shareholder value and rapidly reducing GE's swollen payroll. GE's shareholders have seen their investment increase by more than $300 billion, growing at a compounded rate of more than 23 percent, during Welch's tenure.

In 1998 the GE stock price increased by 39 percent. In that year Welch received $10.9 million in salary and bonus and was granted restricted stock and options valued at

$41.1 million at the time they were issued to him. In addition to this compensation ($52 million), he also derived income in 1998 of $46.5 million from exercising options on 660,000 shares previously granted to him. Exercising a certain number of these options is more or less an annual event for Welch. So his annual income was about $93 million for 1998. Welch owned 2 million shares of GE stock outright (worth about $200 million before capital gains taxes), and an additional 4.7 million shares that were available as restricted stock or stock to be issued through options (valued at $260 million before taxes).[14] Still, mighty Neutron Jack, for all he had done for his stockholders and for all the stockholders' board of directors had done for him, was a bit too short to make the *Forbes* 400 list in 1999. He still has a couple more years to try, however, before he has to retire.

Irish Tony

Anthony J. F. O'Reilly, once a star rugby player for the Irish national team, took over as CEO of H. J. Heinz Company in 1979 at the age of forty-three. In 1998 he gave up the CEO job after nearly twenty years at the helm but remained as chairman of the board. During the time when O'Reilly was CEO, the company's stock price increased at 17.3 percent per year, about the same rate of increase as the Standard & Poor's food group index. The stock rose sharply soon after his appointment as CEO, from below $3 per share to close at $13.50 in 1986. It closed at $23 in 1989, then languished there for six years until finally breaking out in 1995, when it closed at $33. During this period, when O'Reilly's compensation was reportedly among the highest received by any American CEO, he was often prominently featured on lists of the country's most overpaid executives.

During 1998 O'Reilly received approximately $3 million in compensation. On December 31, 1998, he owned 6.2 million shares, worth $350 million, and options to purchase an additional 750,000 shares that were worth about $6 million. After retiring as CEO he was to receive annual compensation of at least $500,000 per year, plus such bonus as the compensation committee of the board of directors decided to recommend, plus $1.2 million in annual retirement benefits. Further, O'Reilly, who has retained his Irish citizenship, has a number of significant business interests in Ireland and is a partner of a law firm in Dublin.

O'Reilly's compensation was determined by a committee of six nonexecutive members of the company's board of directors. It reviews the CEO's salary, annual incentive bonus, and options grants in comparison with the compensation received by ten peer group companies and takes advice from a compensation consultant. Compensation is also "based on payment for performance in achieving predetermined goals that contribute to corporate earnings, with the objective of enhancing shareholder value." Performance goals for the company's executives are established by the compensation committee. Of the six members of the compensation committee in 1998, two are former senior officers of major corporations who were appointed to the board after O'Reilly became CEO. They were in their early seventies at the end of 1998, but the other four committee members ranged in age from seventy-seven to eighty-one. The average age of the six committee members was seventy-seven, making it perhaps the oldest board committee in America.[15]

At the end of 1998 Heinz's market capitalization was $16.5 billion, up from about a billion when O'Reilly took over. Overall O'Reilly has contributed to the creation of about $15 billion of market value for Heinz over twenty years, of which he received about $350 million (2.25 percent), plus a generous amount of cash to live on for the rest of his life. Was that a fair amount of the gains to be distributed to the man in charge? For a long-term performance that only equaled the average of twelve food companies, could the board have got someone just as good to work for less?

Coke paid Goizueta 1.3 percent of its $100 billion market appreciation during his tenure. Disney had a market cap gain of $60 billion as of December 1998 during Eisner's watch, of which 1.1 percent was given to him. Sandy Weill and John Reed, co-CEOs of Citigroup, between them owned about $1.5 billion of equity in their company, which saw its market capitalization increase by $150 billion by 1998, a combined percentage of about 1 percent. Hank Greenberg presided over the creation of more than $150 billion of stockholder value, of which he benefited to the extent of about 0.8 percent. In Jack Welch's case, the stockholders got a real bargain. More than $300 billion of market value was created with only 0.17 percent of it ending up with the CEO. That leaves Irish Tony as the best paid CEO of the group, in terms of what he contributed to shareholder value—his stock holdings, per unit of value of shareholder increase created, were thirteen times as large as Jack Welch's.

ALL THE REST

The six men profiled presided over the creation of an enormous amount of market value, almost $1 trillion over two decades, or about 8.5 percent of all the growth in market capitalization of U.S. stocks since 1980. Between them they captured for themselves an average of 1.3 percent of the gain in their companies' stock market capitalization for their services. Most of their shareholders were glad to have the deal they got, though periodically all of these CEOs have been on the list of overpaid corporate executives prepared in conjunction with annual compensation surveys. *The Wall Street Journal*'s 1998 survey of 350 well-known publicly traded companies, which was prepared by consultants William M. Mercer, Inc., included fifty-six CEOs (excluding founders or inheritors, but including our six) with personal investments in their companies of more than $100 million.[16] Assuming that of the $10.6 trillion gain in total stock market value from 1980 through 1998, around 1 percent in aggregate was paid to CEOs, then that would represent about $100 billion of increased personal wealth for them. Perhaps another $200 to $300 billion has been accumulated by other senior managers of all these publicly traded companies. Altogether a third to half a trillion dollars has passed into the hands of America's hard-working, methodical, and often colorless managers of publicly traded companies.

Many of these corporate managers were from the technology, consumer products, pharmaceutical, and finance industries, where a great deal of the market value increase that has taken place over the past two decades occurred.

The hired hands that have run the companies founded by others have been paid extremely well for their management efforts, though they have been paid only a small fraction of the gains actually recorded by shareholders. Never before has the American managerial class done so well, propelling for the first time hundreds of their number into the ranks of the very rich, and thousands into the ranks of the ordinary rich. American managers make far more money than their European counterparts (as recent mergers between Daimler Benz and Chrysler, Deutsche Bank and Bankers Trust, and British Petroleum and both Amoco and Atlantic Richfield, clearly revealed). CEO pay, too, is at an all-time high in relation to the average factory wage earner—a ratio that in 1998 was about 200, up from about forty-five in 1965—a fact not missed by journalists, union negotiators, and government officials.[17]

Pay-for-Performance

Large parts of the American public, however, are convinced that "executive compensation" is a term only to be defined as excessive. All of the major business newspapers and magazines publish annual compensation data, one of the principal purposes of which appears to be to rain scorn on greedy CEOs, intimidated boards of directors and their compensation committees, and all those involved with the process of setting the rules. Compensation abuses, when they occur, are widely reported in the media as if they were normal business behavior, and watchdogs and vigilantes have sprung up among institutional investors and regulators as a result. They lobby for improved transparency in compensation arrangements and attempt to draw shareholder attention to potential problems. On the whole their efforts have been worthwhile and have contributed to numerous improvements in the disclosures about executive compensation that enable the rest of us to see what's going on. These efforts force companies to face full disclosure of their compensation actions and should be continued. But the fact is, most investors are either indifferent to the complex issues involved in properly understanding executive compensation or vote to support management when it is challenged on these issues. Most investors seem to believe that if the management team can get the stock price to rise over and above that of their peers, then they ought to be paid well for it. And the best way to pay them is to provide strong wealth incentives in terms of ownership of company stock for getting the stock price up even further, so their interests and those of the shareholders are closely (if not exactly) aligned. What shareholder of IBM, for example, would quibble about the fact that Lou Gerstner, brought in as CEO in 1993 when IBM was about to take its last rites, now owns more than $500 million in IBM stock and options? The stock is worth that much mainly because under his leadership (after others had failed) the business was turned around and became a strong technology company again.

But the experiences of Gerstner and the other CEOs mentioned do not enable us to duck a number of important questions: Are we getting the performance we are paying for? Is the negotiation between agents of management and the representatives of shareholders a fair one in which neither side has a built-in advantage? And is the market indifferent, in terms of the valuation, to a company that repeatedly pays too much to its managers? Lots of efforts have been undertaken by academic observers to study these things, though a full set of results is not in as yet. But preliminary indications are that each of the questions should be answered no. If a company repeatedly gets its compensation equation wrong, then it will probably have to pay a price for it. It's basic market law, going back to Adam Smith.

The boards of directors of all public companies maintain a committee for recommending the compensation packages of management. A few companies insist that the CEO be a member of this committee, though most see that doing so creates a conflict of interest. The committee is usually made up entirely of nonexecutive directors, called outside directors because they are not employed by the company, and therefore are independent to an extent that no employee director, an inside director, could ever be. The committee is also usually chaired and led by a long-serving director who knows the company's culture and its history, and who is considered loyal to management. Its task is to hire consultants, study the compensation arrangements of peer group companies, assess the company's performance relative to the peer group, and make recommendations for the compensation of the CEO and other top officers. Periodically the committee resets rules to account for the latest tax arrangements and rethinks compensation requirements to emphasize, for example, long-term results, or to tie the standard more directly to accounting measures, such as earnings, or to the company's stock price. Formulas can be devised, especially for salaries and bonuses, but not so easily for longer-term results for which rewards in terms of a greater equity interest are more appropriate.

In principle pay-for-performance is generally thought to

be a good, solid, American free-market kind of idea. But it is much more difficult to implement than most people think. Accordingly three kinds of errors get made, and almost always these favor management.

Compensation committee members are not experts, and they must rely on others, mainly consultants, who are. The consultant's job is to study the compensation packages of peer group companies to enable the members to eyeball where their man fits in, and to make adjustments so he is not being underpaid. (It is always assumed that if he should ever be underpaid, however briefly, he would quit the company and the committee would have to find someone else.) The system generally comes up with a periodic need for an upward adjustment of the package that their man has. This may be because he really is underpaid (in terms of, say, salary and bonus but not, perhaps, in stock participation), or because the peer group has been chosen to favor those with generous plans. (Disney is in a lot of peer groups.) The committee then has to ask what performance is it that they want to reward, for which they may go back to the consultants. What does the peer group do? Are we competitive? Some companies tie accounting performance to cash compensation (which may amount to less than half of all wealth-creating compensation) and judge stock option grants and related compensation programs some other way—how did we do relative to the peer group? If everything is tied to a peer group average, then just beating an average result by a little may be seen as a significant achievement when it is not.

Manipulating the System

On the committee, no one wants to be the resident spoil-sport or the pain in the ass who is always questioning people's performance and their pay packages. The board, usually made up of persons invited to join by the CEO and who are grateful and pleased to be members, wants to be supportive of management. But this willingness to please, together with a reluctance to criticize, may cause the committees to err on the side of being too generous, especially on the nonformulaic part of the compensation package. In 1991 Roberto Goizueta was granted a million shares of restricted stock, not options but the stock itself, worth more than $80 million, because Herb Allen, a Coke director, proposed it to reward outstanding performance, and the others wanted to be supportive.[18] Coke's stock price had done very well, despite a couple of blunders ("new" Coke, Columbia Pictures), as a result of decon-glomerating, stock repurchases, the opening of markets in Eastern Europe, and because Warren Buffett became an investor. In Goizueta's case the pay may have been disproportionate to the performance. He died six years later owning 11 million shares that he received through subsequent grants and options.

Compensation committees can also be excessively generous in awarding reload options and in allowing options to be repriced after issuance. Executive options usually have a life of ten years and are exercisable at a price equal to the market price at the time of their issuance. The option itself has a value, one that can be calculated using the Black-Scholes formula, for which Scholes was awarded the Nobel Prize in economics (Black had died by then). The formula takes a number of factors about the stock into account, especially its volatility. It then generates a value that the market ought to be willing to pay to have the chance, *for ten years*, to convert into stock by only paying the exercise price set at the time of issuance. To change any of these terms after the option is granted is to change its value.

Allowing stock options to be repriced once they are issued can be a seriously overgenerous use of them as a compensation device. Repricing occurs when the exercise price is lowered to match a declined market price. If the stock price drops (usually because of some action associated with management's performance, but sometimes because of general market conditions) the options are supposed to be worth less. To reprice them (presumably to keep valuable managers from being disillusioned into leaving) is to restore their lost value and remove the risk of being a stockholder from management (but not from anyone else).

Take the case of Cendant Corp., a company created by the merger of two consumer services businesses in 1997. One of these, HFS, Inc., was headed by Henry Silverman, a former Drexel Burhman executive since turned into a successful financial entrepreneur (a *Forbes* 400 member). The other company, CUC International, a direct marketer, was headed by a man named Walter Forbes, who became chairman of Cendant, Silverman being the CEO. Within three or four months Silverman's people discovered that CUC's cash was overstated by $100 million or so, an oversight that certainly seemed too big to have been missed. Cendant's stock dropped from $42 to $14. Silverman was furious and forced Forbes to resign, though he did so with a multimillion-dollar severance check. Forbes said he didn't know anything about the fraud. Silverman then began the task of picking up the pieces. He was, after all, the biggest shareholder of the company. He held 46.3 million in-the-money options in Cendant stock valued at $800 million at year-end 1998 (after the fraud was discovered), including 17.2 million options that were repriced by the board in September 1998 to the market price then prevailing, and in some cases at a 50 percent premium above it.[19]

If there is no reason for doing this except to keep a CEO from threatening to leave, then it is completely in opposition to pay-for-performance rules, and indeed starts to look like blackmail or exploitation. Repriced options, as in the case of Cendant, are pay to managers only for *bad* performance, or for general bad conditions that affected all shareholders. After such a fiasco as the CUC International merger, should the Cendant shareholders want Silverman, who arranged the merger, to be rewarded? Surely with all the options he already had he was not likely to get up and leave. If the Cendant stock price simply returns to where it was when the fraud was discovered, Silverman could make approximately $300 million, but the shareholders that stuck with the company during this period will have made nothing. Why should the managers responsible for the disaster get a better deal? If you want to keep your CEO after a market "accident," then encourage him to be worthy of a new grant (for performance in adversity) that would be issued with an exercise price at the current market price, which should look cheap in the future if the CEO is successful. It is no wonder that institutional investor watchdogs search out repricing abuses and try to call stock holders' attention to them. Unfortunately instances of repricing occur all the time, and although well disclosed, they are seldom disturbed.

Finally, compensation committees can make the error of being too lax. Are they too willing to look the other way when the lawyers shred any remaining real performance features from their executives' contracts and add a myriad of little details in which many devils lurk. One wonders just how vigilant the Heinz board's compensation committee (the one whose average age was seventy-seven) was in running down all the details of O'Reilly's compensation. If lax and unvigilant, how can the compensation negotiations between manager and shareholder not be biased toward the manager?

Seeking the Balance

Despite some evidence of significant compensation abuses, the general opinion seems to be that the overall effect of such behavior on American corporations is both modest and tolerable. For the most part the investing public thinks that when executives do well the shareholders do, too, and therefore excessive compensation is not a big deal. It is, after all, only a transfer of wealth, however involuntary or as the result of indifference, from shareholders to managers, and the public should not be concerned.

Maybe so, but the system is increasingly subjected to a corrupting influence in which those who wish to manipulate the system can do so with impunity, at the expense of the vast community of American shareholders that is more than half made up of savings and other financial institutions. The system has adopted practices in which constant repricing of executive compensation based on peer group averages slowly but steadily pushes compensation costs up regardless of performance. The quantity of shares reserved for executive compensation (through options, restricted stock grants, or other plans) has continued to grow to levels that now represent substantial potential dilution of shareholder value. And accounting practices do not require full reporting of the actual costs of issuing options and other compensation arrangements, so that now more than a third of total compensation expense (more in many cases) is off the books. There is not much effort to adjust companies' earnings per share to reflect these costs which were incurred in particular years, presumably in exchange for performance. These things tend to obscure or distort the valuation of companies in the market, but in the end the market finds out.

Take Merrill Lynch as an example, although you could take any of the stocks that did well in the 1990s, especially including the technology stocks. In 1998 if you looked carefully at the footnotes to its financial statements, you would realize that Merrill (which had a bad year in 1998, when earnings per share declined by 38 percent) paid out 52.4 percent of its net revenues (gross revenues after interest expense) in cash compensation. Merrill is a large, predominantly retail organization, which has a reputation for managing well and not overpaying its employees. Yet here they are, paying out the same percentage of net revenues as the pure investment banks, which arguably have more demanding personnel requirements. Further, Merrill had authorized and issued 145 million restricted shares or stock options for executive compensation plans (not all of which were outstanding), an amount equal to *40 percent* of the total number of Merrill Lynch shares outstanding at the end of 1998. The effect of the dilution upon the exercise of already outstanding options would have reduced Merrill's earnings per share from $3.43 to $3 (−12.5 percent), or to $2.77 (−19 percent) if future options expected to be outstanding were taken into account. Merrill tries to limit the dilution effect by purchasing its shares in the market when it is permitted to do so (to make available shares for the future exercise of options without issuing new shares to do so). This means spending corporate cash on the program, perhaps without full consideration of whether the money might best be used for something other than supporting its executive compensation program. In the three-year period ending in 1998, Merrill repurchased 50 million shares in the market while issuing 38.5 million new shares to employees through restricted stock or options programs. At the end of 1998 Merrill's stock was trading at 19.4 times 1998 undiluted earnings per share, and twenty-four times fully diluted earnings per share. Which multiple should be used to assess Merrill's true value?

Future dilution in earnings per share affects the stock price. The more dilution, the less the stock market is going to like it. Maybe this factor explains a significant part of the discount that many financial services shares trade at, relative to the S&P 500 index. Most investment banks follow Merrill's practices (remember how the compensation committees work) of high cash compensation and significant options for top performers, and increasingly other large banks and financial securities companies are doing so also. But in the end the market seems to know and chops some value off the company's share price. General

Electric, by comparison, traded at forty times earnings at the end of 1998; it had 3.6 percent of its outstanding stock reserved for options already issued. Potential dilution of GE's 1998 earnings per share as a result of options issued would be less than 4 percent. In 1998 41 percent of GE's revenues, by the way, came from financial services, so the comparison with Merrill Lynch and other financial services companies is not far-fetched.

Compensation arrangements don't have to be those that Merrill and many other companies employ, especially if getting the best outcome for stockholders is the objective. There can be other ways. But the most competitive industries will tell you that getting the best people is the most important part of their success, and these people require the most competitive pay packages. This is what really matters—that the companies perform well so future generations of corporate managers can also aspire to big money because they earned it. But along the way many companies should clean up their acts. It could be in their interests to do so.

CHAPTER 5

The Entertainers

A star is someone rich and famous. More than that, a star is a supercelebrity, a special person that the public knows and gladly pays money to see, or hear, or watch perform. Ordinary celebrities are people other people are interested in, even fascinated by. Such people are often able to capitalize on their fame, however transitory it may be. Even Monica Lewinski came to be a celebrity for a while and, if nothing else, got a lucrative book contract out of it. Stars, however, make a living out of being celebrities.

Stars and celebrities live inside the extended boundaries of the entertainment industry, one that generated nearly $200 billion in revenues in 1998. This industry has been shaped by prosperity, which has generated increasing amounts of time for leisure activity and the money to enjoy it. The industry has also been expanded by new technologies and media forms that provide access to a growing variety of different forms of entertainment. People have to pay for the entertainment, of course, which they do either directly or through consumption of products that advertisers are attempting to sell, so as a result the industry is dependent on the general economic health of the country.

The entertainment industry principally consists of filmed products (movies and TV shows), recorded music, radio, TV and cable broadcasting, and all kinds of sporting events. Also included, but less important, are book and magazine publishing, and live performances. It's a large industry, with many crossovers from one media segment to another. The movie industry makes TV sitcoms, too. Rock stars make movies to promote album sales—otherwise they live on the road selling tickets to their concerts. Athletes gain recognition by being on TV, which can be parlayed into other media. Many athletes write autobiographies and appear as guests on talk shows. They would also like to sell you sportswear, how-to videos, and branded athletic equipment. The number of people working in such a large industry is vast, but the number of stars, those that broadcasters and advertisers really want to put on the air, is only a tiny percentage.

Most stars are highly talented individuals from the world of entertainment and professional sports. They perform in ways that dazzle the rest of us, as Barbra Streisand has done with her singing and Michael Jordan with his jump shot. Most of the rest of us have few such talents of our own, so not only do we recognize extraordinary talent when we see it, we tend to be captivated by it. Extraordinary talent, however, has to be very rare—one in a million, or even ten million—or it's nothing special.

If it is true that only 1 percent of high school students plays as starters on varsity teams, and only 1 percent of these do so in college, and only 1 percent of the college players makes it into the pros, professional athletic talent is certainly statistically rate. But if only 1 percent of the pros makes it to the halls of fame, then the odds of any of us being a star athlete like a Jordan or a Wayne Gretzksy or Jack Nicklaus (the preeminent players of their generations) may not be any better than about 1 in 10 million. Talent so rare should be worth paying money to watch. And if there are enough people interested, and ways for them to witness the performance, and enough money out there for the willing to pay to make it all happen, then the lucky performer may end up very wealthy.

ECONOMICS OF STARDOM

But even so, it takes more than pure talent to make the grade. A real star is someone among the top one thousand or so of all persons in the public eye, those most frequently subject to media exposure. This may be all the celebrities an eager public can keep track of, but it is less than 0.0004 percent of the American population. Within this fortunate group, however, financial success comes from creating value from celebrity, value proportionate to one's popular appeal. The more appeal you have, the more, and the more often, people will pay to be in your presence or to purchase products associated with you. Your name becomes a brand, which has to be managed like any other brand. Managing such a brand, one that depends on talent, success, and persona, is a delicate thing. Some do this extremely well and create a variety of different markets for their brand, the more the better. They know when to push their products and when to withhold them. All such activities are designed to maximize the potential cash flow that can come from high celebrity standing during what may turn out to be only a few years of opportunity. Crowd appeal is a fickle thing, and many once-successful performers lose it after a few years. Only a very few, like Frank Sinatra, have been able to maintain large-scale audience appeal for long periods of time. Everyone else is at the mercy of a whimsical market that can love you one day and drop you the next. Stars have to make the most of a limited window of opportunity.

Windows of Opportunity

Forbes publishes, among its many lists, a list of the top one hundred American celebrities, ranked by some sort of measure of star power. The list is arbitrarily made up of forty top entertainers and producers, forty athletes, and twenty authors and celebrities from other worlds, all ranked (in the *Forbes* way) by their incomes. The top twenty had an average income of $75 million in 1998, the bottom twenty of $11 million. Virtually all of their income was taxable at regular rates, and there were few opportunities for stock options, capital gains, or other forms of wealth-building that are common among corporate executives.

An average star, for example, might expect a ten-year period in the limelight. Within this period, the star's income would break into the million per year class and rise rapidly to, say, $20 million, before declining back to the one-million level. Considering full tax rates, and substantial payments to agents and others advisors, let's assume that the star is actually able to retain 50 percent of the cash flow and that this cash flow could be invested at 10 percent. The ten year payment stream, then, would have a net present value of something around $23 million, which could generate an annuity of about $1 million in revenues from tax-free bonds. A million a year in after-tax income is nothing to sneer at, but it may not be all that we associate with true stardom and the low probability of achieving it. Indeed it appears that the top hundred CEOs of American corporations in 1998 earned as much on average as the celebrities did. Surely, however, they did more to increase their wealth through options plans and other devices. The celebrities may have one-in-a-million talent, which no one believes the standard-variety CEO has, but the CEOs probably end up with more money.

It is also worth pointing out that statistics do not apply to individuals. If you should be a potential big star, just entering your window, you do not really know whether you will do as well as the average star or not. Your appeal may not last as long as others or generate as much income. Going in you might actually be convinced that your particular chances of netting out at $23 million were much less than 100 percent, say, more like 30 percent. In such a case the expected value (the probability times the value of the outcome) of your time in the spotlight would drop to $7 million. And remember, you are already discovered, a star-to-be, which only a tiny percentage of star hopefuls ever get to be. If you go back in time a little further, before you got to be starlike enough to have a window of opportunity, the forward-looking probabilities fall off even further. Even considering all the money that stars get, when you also consider the probability of getting it, most people, regardless of talent, might find themselves with a higher lifetime expected value from careers as an insurance salesmen.

For stardom to turn into wealth requires that the net cash flow thrown off from selling the brand be managed efficiently and reinvested productively. If you get to be a star, and do all of these things well, you ought to be able to retire wealthy. Not all do so. Few stars are well educated, practical, and conservative people who understand both the limitations of their fame and the importance of thrifty habits and good investment management. Few also have had any training in the mundane fields of accounting, investments, and tax planning, though increasingly services are provided in these areas by agents and other advisers.

The great commercial advantage of being a star, of course, is the leverage. There is only one you but there is a potential audience of tens of millions that can now be accessed through the various entertainment media. And today, by distributing it in hundreds of countries outside the United States, the market for your product can be greatly expanded.

But it has not always been this way. How wealthy stars have ended up also depends on other things. Byron Nelson may have been the best professional golfer of his generation. (Bobby Jones was an amateur.) He won most of the big tournaments and, in 1949, managed a string of eleven tournament victories in a row. In that year he made a total of $63,000. In his entire career he probably earned less money than dozens of professional golfers do now in a single year. The golf business just wasn't much of a business when Nelson played, because the sport wasn't widely popular and there was no television to broadcast it on. Surely no one ever thought of putting golf matches on the radio. There were few sponsors for the big tournaments, no market for videos or golf schools or opportunities to put their names on fancy courses in resort communities with condos, so guys like "Lord" Byron (and his contemporaries, Ben Hogan and Sam Sneed) had to go without. Indeed most of the growth in the professional golf business has come in the last twenty years. In 1970 the total purses paid out on tour was about $7 million; by 1998 the amount had grown to $130 million.

Even the great Babe Ruth didn't die rich, coming as he did before television. And great athletes before baseball (the first professional league game was played in 1876) virtually did not exist—there were few sporting competitions, and with the possible exception of boxing, no opportunities to become famous at all. Before the movies, entertainment stars were mainly singers and writers, who lived off their ticket and book sales. Certainly they were more famous then than they were rich.

A lot depended, too, on the amount of exposure stars could get once they were known. The modern entertainment industry (music, TV, and movies) has been able to reach more people than ever before. Today's movie stars, such as Harrison Ford, have probably been seen at least once by virtually all the 280 million people living in the United States and at least that many outside the country. Over his long career, in the *Star Wars* and *Indiana Jones* series and in many other films, he has probably been seen by several hundreds of millions of ticket buyers. Clark Gable was perhaps a more famous actor in his time, but he couldn't have been seen by even a tenth as many people during his lifetime. In 1998 Harrison Ford made $58 million in income, a few pennies each from all of his viewing audience.

How much stars can earn also depends on the business deals they make. Most entertainment stars are paid a flat fee for what they do, others agree to a percentage of revenues. Some perform a variety of services in a movie (e.g., actor, director, screenwriter, producer, even investor) and are paid something for each. And entertainment stars get a variety of lavish personal expenses as part of their deal, paid for by the film's producers and backers, so they can live well for very little when they are working. Star athletes can negotiate long-term contracts and, when the contracts expire, become free-agents able to sell themselves to the highest bidder. They also, when they are famous enough, attract product endorsement contracts, guest appearances on TV shows, book contracts, and a variety of other opportunities to generate more income. Tiger Woods, for example, made $27 million in 1998, of which $24 million was from endorsements.

ENTERTAINERS

Mary Pickford was the country's first movie star. She began her career in silent movies in 1909, when she was seventeen years old and the movie industry was just coming to life. She made movies with the legendary director D. W. Griffith early in his career, and the two made the careers of each other. She was the stereotype of a beautiful, childlike, and lovable female character. She was by all accounts a hard-working, highly professional actor, and she remained a hot property during her entire career, which continued until 1933 when the silent movies were replaced by talkies. She was married to the first of the great swashbucklers, Douglas Fairbanks, and the two of them maintained a storybook marriage for sixteen years that continuously assisted their careers. She is said to have been "the face that launched one hundred million film fans," and was the first woman in America to earn more than $1 million in a year from her own endeavors. She was also the brains behind the effort to organize United Artists, a corporation that would employ the principal actors and sell their services to the studios producing the movies. She was thought to be a very shrewd businesswoman and investor and made a huge fortune for the Fairbanks family and for her business partner, Charlie Chaplin. She died in 1979, having lived as a star for most of her eighty-seven years.[1] She was talented, fortunate, hard working, and professional. But more importantly, she was also a brand-marketing expert, a courageous dealmaker, an enterprising opportunist, a careful investor, and a generous contributor to charities.

After Mary the movie industry developed very rapidly when the talkies were introduced, and it has continued to grow despite the inventions of radio, television, cable, video rentals, and the Internet. As the audience increased, others coming along got the benefit of it. First there was a posse of Western stars, including Tom Mix, Hopalong Cassidy, Gene Autry, and Roy Rogers.

Selling the Brand

Autry and Rogers were the most successful of this group. They capitalized their stardom into fortunes worth hundreds of millions of dollars. Unlike their rivals, both were vocal, which meant they could play in a whole new genre of films, the musical western, which would introduce many popular new ideas, such as colorful outfits, singing ranch hands, and cowgirls. But they were both aware of their brand names and marketed them aggressively, offering a variety of branded products such as records, sheet music, radio shows, children's books, clothing, and toys.

Roy Rogers, "King of the Cowboys," performed in Western movies from 1935 until the early 1950s, when he turned to a weekly television show featuring himself and his wife, "Queen of the West," Dale Evans. This show ran until the early 1960s. Roy Rogers was probably the first movie star to diversify into an unrelated business line that could still benefit by identification with the brand. This was the move into the Roy Rogers fastfood restaurant chain, developed with the Marriott corporation and later sold to Hardees, which carried on making money for Roy and Dale long after they were both too old to perform themselves. Roy died in 1998, at eighty-six, but you can still visit the Roy Rogers Museum or its website, or buy his records and keepsakes. The brand name franchise goes on beyond even the grave.

Gene Autry, "The Singing Cowboy," had a similar career, though reportedly one that was more successful financially. He had all the business angles to promote his brand that Roy Rogers had, but he also invested heavily in Los Angeles real estate and owned the California Angels baseball team. Autry was perhaps the first star to parlay his sizeable earnings into a real fortune just from investments. He also died in 1998, at ninety-one. You can still visit his museum in the town of Gene Autry, Oklahoma and several very active websites.

After the cowboys there were a number of big Hollywood stars in the 1940s and 1950s who lasted a long time and worked their brands for as long as they could. Bing Crosby, the singer and actor, was one of the richest. He made dozens of movies and records, and had radio and TV shows. Frank Sinatra came along about a decade later and was just as successful. Then there was Elvis Presley, and the Beatles, and Barbra Streisand, all of whom were in both the music and the movie business.

And Owning It, Too

In 1999 the only performer to make the *Forbes* 400 list was Oprah Winfrey, forty-five, the first woman to ever earn more than $100 million in a year. Oprah is an actor, a producer, a TV-show hostess, and a savvy investor. She was listed as being worth $725 million. She may become the first black billionaire in America someday, but she was probably among the least likely to do so. She was raised in Mississippi by a tough old grandmother. She was a highly verbal child, a beauty, and a natural performer. She talked her way onto a radio disc jockey's show in Nashville, and was instantly successful in attracting an audience. Then she moved to TV, first in Baltimore, then in Chicago. She dreamed of being like Barbara Walters and learned to interview people very empathetically. She moved to daytime TV and hosted a show for women that was immediately successful. She took on highly emotional subjects, like trauma and sexual abuse, and introduced much controversial content in her show that was new to television. Her audience loved her. She made movies, too, winning an academy award nomination for her performance in *The Color Purple*. But as she was still an employee of an ABC-affiliated company, her show could not be syndicated beyond the network. So in 1986 she quit, hired a tough, streetsmart agent, and signed on with King World Productions, which would syndicate the new *Oprah* to 138 stations across the country. The show quickly ran away with the daytime television market, which was then bringing in $2.5 billion in revenues. Oprah's draw was so strong, she (like Mary Pickford and, later, Lucille Ball) was able to form her own production company, called Harpo ("Oprah" spelled backward). A production company, or studio, produces shows that are syndicated by the distributor, in this case King World. Profits from the ownership of the show would thus be shared between Harpo and King World. She also signed a contract with ABC for six primetime TV movies and recently extended her talk show in the 1999–2000 season for an estimated $120 million per year, plus stock options in King World that could make her one of the company's largest stockholders.[2] In addition, in 2000 she announced a new magazine, called *O*, a cable TV investment in Oxygen Media (a cable and website network for women), and a website of her own, Oprah.com. She certainly had all the qualities necessary for success as a celebrity—the basic talent, the vision of a brand, the ability to maintain and market her celebrity, the business sense of her own value, and ultimately, the ability to secure ownership and control of it.

The top-earning entertainer in 1998, however, was not Oprah (she was second) but Jerry Seinfeld, whose money was largely derived from ownership of his own TV show, the one about "nothing." Seinfeld was reported to have earned $225 million. After Jerry and Oprah, the list falls off sharply to film stars Harrison Ford, Robin Williams, and Mel Gibson, all in the $50-million-plus range. Musicians in this range in 1998 included the Rolling Stones, Master P (a rap artist), Celine Dion, Garth Brooks, Sean (Puffy) Combs; cartoonist Mike Judge also made the cut. The fortieth-ranked entertainer, in terms of 1998 income, was Julia Roberts, with $28 million. The income curve, however, starts to fall off sharply after Julia. The 100th-ranked entertainer is in single-digit millions, and by the 500th ranking the entertainer is probably only a bit further along than he or she was when they were waiting on tables somewhere. A brand sells or it doesn't, but it desperately needs a chance to be recognized and more than a little help in first getting established.

Assembling the Package

The producers know this and work the system to their benefit. They assemble expensive branded and/or inexpensive unbranded talent and put it together into a vehicle to be packaged and sold in multiple ways to the entertainment market. They control the vehicle itself (the movie, music album, concert tour, whatever), the budgets and the contracting (the ever-so-complex division of the gains). A moviemaking project includes, in addition to acquiring the property itself, a variety of other tasks: financing, manufacturing the film, distributing, and marketing and advertising. Producers hope to make a substantial development profit, much like a real estate developer makes a profit from similar activities in putting together a shopping mall or similar project (in the entertainment business, developers are called producers).

Producers work to assemble as many packages for the market as they can. They are risky endeavors, like venture capital investments. Most are only barely profitable, many are flops, and very few are extraordinarily successful. So most producers, or the studio organizing the packages, want to diversify the risk through a variety of syndication and other risk-sharing mechanisms. These are complicated, so a battery of specialists is involved in almost every aspect. The projects are also expensive (the average total cost of 240 films produced in 1996 was $60 million) and, therefore, very capital intensive and highly leveraged. Movie production is closely tied to interest rate movements and the availability of funding from a variety of different sources, including junk bonds, limited partnerships, and the stock market. Films earn money from being shown, first in domestic theaters, then in foreign theaters, pay per view, worldwide home video, pay TV, foreign TV, network TV, and syndication to cable and other networks. But they have to be heavily promoted, advertised, and hyped to attract the public. Even so, no one knows when the film is made whether or not anyone will wish to see it.[3]

In the early 1980s the film industry was scrambling for talent, for stars to make new movies that could shore up their market share against increasing competition from cable TV and videos. Michael Ovitz, then chairman of Creative Artists Agency, was the agent for much of the industry's top talent. Ovitz knew how to work the town and auction off his charges for the highest possible price. He even put film deals together himself, on behalf of his actor clients, a role normally left to experienced producers. Few of these deals were successful for the studios, but the artists did very well. Margins and returns declined sharply. But many of the studios changed hands into conglomerates managed by tough-minded controllers. Time Warner (Warner Brothers), Viacom (Paramount), News Corp. (Twentieth Century Fox), and Disney were hardening to the idea that the stars should have all the money, and they began to crack down on costs, cancel expensive projects, and replace stars with unknown actors to raise returns. Stars that were used to working for $10 or $20 million a picture found themselves being offered less than half that amount if they wanted the part. Most did.[4] Ovitz left the agency business in 1995 to join Disney as president, replacing Frank Wells who had died. Michael Eisner believed Ovitz knew the Hollywood game better than anyone, but in the end he didn't do Disney much good. He was let go after less than a year on the job (pocketing a $100 million separation package).

The most spectacular of the big-time movie producers at the end of the 1990s was Steven Spielberg, who was an exception to all the rules. He had a long list of box office successes, beginning with *Star Wars* and including the *Raiders of the Lost Ark* series, *Schindler's List*, and *Saving Private Ryan*, all huge moneymakers. Speilberg's income in 1998 was reported to be $175 million, and his net worth about $1.6 billion and still rising fast. Another nonacting star was George Lucas, a special-effects and distribution genius who was Speilberg's collaborator in the *Star Wars* and *Raiders* movies, who was worth $2 billion. Lucas certainly understood his market. The original three-part *Star Wars* series, produced in the early 1980s, was tweaked up and re-released in the mid-1990s. Then he devised a new series that would cover the time before the original trilogy, a prequel to it, with a happy mixture of new characters and old ones (when they were young). It, too, was a blockbuster success.

David Geffen was the music industry's top producer in the 1980s. He was a college dropout who finagled a position in the mailroom of the William Morris Agency, then talked his way into the music business, signing up a few minor performers and doing well promoting them. In 1970 he started his own record company, signed up Linda Ronstadt, Joni Mitchell, and the Eagles, and later sold the business to Warner Brothers, where he met entertainment industry legend, Steve Ross. He worked for Ross briefly as a vice chairman of Warner Brothers, then accepted financing from Ross to form a new record company, which was a big success with performers such as Gun 'N Roses, Aerosmith, and Cher. In 1990 Geffen sold the business to MCA for ten million shares of stock. Subsequently MCA was acquired by Matsushita at a significant premium and Geffen was on his way to becoming Hollywood's first music billionaire.[5] After the sale Geffen continued to dabble as a producer of films and Broadway productions, and in the mid-1990s he joined Steven Spielberg and Jeffrey Katzenberg, who had left Disney in an ugly public dispute with Michael Eisner (just before Ovitz arrived), in forming a new multimedia production company, Dreamworks SKG. Its three founders, with a combined net worth of over $4 billion, would know no limits. In 1996 Dreamworks raised $1 billion from a large group of starstruck investors who did not believe that anything these three worked at wouldn't be a big hit. At first it was slow going, however, but then it got better. Spielberg's Oscar-award-winning movie *Saving Private Ryan*, which Dreamworks had to share with Paramount, was the group's first hit, but other efforts like the animated *Prince of Egypt* were duds.

ATHLETES

A significant number of our top entertainers are over fifty years of age. After all, it takes awhile to get established in the business and to get the brand name working effectively. Other entertainers, however, may find that their careers depend on their looks or youthfulness, and that they are in danger of becoming faded brands before they know it. The real economic value in being a star is in keeping the brand on the shelf. Athletes, of course, have a hard time with this. Even if they don't get injured, they are usually too old to compete after forty. They have to make their money while they can.

Endorsements Make the Man

The best brand name in athletics in the late 1990s was without doubt Michael Jordan. Though he was able to earn a $31 million salary from the Chicago Bulls, for which he was the franchise player until he retired at the end of the 1998 season, his real income, nearly $50 million, came from product endorsements. Earning nearly $80 million in 1997, Jordan was the highest paid athlete ever. But after retirement from basketball his income would drop considerably, though Jordan is a skillful brand manager and will surely think of something to make up for the lost salary.

After Jordan on the list of high-income athletes in 1997 were boxers Evander Holyfield and Oscar de la Hoya. Holyfield had a very big payday the night Mike Tyson bit his ear off, earning $33 million. This kind of payoff, of course, is available only from a much-hyped championship match; most professional boxers never see anything of the kind. The boxing audience is not large, nor does it attract endorsements, but everyone turns out for a top fight, which is offered only live and on pay-per-view TV. Holyfield's total income of $54 million included only $1 million of endorsements, the rest being in the form of payments from previous fights. Even Mike Tyson earned $27 million in 1997 (more than Tiger Woods), though this, not surprisingly, included no endorsements. However, popular forty-eight-year-old George Foremen, who collected over $10 million from fights in 1997, also earned nearly $5 million more from endorsement of a countertop cooker, a "lean, mean grilling machine." Boxers may not be associated with a particularly glamorous sport, with lots of brand management opportunities, but there has probably never been any athletic brand name as well known and admired as Muhammad Ali's, though he was not a significant endorser of other people's products.

After the boxers, in 1997, came the race-car drivers, Mike Schumacher and Dale Earnhardt. Schumacher is a Formula One king with big earnings from racing and $10 million more from endorsements. Earnhardt is a stock-car driver with $16 million of endorsements against $3.6 million of racing income.

Then there was a slew of other basketball players: Shaquille O'Neal, Grant Hill, Horace Grant, David Robinson, Alonzo Mourning, Juwan Howard, Hakeem Olajuwan, Dennis Rodman, and Reggie Miller, all of whom managed to aggregate income of more than $10 million. The contributions to this income, provided by their respective endorsements, however, was far from evenly distributed. O'Neal and Hill each collected endorsements worth more than $12 million, and Rodman, then the colorful bad boy of the Chicago Bulls, picked up $6 million.

After Tiger Woods, golfers Greg Norman, Arnold Palmer, and Jack Nicklaus were the best paid in their sport. Palmer had $16 million of endorsements in 1997, Norman $13 million, and Nicklaus $9 million. Palmer and Nicklaus, however, had been receiving significant endorsement income for twenty years or so. Golfers seem to be naturally good brand managers. After the golfers, the *Forbes* top forty athletes for 1997 picks up a variety of baseball and hockey players, and ends, in fortieth place, with Brett Favre, the star quarterback of the Green Bay Packers and the only professional football player on the list. His total income was $9.2 million, of which $3.6 million was from endorsements. The *Forbes* fortieth ranked entertainer, on the other hand, made nearly three times as much. Everybody likes movies and music, not everybody likes football, and Favre had only been at the game professionally for six years in 1997. Most likely he would have only another ten years or so as a star, assuming he was not injured or cut.

Sports Economics

Sporting teams that are organized into a league actually operate as a cartel. They can restrict entrance into their league, and they set the rules, not only of the game itself but who can play the game and how competitive practices involving recruitment and compensation for players are regulated. College sports are different from professional sports, but only in the details. The idea is to create a league of a finite number of generally evenly matched teams that people will pay to watch play against each other, year after year. The people will turn into fans if the quality of play is good and consistent, and the games are exciting and the rules observed. The more fans, the bigger the market for the product and the more the revenues that can be generated. But to make it all work, the leagues have to have power to increase the number of teams, to regulate transfers of ownership of teams, and to negotiate broadcasting contracts and allocate the money received among all of the teams in the league. This is not as easy as it sounds. Despite the high popularity of tennis and soccer, and most women's sports in the United States, economically successful professional leagues have been difficult to establish.

The big four professional sports in America in the late 1990s were baseball, basketball, football, and ice hockey. In total, these four sports generated attendance of over 100 million in 1995, with baseball accounting for about half, though the growth rate in baseball attendance for the previous fifteen years was only 1.7 percent.

But many more people take in the games on radio or television. In 1995 1,742 hours of broadcast television time was allocated to sports. Of this, 27 percent was for football, 19 percent for basketball and 17 percent for golf (not a "major" sport, but a rich one in terms of advertising). Baseball received 7 percent of the broadcast hours, tennis also 7 percent, auto racing 4 percent, and ice hockey 2.4 percent. In addition, cable television managed to fit 7,200 hours of sports onto its (more narrowly and locally focused) networks in 1996. About 29 percent of these hours were for college basketball and football, 18 percent for major league baseball, and 11 percent for golf. The total of the two types of televised sports programming combined is 8,944 hours of sports TV per year, which divided by 365 days, gives us a little more than twenty-four hours of sports per day for 1995. A true sports fan couch potato need never stir.[6] The television broadcasting contracts bring in billions of dollars to the leagues, in amounts that have been rising steadily as advertisers fork over more and more money to reach viewing audiences. The leagues distribute these revenues among their teams.

The ownership structure of sports businesses is not like other industries. In 1998 there were 116 major league teams in the big four sports. Of these, eighty-four were all or partly owned by sixty-six different publicly owned corporate investors. Nineteen of these were media, entertainment, or communications companies, and seventeen more were from a variety of manufacturing or general industrial firms. Of the rest, fourteen were financial services companies and thirteen were consumer products or retail firms. Four of the teams, the Boston Celtics, the Green Bay Packers, the Vancouver Canucks, and the Florida Panthers were publicly owned.[7]

For the team owners the share of TV receipts is a big

revenue item, without which most of the teams couldn't exist. They also get revenues from ticket sales, parking, stadium luxury boxes, and other concessions, but they have to foot the bill for the team's payroll and expenses. Teams that own their own stadiums have much better underlying economics than those that do not. Those that don't often try to persuade local and state governments to build a new stadium for their team (which would provide the owner with a better contractual deal). Such projects are usually financed with tax-free municipal revenue bonds, which the city or state is obligated to repay. The issuing authority would lease the facility to the team to cover the obligation, and justify doing so on the grounds that new jobs were being created and people would move to the area to attend events. There is very little evidence that such justifications are legitimate, but cities and states are still attracted to the idea of having a local major league team. Also, many owners have adopted the practice of leasing facility naming rights to corporate sponsors who will pay to have the facility named for the company, as in the Continental Airlines Arena at the Meadowlands Sports Complex in New Jersey. At the end of 1997, approximately one third of all major-league sports teams had entered into naming rights agreements. Some of these were quite valuable. Staples, the office products retailer, for example, agreed to a twenty-year name-lease for the Staples Center, for the Los Angles Lakers (basketball) and Kings (hockey), for payments with an estimated value of $100 million.

But the biggest headache for the owners in all sports teams was their relationship with the players, and it had been for a long time. In 1970 baseball players forced a union on their owners, and economic values began to shift from owner to player. Further, in 1976 the Supreme Court disallowed the "reserve clause" in baseball players' contracts, which required the player to negotiate with the team owner, and no one else, when his contract expired. The players, inspired by their union, then forced a new system on the owners in which they could become free agents once their original contracts expired and could negotiate with any team in the league for their services. When a new player first signed on, he usually took what he was offered and was grateful for the chance, though in recent years signing bonuses and lucrative salary arrangements have become more common for outstanding players. After playing a few years the player could establish his true value to the team, so that when his contract expired, he could expect the owner to match that price or let him try his hand at negotiating elsewhere. But in reality players discovered that they could usually extract a premium value for their talents by selling them to another team rather than staying put. Competition for players, special needs of teams, and some other factors were responsible for this, including the retention by the players of highly skilled agents to represent them.

In the end the outstanding players did very well by the free agency system, as several teams would bid for them when their contracts were up. Such players, after all, could sell tickets to games and maybe help the team win a title. But the free-agency system was less attractive for less-good-players, ones who were being marginalized by younger players or who were thought to be too expensive to keep on for just a few more years of service. The union was able to negotiate a minimum salary rule in baseball to assist these players. As a result of these developments, the economics of team ownership declined in baseball.

In some markets, like New York, the money coming in was good enough to be able to spend it freely to acquire top players, and the Yankees, which did so, became perennial winners. This was not thought to be fair to teams in less highly populated markets, and was considered a threat to the effort by the league to maintain teams of approximately equal quality. So a mild form of payroll cap was added by the league (in the form of a tax to be paid by teams exceeding limits) to keep things more even. Also, the economics of baseball were being disturbed by the increasing number of acquisitions of major league teams by companies involved in the media, entertainment, and communications industries. The Atlanta Braves were owned by Time Warner, the Chicago Cubs by the Tribune Company, the Anaheim Angels by Disney, the Cincinnati Reds by Gannett, and the Pittsburgh Pirates by CBS. These companies have many reasons to benefit from owning a sports team and do not necessarily require that the team itself be profitable, as long as profits can come from other activities, such as broadcasting the games. This created conflicts of interest between owners and destroyed much of their negotiating solidarity. This put a lot of pressure on independent owners in the late 1990s to sell, which many of them did.

Owning a Team

By the end of 1998 all the sports leagues had shared some if not all of the changing economic characteristics experienced by baseball owners.[8] Baseball had done the most to destroy its own economics, it was agreed, and hockey had not yet been able to develop them very much. Basketball and football did better at marketing themselves and in controlling player demands. According to *Financial World* magazine, which publishes a somewhat controversial list of team valuations for all major-league teams, the average major-league hockey team was worth $90 million in 1997, up from $50 million in 1993. For baseball the average major-league team was worth $133 million in 1997, up from $109 million in 1993. Basketball teams averaged $150 million in 1997 ($71 million in 1993), and football teams, worth the most, averaged $202 million in 1997 and $129 million in 1993. Most had about doubled in the four-year period, but baseball teams had lagged the others. *Financial World*, however, still estimated that George Steinbrenner's New York Yankees were worth about $240 million in 1997. Steinbrenner had paid $8.8 million for his interest in the team in the 1970s. Some sports bankers have indicated the market value for the Yankees, America's best known sports franchise, would be several times the *Financial World* estimate.[9]

For years, though, the thought was widespread that the only way to make money owning professional sports teams was to pay too much for them in the first place, in hopes of being able to sell them later to someone who would pay even more. And there was always someone, it seemed, among the country's richest families, who would pay almost anything for the "privilege" of owning a team. Well, maybe there would be. But billionaire sports buff Wayne Huizenga, founder of Waste Management Corp., Blockbuster Video, and Republic Industries, wasn't so sure. Huizenga is the owner of the Miami Dolphins football team, the Florida Panthers hockey team, and the Florida Marlins baseball team. After winning the World Series in 1997, Huizenga claimed that he had lost $75 million in the previous five years on the Marlins, and he wanted some of it back. So he shopped the team, but without finding someone ready to pay his price. Instead he decided to recover his investment by selling off the high priced players that he had accumulated in his bid for the championship. The fans, of course, were horrified.

Huizenga's experience notwithstanding, there still seemed to be a very active market for teams in the late 1990s. In 1997 Microsoft cofounder Paul Allen paid $200 million to own the Seattle Seahawks, his hometown football outfit. In 1998 LBO investor Tom Hicks invested $250 million to own the Texas Rangers baseball group, and later that year banking billionaire Alfred Lerner came up with $530 million for the new Cleveland Browns. In early 2000 Robert Wood Johnson IV (great-grandson of the founder of Johnson & Johnson) agreed to pay $625 million for the New York Jets, a team with a poor record, no stadium of its own, and a famous coach who had just resigned. Even this terrific amount was exceeded by the $700 million for a new and as-yet-unnamed NFL franchise in Houston a few months earlier.[10] These were very big numbers in relation to the teams' earnings and apparent financial prospects, and to *Financial World* published valuations, which only took into account actual and projected cash flows. Cash flows, of course, were rising because each team shared in the growing amount of TV revenue, though some observers claimed the Jets were even then worth only $250 million. These valuations, however, did not figure the intangible value of owning your own team into account.

How large this intangible could be was demonstrated in early 1999 when Howard and Edward Milstein, along with Daniel Snyder, bid $800 million for the Washington Redskins, which was being sold by the estate of the late Jack Kent Cooke. The price was thirty-six times the net income of the team in 1998, and four times the *Financial World* valuation. Howard Milstein is a wealthy real estate investor who had earlier bought a hockey team. "For all of us, this is the most exciting thing we have ever done, or will ever do," Howard said. The group planned to borrow $400 million, collateralized by other assets, from Société Générale, a French bank with major interests in financing NFL deals.[11]

MOGULS

The real stars of stardom, the economic stars, never appear on camera and are not well known to the public. These are the media and entertainment industry moguls who control broadcasting, cable TV, movie studios, publishing, and various other channels through which stars get to become stars. Altogether there were sixty-four individuals that *Forbes* had identified as media folk among its 400 richest people in America.

The richest of these was John Kluge, eighty-five in 1999, the founder of Metromedia Co., who was thought to be worth $11 billion. He formed Metromedia in 1960, then amassed a large collection of radio and TV stations and a cellular network. Thirty years later he began selling the broadcasting and cellular properties, and has converted his holdings into fiber-optic cable networks, and, improbably, into low-tech chains of steak houses and coin-operated laundries. For all practical purposes, however, he is now out of the mogul business.

Summer Redstone, seventy-six in 1999, is still in it, big time. Redstone inherited a drive-in theater business in 1954, expanded it to a chain of 1,200 movie theaters, bought Viacom in 1987 in a leveraged buyout, then Paramount Pictures for $10 billion, Blockbuster Video (from Wayne Huizenga) for $8.4 billion, and in late 1999 he acquired CBS broadcasting for $39 billion in stock. These companies, however, all had to be sorted out when he bought them. Their costs were cut drastically, many parts and pieces were sold, and new deals and joint distribution arrangements negotiated. The fiesty chairman of Viacom, Inc., was worth an estimated $9.4 billion in 1999.

Australian born Rupert Murdock ($6.8 billion) is chairman of News Corp., a multimedia and entertainment empire spanning the globe. The group is into newspapers, publishing, television and satellite broadcasting, movies (Twentieth Century Fox), sports broadcasting, and team ownership (Los Angeles Dodgers). If anyone can make you a star, Murdock can. But Murdoch is well known as a very tough businessman, so you would have to believe there would be a very full price to pay.

Kirk Kerkorian (MGM); Michael Eisner (Disney); Mike Bloomberg; and Ted Turner, who sold his cable TV business to Time Warner, have already appeared in previous descriptions. They are all starmakers, too, and much richer than any of the stars.

So are the Newhouse brothers, Sam and Donald, the sons of publishing giant Sam Newhouse, Sr., who died in 1979. The brothers share a $9 billion fortune and a vast newspaper and magazine empire, with some cable networks thrown in. Cable TV entrepreneurs John Malone and Amos Hostetter, at around $3.5 billion each, continue to make deals. Altogether the top ten individuals in the U.S. media and entertainment business had accumulated fortunes of over $50 billion. You can catch a lot of stars for $50 billion, perhaps all of them.

The past twenty years has been especially kind to media entrepreneurs, who succeeded because of a combination of leverage, guts, and good luck. Most of them have made virtually their entire fortunes during this time, and several have had to struggle to retain it on several occasions. They were the biggest stakeholders in the future, having placed the largest bets. The economy and the financial markets cooperated, and today they own or control the film studios, the cable networks, the independent radio and TV stations, satellite transmissions systems, and various print media and sports businesses. They don't personally select what programs are aired on their systems, but they have lots of influence, and thousands of stars and star-hopefuls pass through their grasp. They have power that makes the moguls of Hollywood's earliest days seem trivial. Ultimately they demonstrate what many students of wealth already know, that it's better to own a system that services the needs of tens or hundreds of millions than just to be one of the products which provide the service, no matter how good at it you may be. Michael Jordan would have to work for 140 years at the level of his 1997 career peak income (after taxes) to catch up with the fortune of Rupert Murdock, who probably couldn't sink a twenty-foot jump shot if you gave him a week to do it.

CHAPTER 6

The American Wealth Culture

The American political and economic system that has produced so much wealth and opportunity for its citizens over its history is a phenomenon unequaled in any other society in the world. But our present system didn't just appear out of nowhere. It emerged, after a lot of struggle, from a long line of contributions of many individuals and evolved through many economic and historical events that are uniquely American. Starting as a former colonial society of thirteen relatively small states, three million people, and no money, this country managed in 250 years to attract all the human talent and financial resources it needed to become the world's greatest economy. The attracting of resources is the hard part. Hundreds of other countries, all evolving their own way, have failed to even come close to this achievement. So there really is, at our roots, something special about this country that is often not fully appreciated, something that seems to explain why so much of the wealth in America was earned or brought here, and why old money tied to social class and station is just not that important. Our society values and respects wealth and the achievements that it represents, but not above all else. As a wealth culture, we are quite different from all other countries.

We are different in terms of our history and path of development. But we are also different in terms of what we have become.

THE STOCK MARKET CULTURE

The stock market became the principal mechanism for measuring and realizing wealth in the late twentieth century. Before then, even though the stock market had a long history in America, personal wealth was often tied to real estate, farmland, private businesses, and savings instruments. Before the 1960s stock ownership among the general public was limited and not very widespread. After that, institutional investors increased their influence in the markets by managing growing amounts of pension and mutual funds on behalf of ordinary citizens, but the citizens themselves were still fairly distant from the market. However, during the last twenty years of the century, this could no longer be said. The stock market had become too large, and the citizens' personal wealth was too much involved with it, for it not to have become highly important to the average household.

In late 1999 there were nearly ten thousand American companies that were owned by public investors. These investors included both individuals and institutions, and among them were several thousand mutual funds. The market value of shares of these companies was about $17 trillion in December 1999, up from $1.4 trillion in 1980. Around fifty million Americans owned stocks or mutual funds directly in 1999, but 60 percent of all stocks were managed by professional institutions (including pension and mutual funds). This large pool of investors traded their stocks actively, providing liquidity and a continuous market for all. Investors confidently and readily bought and sold shares in the market, which was widely believed to be transparent, honest, and well regulated. In 1999 more than $20 trillion of market value in stocks was traded in the market.

The stock market was the principal vehicle for issuing new shares to raise equity capital for companies, but it performed a variety of other functions as well. Corporations may also buy their own stock back in the market when they have a surplus of funds. And the stock market has become a clearinghouse for the purchase and sale of control of corporations. Most mergers-and-acquisitions transactions occur now in the stock market, when one company publicly offers to acquire the shares of another. Also, company executives increasingly rely on the market for important portions of their compensation, by being willing to be paid in options to purchase shares of stock traded (or to be traded) in the markets. Owners of nonpublic companies use the stock market as a proxy for valuing their holdings. Real estate values, both residential and corporate, are closely correlated to the stock market. So are the prices of fine art and other luxury goods, even good tables at New York's finest restaurants. If there were a single proxy for measuring wealth in America at the end of the twentieth century, it would have to be the values established in the stock market.

This might also have been true in 1929, after the frantic bull market of that time which first attracted retail investors into tech stocks and pyramided mutual funds. But in 1929 not as many Americans invested significantly in the stock market, nor were so many Americans rich. But in the 1980–2000 period, it was the stock market that spread the wealth then being generated far afield. The stock market, not some political (or religious) utopia, has quite unexpectedly turned out to be the "shining city on the hill" proclaimed by Ronald Reagan, where millions of Americans would come to reside.

SPREADING WEALTH

The household sector participated extensively in the stock market gains of the 1980s and 1990s, and it was largely through this participation that its wealth holdings rose to $37 trillion by December 1999. A 1998 *Survey of Consumer Finances* prepared by the Federal Reserve reported that 49 percent of households reported an exposure to equities, through direct ownership or through mutual funds. This was up from 32 percent in 1989. The direct equity investments of American households, combined with their investment in defined contribution pension funds, represented about 60 percent of all common stock outstanding at the end of 1998. This level of participation in the benefits of stock ownership apparently was enough to leave the general population in the United States fairly relaxed about the burgeoning of wealth throughout the country. Indeed

THE AMERICAN WEALTH CULTURE

the growth in self-perceived wealth of the American household sector resulted in some of it being cashed in to increase consumption, which in turn helped boost GDP growth by a few percent.[1]

Before the 1980s the great majority of Americans appeared to believe that it was alright to *be* rich, and that no one who wanted to work hard at becoming rich should be precluded from doing so, but few Americans felt that they *were* rich; or even rich enough to be though of as well off. Since then, though, a great deal of new wealth (measured by rising market values) has been created, and participation in this new wealth has been much more democratic than ever before. At the end of 1999 the average household had eight times as much money invested in insurance and pension reserves than in 1980, ten times as much in corporate stocks and mutual funds, and three times as much in fixed income assets. Homes were worth three times as much, and privately owned businesses (probably valued too conservatively) at least twice as much. During the previous twenty-year period, from 1960 until 1980, real household wealth also doubled, but the principal sources of increase were in the values of homes and private businesses.[2]

By 1999 the average family had to consider itself a serious investor. Some had had their first experience in making money though investments that were essentially passive, some so passive (such as pension funds) they hardly knew what was in them. Some bought stocks or mutual funds they had selected themselves and made money because they went up. By the end of the 1990s many ordinary investors had become customers of discount brokers, and some (not many) had become daytraders, using Internet connections to trade for themselves in especially volatile stocks. For many of them it was fun, like playing slot machines. For others it was a realization that the stock market could be a separate source of income for them, one that was not tied to the job they went to every day. If things worked out, they would have a nest egg to retire on or to use in the event they were laid off or became incapacitated. After participating in the long market rise of the Reagan and Clinton periods, few, if any, seem to be looking over their shoulders for a better time gone by. Almost all would have to admit to being better off than before the period began.

Partly this is because Americans have also accumulated nonfinancial wealth at a great rate in recent years. Their standards of living are higher than ever, thanks to higher incomes, but also to technology improvements that have brought down the cost of electronic and computer devices, improvements in medicines and health care, and in the availability of low-cost travel and education.

Americans have many other wealth-equivalent benefits. Their bank deposits are insured, at least up to $100,000 per account. Their accounts with stockbrokers are insured. They have radio and television, which provide free access to multiple sources of information and entertainment twenty-four hours a day. For a little money they can get cable television or an Internet hookup. They can get around on free roads and highways, educate their children, and take vacations in stupendously beautiful national parks, all at affordable cost. The taxpayer, of course, pays for these features of American life, but tax burdens are not distributed evenly. The rich, despite the availability of a few deductions that most people cannot employ, still pay more of the country's taxes than do the nonrich. The IRS reported in 1995 that almost 60 percent of those earning $200,000 or more had effective, all-in tax rates of 25 percent or more (38 percent had rates between 25 and 30 percent). True, the marginal tax rate paid on the last dollar of income of those in the highest bracket was over 40 percent, but the average American had an effective tax rate in 1995 of less than 14 percent of gross income. The average guy, of course, gets to use the airways, the highways, and the rest of the public goods offered to American residents for a relatively lower cost than that which is charged to the rich folks.

In a *Wall Street Journal/NBC News* poll of two thousand adults reported in March 1998, neither envy nor resentment of the rich was pronounced. Slightly fewer than 30 percent of respondents said they admired rich people, while only 6 percent said they resented them. Also, 68 percent of those responding to the poll said they believed in the free market and competition, 60 percent characterized Americans as "ambitious and striving to get ahead," and 24 percent claimed that they expected to become millionaires themselves during their lifetimes.[3]

The 1998 Federal Reserve *Study of Consumer Finances* showed that more than half of the wealth of the top 1 percent of Americans (which arbitrarily defines the rich for the Federal Reserve) came from entrepreneurial sources, particularly people who own their own businesses. It also noted that those who are rich (or not rich) are not always the same in successive surveys. There is a lot of mobility, the study reported, into and out of the top 1 percent, which is mainly comprised of older, successful people and their inheritors.[4] Mainly, perhaps, but not entirely. Young people are getting in on the act, too, as the dynamic new companies many of them work for go public and make sudden millionaires out of them. For example, *Barron's* ran a list of seventy-seven people who had made over $100 million each in initial public offerings during just the six months ended June 1999.[5] The number who had made a mere $1 million, of course, was far greater. Almost all of these people were not considered millionaires before their IPOs, and were certainly overlooked then by millionaire-counters Danko and Stanley.

The typical American citizen appears to be content with the early twenty-first century economic system in the United States, a system seen by many as a model form of free-market, democratic capitalism. The citizen believes that the system works better in America than in other countries, and that most of those who become rich in America do so through their own efforts, not because they stole the money, or exploited others less fortunate, or benefited unduly from the influence of powerful friends. There still may be some problems with money earned at other, darker times in our history, and perhaps some resentment of those who inherit large amounts and choose not to work or contribute anything useful, but not so much for money being earned under the present system. The average person appears to accept and respect those who gained their wealth "the old fashioned way, by earning it." Most Americans are comfortable with the understanding that the most successful are those who wanted success more and paid the price for it. Few today, in the interest of social justice, would seem to support limitations on wealth-making, for fear that they might restrict their own children or grandchildren, whose opportunities they certainly do not wish to see limited at all.

MONEY IN YOUR LIFE

As the twentieth century closed down, it was difficult not to notice all the many signs of wealth on display. Builders and contractors were booked ahead by a year or two. Parking lots were crammed with expensive cars, stockbrokers called every night during dinner hour, and there was at least one fundraiser you could go to every week. A magazine entitled *Billionaire* appeared on newsstands. This magazine, which was a special edition of a regularly appearing magazine called *Millionaire*, was devoted to advertising all sorts of extreme-luxury goods, from large yachts, to homes in exclusive, gated communities, to gold-plated plumbing fixtures, hand-sculpted pool tables, and cowboy boots made from the skins of stingrays.

But living with money requires first getting hold of it to spend. You can spend your salary and your bonus. But you can't spend your stock options or the shares you own in your company, unless you exercise your rights to do so and sell in accordance with regulations that limit what you can do. If most of your wealth is tied up in stock that you can't sell at all, or sell more than a small amount of, your wealth is still out there, waiting to be harvested. While it's waiting, it is exposed to all the risks that you have been worrying about for years. And, of course, most of your eggs are in this basket. So to get the use of and the unrestricted benefit from owning your stock, first the money has to be gathered up and gotten control of and put into something safe. You have only truly harvested your money when you have sold the business you set up for cash and invested the proceeds (after tax) in a nicely balanced portfolio of blue-chip securities. You can partly harvest by doing an IPO and in time selling some of your stock or by having your company buy some of your stock back from you. There are various ways to do this, but you aren't really and safely rich until the harvest is in. Once it is, your life is changed and you can become a big spender if you like.

Spending It

In January 1999 Cornell University economist Robert Frank published a book called *Luxury Fever* about American spending habits in the late 1990s. He was appalled by what he found: a grotesque second coming of the financial excesses of the Gilded Age of approximately a century before. What appalled him was the waste of financial resources that was the result of reckless, competitive spending. Folks were not just trying to "keep up with the Joneses," who lived down the street; they were trying to keep up with anyone in the country whose lifestyle was more flamboyant than their own, an impossible task. Modern communications have made us aware of other people's money in a way that we have not experienced before. And being inherently competitive and endlessly seeking attention, we Americans, according to Frank, have come to be entrapped in a spending cycle that makes little sense and is harmful to the economy as a whole. The same thing happened in the 1890s, we are reminded, when Mrs. Vanderbilt and many others like her entered into serious competition building mansions on Fifth Avenue and in Newport, while their husbands built bigger and faster yachts. This is nothing new in human history, Frank also notes, as wealth has always been showy and competitive since it first occurred. He wants to do something about it, however, such as having the government impose a progressive, ultimately massive consumption tax on those who spend too much, so the money can either be saved instead of spent, or otherwise redeployed by the government into useful social programs.

One thing Professor Frank is sure to know, as an economist, is that when the money is there, a lot of it is going to be spent, regardless of the sales tax. And people will spend it somewhere else, of course, if spending it here becomes too expensive. A small portion of the wealthy always can be counted on to spend excessively; that is, someone has to be in the ninetieth percentile of spenders. But a great deal of what Frank regards as luxury fever is actually taking place at midlevels of wealth, out there among the five million or so American millionaires. Many of these people feel wealthy as a result of their successful investments or increased pension fund values, and accordingly spend some of their capital gains knowing they still have money in reserve. In actuality this may not be excessive or irrational behavior at all, even though statistically it might appear to be if the expenditures equaled a high percentage of their ordinary income. Such spending patterns screw up the national savings figures, too. These reached a low point in mid-1999, making us all look like mindless spendthrifts, when in fact the wealth of our households (even after our excessive spending) was increasing significantly.

Further, what we call spending often is not spending at all, but investing. Bill's Gates "spent" about $60 million for a lavish house on the shores of Lake Washington, near Seattle, an amount he can easily afford, by the way, so therefore not an "extravagant" amount for him. But the house is really not an expenditure, it is an investment, perhaps one that will be hard to sell for what it cost (but who knows?), but an investment nonetheless. Gates should expect some return of interest and principal from the investment, but he is probably willing to forgo some of this in exchange for satisfying all his particular requirements in a house. This is also true for investments in other luxuries, such as art, airplanes, and fancy cars. You always get something back in such investments, aside from the psychic income. Sometimes these assets rise in value as much as other assets do.

The spending habits of the rich have received a great deal of attention from marketing experts and psychologists in recent years. A 1994 *Town and Country* magazine study of wealth in America revealed four categories of affluent consumers: "stylish" (27 percent of the sample group), mostly brand-and prestige-conscious females; "adventurous" (27 percent), mostly try-anything single males; "conservative" (29 percent) family-oriented, quality-minded folks; and "utilitarian" (16 percent) value-conscious, no frills males.[6]

Lois Carrier and David Maurice, two financial planners, wrote an article in 1998 about "the money personalities" of some of their clients, in particular compulsive spenders and hoarders. They concluded that money behavior is learned in the home, and there our personalities are conditioned at an early age to relate to money and to rationalize either having it or not.[7] Juliet Schor, who has studied "overspent Americans," also has concluded that the behavior is learned from childhood experience.[8]

Stanley and Danko, authors of *The Millionaire Next Door*, also go along with the idea of learned money behavior. They claim that the typical millionaire next door (one of our five million) is a self-made entrepreneur who began accumulating wealth at an early age by practicing frugality, common sense, and notably nonlavish consumption habits. They do keep up with others, but these are people they know, not ones they imagine or see on television. These patterns suggest to us that the proportion of the population that engages in excessive spending is offset by a similar proportion that hordes. Those in the middle, where the majority is, behave about as they always have. It's the median level of money they have to spend that has changed. Maybe too much of it, for Professor Frank's taste, gets spent on stingray boots.

Power Trips

Money is power, but what is power beyond the right to boss around people who work for you? Real power is the ability to control events and the actions of important institutions. A lesser form of the same type of power is to influence, if not control, these events and actions. This is the stuff of government and major public institutions, whose actions can more clearly affect the lives of those about you than running a large soap company or an insurance brokerage can. Money, of course, can be used to buy power and influence in various ways and amounts—by acquiring political or high appointed office, for example. But this is not a simple process, and it doesn't always work out.

There are a lot of rich people prepared to finance presidential candidates in the hope that there might be something in it for them once the fellow is elected, a Washington job perhaps, or an Ambassadorship, or access to the administration to discuss a complex regulatory matter. Indeed, there are so many rich contributors (just look at the stupendous amounts raised for the 2000 campaigns) that it tends to make it difficult for rich individuals to get really noticed, and accordingly many are not. However nice it may be to spend the night in the Lincoln bedroom, or to attend a White House gala, such niceties are not especially powerful or influential.

Sometimes, too, the candidate is doing so well he doesn't need to beg so hard for money. This may be a rare thing, but Ronald Reagan rose to the presidential nomination hardly knowing anyone on Wall Street. Bill Clinton raised more money than he could ever use because he liked doing it and seemed to be very good at it. And no candidate ever had an easier time raising campaign money than George W. Bush. Even Bill Bradley, who eschewed contributions from the rich, was able in his brief challenge to Al Gore to raise quite a bit of money without promising Paris or London, or the Secretary of the Treasury, to anyone.

The rich people who succeed in the political business are mainly those who are willing to work within the system to help the candidates and office holders to accomplish their political aims. Averill Harriman was a rich man who contributed a lot to Democratic interests and candidates, but he did it for nearly fifty years and served in many

lesser posts along the way. In midcareer he ran successfully to become New York's governor. (Nelson Rockefeller,
another very rich politician, succeeded him as governor.)
Harriman's wife, Pamela, was an early Clinton supporter
and fundraiser; she was rewarded with an appointment as
Ambassador to France. A number of the major cabinet
posts (State, Treasury, Attorney General, and Defense)
have gone, over the years, to wealthy but also savvy contributors who were also active over time in a wide variety
of party affairs.

Wall Street people are particularly good at fundraising,
so that's what they are usually asked to do. After all, more
out-of-state money for political campaigns is raised in
New York than anywhere else. If things work out, the
funds-raiser gets an invitation to take a job that may be as
visible as it is powerful, though often the person discovers
the job offered is neither, as perhaps Donald Regan, once
head of Merrill Lynch, learned during his time in the Reagan administration. In any presidential campaign year
there are prominent Wall Streeters and corporate CEOs
locked into each candidate's camp. Of course their firms
want to have someone from their midst become persona
grata to whichever administration comes to power. Most
of these big shots, however, seem to just like hanging out
with famous politicians, getting to drop a lot of prominent
names, and, for the intellectually curious, participating in
what one officeholder called the world's most fascinating
array of policy issues.

Two one-time senior partners of Goldman Sachs were
appointed to high office in Washington after years of loyal
fund-raising for their parties. John Whitehead was Deputy
Secretary of State in the Reagan years, and Bob Rubin be-

came Clinton's Secretary of the Treasury after serving first as head of the National Economic Council. Some others from Wall Street, like lawyer Cyrus Vance, or bankers Douglas Dillon, Paul Nitze, and Roger Altman, among others, started their political careers with junior jobs in Washington, only to return later in different administrations in more senior positions. Vance was in the Johnson administration before becoming Secretary of State in the Carter Administration, and Dillon and Nitze had high positions in the Eisenhower and Kennedy years. Altman, who held a junior position in the Carter administration, was Deputy Secretary of the Treasury in Clinton's, and surely would have been Secretary of Treasury if he had not become involved in loyally, but inappropriately, passing Whitewater information on to the White House staff. Each time one of these people takes a Washington office, they bring a few trusted souls with them, who in turn learn how to operate in Washington's peculiar ways and become available for more senior positions during a future administration.

Many contributors who are fascinated by the goings-on of high political office, however, are not especially interested in holding office themselves. They are not about to quit their lucrative day jobs for something as ephemeral, and more recently as dangerous, as a subcabinet position. But they like the scene, and befriending senators and governors, not to mention presidents, is heady. They help raise campaign money, and the officeholders invite them and their spouses to dinner parties with the politically powerful people of the moment, and they get to say what they think about foreign aid or the Russian economy or health care. They get to know the right and fashionable people in political circles, and to show them off a little to their friends who are on the outside. There are lots of people like this, rich political groupies, who participate in the campaigns vicariously by providing the millions needed for each and every one.

A few, a very few in fact, decide to go a step further and actually run for office themselves. With the cost of campaigning as high as it is, it helps a great deal to have money of your own to spend, a fact not often overlooked by party officials looking for a nominee for a tough election fight. It takes money to win elections, and if it's your first try and people don't know you at all, you probably have to spend your own money to overcome your obscurity. That alone won't get you into office, but people do not elect folks they never heard of to high positions. Having the capital to jumpstart your efforts is a big advantage. One recent study claims that more than 50 percent of state legislators are lawyers (presumably at least upper-middle-income people), and almost all of the nation's governors and presidents have been from the very wealthiest segment of society. (This study goes on to conclude that their income level does not make them representatives of the ordinary middle- or lower-income families that are the majority in America, and therefore the system develops voter apathy.)[9]

Harriman and Rockefeller both were able to gain office in New York State, as was Pierre "Pete" DuPont in Delaware, because of the great wealth at their disposal. Nelson's brother Winthrop Rockefeller was governor of Arkansas. In 1999 Nelson's nephew Jay was a senator (and former governor) from West Virginia, and his nephew Winthrop was lieutenant governor of Arkansas. The Kennedy family might be unknown to us today had it not been for the considerable wealth of Joseph Kennedy, all of whose surviving sons, John, Robert, and Edward, were elected to prominent offices (as have been many of his grandchildren). Personal wealth has made a difference in a number of U.S. Senate seats, including those held in 1999 by Senators Bill Frist (TN), Frank Lautenberg (NJ), John Kerry (MA), and John Warner (VA). Frist and his brother, Thomas, were founders of HCA Corp., which later merged into Columbia HCA Corp., and Lautenberg was the founder of ADP Inc., a company with a market capitalization of $26 billion in 1999. Lautenberg was once challenged for reelection by Peter Dawkins, a former Army officer who was a Lehman Brothers executive. If you have the money, the patience, and an attraction to the grubby, mundane, day-to-day content of running for and holding political office, you have a big advantage over all those who don't have the money. The Supreme Court has said that the First Amendment protects individuals from restrictions on spending whatever they want to gain office.

But not all succeed. Ross Perot made a difference to the public debate on the issues but was not successful in his presidential campaign effort in 1992, though it reportedly cost him $62 million.[10] However, this was not a large portion of Perot's fortune (in 1999 estimated at $3.7 billion), and certainly it gained national celebrity status for him for life and a certain amount of respect for his plainspoken, eccentric ways. Steve Forbes's presidential efforts did not succeed in two tries, in 1996 and 2000, despite expenditures of $60 million or so of his largely inherited fortune for the purpose.[11]

In California nearly a dozen millionaires have tried to

spend their way into the U.S. Senate or governor's office in the past decade, including Michael Huffington, a one-term congressman backed by inherited Texas oil money, who ran against Diane Feinstein for her senate seat in 1994. Huffington was widely considered a lightweight, but he spent $30 million of his own money and came very close to winning. One result of Huffington's campaign efforts was that it attracted a number of other millionaire candidates to the election campaigns of 1998. If a weak candidate like Huffington could come so close, they thought, by spending *only* $30 million or so, think what a strong candidate would be like with even more money on the line!

So the 1998 campaigns featured Al Checchi, once CEO of Northwest Airlines and a *Forbes* 400 member, running for the Democratic nomination for the senate seat held by Barbara Boxer. He spent over $14 million in the primary campaign alone. The governor's race was contested by Jane Harman, wife of Sidney Harman, an audio equipment multimillionaire, who spent over $3 million. Darrell Issa, the owner of the nation's largest automobile security company, was a candidate for the Republican senatorial nomination. All of them lost their battles.

In New Jersey, former Goldman Sachs CEO Jon Corzine, dislodged by a coup at his old firm, announced a campaign for the 2000 election for the U.S. Senate seat of retiring Frank Lautenberg. Strongly endorsed by New Jersey's other senator, Democrat Bob Torricelli, whose 1996 campaign Corzine helped finance, Jon claimed that he would be willing to spend "whatever it takes" to win the election and to finance the campaigns of other candidates for other Democratic positions. However, Corzine found himself in a tough race for the Democratic Party nomination with former governor Jim Florio, who spared no effort in accusing Corzine of trying to buy the office.

Corzine recognized that he had to contend with a great deal of voter skepticism, but met it head on. He campaigned vigorously and sympathetically throughout the state, contributed generously to the campaigns of other Democratic candidates, and expressed a number of very liberal positions on social issues not usually associated with Wall Street CEOs. But mainly he spent money on TV ads that saturated the market for weeks on end, many of them sharply critical of his opponent. In total he spent approximately $34 million on the primary alone (almost all of it his own money), an amount well in excess of the previous record for a senatorial primary contest, $8.1 million spent by Charles Schumer of New York in 1998. Corzine won the primary election handily.[12]

Beyond politics, money is powerful if it can provide prestige and influence, especially in great nonprofit institutions, of which there are many in the United States. There is little one can do that is more prestigious than serving as a trustee of the Metropolitan Museum of Art, or as an Overseer of Harvard University, or a member of the board of the San Francisco Opera or the Music Center of Los Angeles County. Another high-prestige organization, Carnegie Hall in New York, led since 1991 by Sandy Weill, is a good example of a modern nonprofit board where money matters most of all.

Weill has been actively involved with Carnegie Hall for many years and was one of the most dynamic forces behind its recent renovation. Since becoming chairman of the board, Weill has reorganized the process by which the board is selected. Two consequences of the reorganization have resulted: Carnegie Hall has raised a great deal more money, and the board positions have become among the most sought after in New York, a city with many prestigious nonprofit organizations. There are sixty-five board positions, about half of which in 1998 were occupied by top corporate executives. The rest of the seats are distributed among philanthropists, musicians, and Carnegie executives.

To be a board member, you have to like music and attend performances. You also have to be willing to do volunteer work on junior varsity committees for a while before being invited to join the main board. But you also have to give generously, and before being considered for membership your financial condition and personal giving history is carefully scrutinized. Then you have to get by Sandy, who sees to the financial compatibility part. In short, this is a conversation in which you are told what is expected of you, in annual gifts (up to $100,000 per year would be nice) and in contributions to special capital campaigns. A few years after becoming chairman, Weill set an endowment fund goal of $75 million, and almost immediately raised half of it from the board, the average director contributing nearly $600,000. New board members are also supposed to use their contacts to bring others into the Carnegie orbit. The net result is that most of the directors are delighted to be on such an effective board, one that does a lot for the arts in New York, offers wonderful music perks, and has a snob-appeal that is unequalled.[13] And, what the hell, you have to give a lot of money away to charity anyway, so it may as well be to these guys. The Carnegie experience was coming to be the norm as the 1990s came to a close.

PASSING IT ON

Sooner or later we all pass on, but our money stays behind. Over the next thirty years or so nearly $40 trillion of American household wealth in place at the turn of the century will be subject to estate taxes, intergenerational transfers, and philanthropic gifts. This is a lot of wealth to pass on, more than at any other time in history. What happens to it once it has been passed on is a subject of growing interest, one in which the outcome does not always follow expectations, especially if you are looking out more than one generation.

Estate taxes are designed to drain off some of the wealth of the wealthy, and recycle it through the government back into the general economy. If you die with an estate of less than $1 million, you won't pay much, if any, estate tax. But if you leave an estate of $20 million and three children to inherit it, each will get only about $3 million after taxes. If this sum is then passed to and shared by your children's children, by the time the fortune gets to the third generation, it will have melted away to less than half a million or so each. This is not exactly travelling from shirtsleeves to shirtsleeves, but unless the children who receive the money can use it to create fortunes of their own, the value and power of grandpa's money soon dissipates.

There are ways to stop this dilution of financial power from happening. The rich can give all their money to a charitable institution or foundation, so its economic power will remain intact. Or they can give all or most of it to just one child so as to keep the fortune intact. They can also investigate ways to minimize estate taxes and to prepare their children to manage the money they receive so as to make more with it than they spend and therefore contribute something to pass on themselves. Most rich people would probably agree that the last one is preferable if they can manage it.

A century ago many wealthy Americans left large amounts of money to children who were not well prepared to handle it. Very few families whose wealth was based on a founder's riches have been able to remain economically potent after the passage of a few generations, though some have done better than others. Those that have done the best (e.g., Morgans, Rockefellers, Fords) have had a favored son that went into the business, learned its details from the ground up, took over as CEO, and in due course inherited most of it. This was to keep the family business intact; otherwise it might have had to be broken up or sold in pieces. The son was expected to further expand the business and repeat the process with his own son, who, in turn, was to pass it on to someone of the next generation if he could. If he could not, he was to sell the company or go public. The family would then retire from management in the company and live on the wealth that its holdings represented. The wealth, however, was then almost always dissipated over many claimants from subsequent generations.

Some contemporary families, notably those of billionaires Hank Greenberg, Lawrence and Preston Tisch, Ross Perot, Leonard Stern, Rupert Murdock, and Sandy Weill, have children working closely with their fathers in common business ventures. Sometimes these sons and daughters have been involved in ventures not directly connected with the publicly traded vehicle most associated with the father, but no one would deny that they had learned a lot about business and finance from Dad and maybe even had some special help here and there.

But even when the children are closely tied in with the family business, it is not at all easy to pass on a famous father's power and influence to a son or daughter to preserve and enlarge in the future. This is especially so in publicly traded corporations, in which succession of the CEO has to pass public scrutiny and an independent board of directors, and nepotism is usually resisted. But nepotism can be a problem in family-owned businesses as well.

Dynasties Are Not Forever

In 1986 Barry Bingham Sr. was the eighty-year-old proprietor of the Louisville *Courier-Journal* and Louisville *Times* newspaper company, a distinguished and profitable enterprise that Barry, an only child, had inherited in 1937 from his father, who bought it in 1917. Barry had five children, including two sons who had died of freak accidents before reaching the age of forty. There was another son, Barry Jr., the heir apparent, and two daughters. Barry Sr. was an enlightened man of his times and had distributed stock in the company to his wife and all of his children, each of whom was also represented on the board of the company. He wanted them to learn about the business and follow his examples of how to act as its leader.

However, this family, like many others, had its hidden troubles and resentments. Barry Jr. was not the first choice to take over from his father; his older brother had been. Still, he was selected by his father to succeed him, and was made chief executive in 1971. Meanwhile Barry Jr.'s two middle-aged sisters had moved back to town and become active board members. Barry Jr., however, felt that they criticized his efforts excessively and his sister Sallie in particular had become a distracting irritant. Sallie was an outspoken New Yorker, a twice-divorced writer and ardent feminist whose career was then on hold. She complained openly about the family's sexism and old-fashioned ways.

A few years later Barry Jr. attempted to have his father remove "the women" from the company's board. They did not show sufficient respect for him, he said, and didn't pay attention to business matters. This created an extended family row, and a year later, in 1984, Sallie told her father she wanted out.

She wanted the company to buy out her stock, she said. She had no confidence in her brother to manage the company and to preserve the value of her inheritance in the future. Many fathers would sympathize with Barry Sr., who responded that he personally had attended to the details of the company succession and that, though Barry Jr. did have some problems, she should not worry about it. Besides, he added, the company didn't have the cash on hand to buy her out and didn't want to take on the added risk of borrowing the money to do so.

Sallie said she was sorry to make a fuss, but she still wanted out and would sell her stock to outsiders if the family wouldn't make an offer. The stress created by Sallie's demands opened other familial struggles, side-taking, and accusations that went on for some time, and the costs and difficulties of the negotiations took their toll on the family's relations with each other. Reluctantly, Barry Jr. asked the company's bankers, Lehman Brothers, to prepare a valuation of the privately held company. They said Sallie's shares were worth between $22 and $26 million, but Sallie hired her own investment banker who told her that her shares were worth $80 million. Barry Jr. proposed a plan for the company to repurchase Sallie's shares for $26 million, a price that he said was final. Sallie offered to sell for $32 million, but no less. Barry Sr., frustrated and discouraged, decided to sell the business rather than continue the dispute. He accepted an offer from Gannet Company for the newspapers and a separate offer for its TV and radio stations and some other properties totaling $440 million. Ironically the proceeds (including her share of a trust that held her parents' holdings) netted Sallie about $80 million, a great deal more than the company's offer to her and just about what her own advisers had said the shares were worth.[14]

In the end Barry Sr. had made a mistake. His daughter was within her rights (she was certainly entitled to look after her own interests) and she, rather than Barry Jr. was proved to be right about the company's value. Barry Jr. had chosen to preserve the family enterprise despite strong indications that it was not in the family's interest to do so. The company was actually worth more to others who might manage it better or more aggressively, so to hang on to it was to depress its value. The family had several stockholders who had no direct interest in the business and wanted their money instead for their own families. The next generation apparently had no prospective CEOs in it, and in any case was large and likely to agree with Sallie that its interests were better served by getting out of the business. But Sallie's initiative had its consequences. It broke the old, aristocratic Louisville family apart, flashed its dirty linen and family squabbles in public, and possibly contributed to the death of her unhappy father, which occurred a short time after the sale was completed. The press had a wonderful time with the story, generally blaming the daughter for stirring up all the trouble and doing her family no good.

Barry Sr. was as stuck in his ways as Sallie was in hers. He believed that his company was an especially good and great one that could preserve its values and high journalistic standards only by keeping ownership and control inside the family. Having inherited from his own father, he had a Bingham Family newspaper dynasty in mind. But was it realistic to believe that his only surviving son would be up to the task?

It was true that Barry Sr. had built a great business by hard work, tough editorial standards, and by being in Louisville during a time of growth and prosperity when the newspaper business was fairly unchallenged. It was also true that this era was closing down to be replaced by one in which newspapers competed with TV, cable, and various forms of instant news. Further, the whole news industry was on tenterhooks awaiting the next, probably expensive, technological breakthrough, such as satellite-communicated computerized typesetting in distant locations. Considering the newspaper's situation and his son's unexceptional business qualifications and aptitude, he may well have made a grave error in choosing his son to head the business during difficult times. And, if he didn't want his wife's and daughters' opinions on these important business matters, why did he put them on the board of directors or indeed give them voting stock?

Barry had an alternative to battling with his daughter

and selling the business to Gannett. He could have taken it public, which would have established a trading market in the stock (which Sallie and anyone else in the family could utilize) and let everyone see the value of his or her holdings. Those who wanted to sell out could do so, those who wanted to stay in the business could, too, subject to the approval of professional management selected by a competent outside board of directors. Barry Sr. might ultimately lose control over his journalistic standards, and Barry Jr. might lose a job, but these events could take a while to unfold and the enterprise they had worked on so hard would still exist and be respected in the industry. But also, each would have permanent, liquid wealth to invest, enjoy, and dispose of as they chose, and no cause at all to tear their family apart. The business, though, would have to be seen as just a business, something that sometime may have to be sold to preserve its value for those who would inherit it. The trade-off, of course, was that there could be no Bingham publishing dynasty lasting long into the future.

Barry Sr. should have realized that dynasties based on inherited family wealth don't work anymore, if they ever did. The last place dynasties seem to have succeeded is probably in Great Britain, where for a long time wealthy families have been able to preserve their names and fortunes. The newly rich of the nineteenth century would join their old-money, land-rich peers by entering the knighthood or the nobility, acquire a great country estate that would cost a fortune to maintain, and then raise their children to act like gentry and never work. This was a pretty simple case of exchanging the dynamics of wealth creation for the static condition of social position. However, in order to preserve the family position, the founder's title, property, and most of the cash, which was needed to maintain the property, would be left to the eldest son of each generation, regardless of qualifications, and his siblings would have to make it on their own somehow. Thus the property, including business holdings and real estate, could be preserved in the family indefinitely and indeed many such intact properties are still around. This form of inheritance, called primogeniture, has been given up in most of the rest of Europe, where ancient use of titles and land holdings are rare and, in many places, not recognized by law. Primogeniture is still allowed in Britain, where old customs continue and the money is still concentrated to preserve the family name. Also, many of the old family estates, called "stone piles" by many of them, have been declared historical sites and cannot be torn down or modified very much. Despite their being uneconomic, these mansions are still taxed and are certainly expensive to maintain. But whatever dynasties are preserved by these practices, they only include one person per generation who inherits the lot, and no one else gets much of anything. Not only do Americans regard this as inherently unfair, they don't see the point in preserving uneconomic old stone piles in the first place. Primogeniture is not illegal in the United States, though it is virtually in disuse and probably could be challenged in the courts by other heirs.

Laurence and Preston Tisch believe that children should be encouraged to take over the business from their parents. They should learn how to preserve and care for it, and to assume the special responsibilities and limelight that comes with it, by being actively involved. There are now three Tisch sons who have taken over running Loews

Corp. from the two elder brothers; that is, three of their combined seven children. They have divided the holdings into logical chunks for each to manage, and apparently they work well together as a team. The Tisch family business is effectively a closed-end investment company that owns a large portfolio of businesses that can be added to or sold. Tisch investors particularly value the investment acumen and viewpoint of the family managers, and perhaps believe that the current generation has been well trained by the last one, considered masters of the value-investing trade. In due course, having learned about business and investments, the children can hire more managers to perform most of the work of managing the companies for them, but they will be capable of closely supervising them and making final decisions. Thus they, like the Rockefellers, can devote more of their time to planning their extensive philanthropic activities, something they have learned takes a lot of effort. But the Tisch sons are only the second generation in the business, and the third is well into the future.

At the end of the twentieth century most successful business founders were able to secure their exits by selling the business or taking it public and, in time, reducing their role in management. This, of course, was possible because of the greatly expanded capabilities of the stock market. Because the markets offer a range of alternatives now, from selling out altogether, doing a recapitalization, or going public, few successful privately owned firms have to force children into the business to protect its value. Though many owners today enjoy having their children working with them, few ever think about forging a true business dynasty. Instead they gravitate toward thinking about what to do with the wealth they have created and how it should be distributed.

And at this point they must ask two of the most important questions of all: "How much do they want their children to get?" and "Who gets what the children don't?"

Spoiling the Kids

A common picture of inherited wealth is one of arrogant, nonworking children and grandchildren who inherit fortunes they have no claim to but birth. They become so dependent on legacies that they never develop their own abilities to support themselves. These are the "spoiled little rich kids" that America disdains. While it is true that subjects for such a picture can be found, not all children of wealthy parents are like this, Franklin Roosevelt, John F. Kennedy, Averill Harriman, and Nelson Rockefeller being particular exceptions. However, it is still the common practice to leave all or a substantial portion of the estates of wealthy individuals to their children, whether or not they are prepared to receive it.

Sam Walton, America's richest man before Bill Gates, followed such a traditional path of wealth creation. He started from very little and loved to work, though he probably never had much choice. If his passion had been to write poetry or teach third grade in an Arkansas public school district, he might not have been able to do so and still support a large family. Sam's passion was business, however, and he was very successful at a relatively early age and accumulated some significant money, the first in his family ever to do so. He knew that money wasn't everything, but it had its uses. It could provide creature comforts that could lower life's stress levels and keep the kids in touch and part of his life. After I'm gone, Sam might have thought, they can give it away if they want to, or do whatever they want to with it. He died in 1992, and was survived by a widow, three sons, and a daughter, most living in or near Bentonville, Arkansas. Each was given a stake in Wal-Mart that continued to grow and was worth about $17 billion in 1999. Each of them gives money to charities and makes investments, sometimes together through a common venture, Walton Enterprises. One son, Robson, is a low-key lawyer who represents the family interests in the company by serving as nonexecutive chairman of the board. John Walton is a college dropout, a Vietnam veteran, and a boat builder who has become involved in educational charities. Jim Walton is a local banker who manages the family's Arkansas-based investment company. Alice Walton ran an investment bank in Arkansas for years before moving to Texas, after a family disagreement, where she raises horses. The Walton children have one graduate degree, ten children, and three divorces between them. Has the money made them happier, better people? Has it made the world a better place than it was when Sam died? It will take a while to know, but it is easy to be skeptical.

Not all wealthy people are in a hurry to pass all of their life's riches on to their children, especially if the riches are clearly outsized. Warren Buffett, one of most original thinkers and outspoken businessmen of his time, claims that he does not intend to leave much of anything to his children, and that they have accepted this fact and have gone on about making their own lives out of their own efforts. Instead, he says, he will leave all his money to a charitable foundation, but he is not intending to fully fund this organization before his death. He will continue to do what he does better than almost anyone—make money—and when he goes there will be a big pile of it left for the foundation, which will be run by good people who know how to give it away. Of course his approach will not allow Buffett to have much say in what his money ultimately gets used for.

But the kids won't be getting it, because giving them that much money could do them much more harm than good, Buffett believes. That's the main point. The money could spoil them (make them act in haughty and superior ways just because someone gave them money they did nothing to earn) and leave them without real friends in a world in which friendships are much to be treasured. It can make them arrogant (thinking they know what is best to do with the money, simply because it's theirs) and cause them to make mistakes and suffer foolish losses. It can make them nervous and insecure, feeling the great burden of preserving every penny of Daddy's money, and it can force the children into needless but nasty conflicts with each other. Buffett may have had the $6 billion Koch family in mind—four brothers who have spent most of the last twenty years and a vast amount of an inherited fortune litigating an endless dispute over a financial settlement that occurred in 1983.[15] Not all children react in such negative ways to inherited money, but many do—especially if they are not trained and conditioned, technically and philosophically, to handle it.

As Buffett knows well, taking on a share of a multibillion-dollar fortune is a big responsibility, one that requires significant prior preparation and familiarization that his children have not received, nor apparently shown much interest in. Buffett is certainly not like everyone else; he was a financial prodigy who spent a lifetime living and breathing investments, which none of his children has done. Like many highly successful dads, he would be a very hard act to follow. Buffett also says he expects to live to a ripe old age, and thus his children would themselves be old at the time of inheritance, not the best of times to require them to learn about handling a great sum of money.

Anyway, says Buffett, what do they need it for? People seek out their own interests and challenges, and rising to your own level as a result of your own struggles is one of the things that makes life rewarding and satisfying, and, yes, happy and fulfilling. Too much inherited money can diminish the value of the children's own chosen endeavors, the income from which might never equal more than a small part of the income from the inheritance. If they really want to be rich themselves, there are ways to do it, and they know what they are.

Philanthropy

American philanthropy is a marvel of the world. In 1999 alone $190 billion, three quarters of it from individuals, was donated to charities, 9 percent more than the year before. More than 40 percent of this money went to religious organizations, about 25 percent to health and human services and social benefit organizations, 15 percent to education, and about 7 percent to the arts. Charitable giving as a percentage of household wealth, however, fell slightly in 1999 to 0.69 from 0.71. In 1998 it had been estimated that approximately 10 percent of all giving was done by the 0.1 percent of the population that earned over $1 million per year.[16] No other country comes close to such generous private support for charitable institutions, in large part because elsewhere charities are regarded as exclusively government functions, especially in countries with high-tax regimes.

In America, charitable contributions are deductible from taxable income and are used to reduce taxes, especially of the rich. Even so, though no one likes paying taxes very much, all the money you give away is gone, but the tax benefit is only about 40 percent, and, in the case of large gifts, that can take a few years to be realized. The total of all American giving to charity was only 2 percent of GDP in 1998, an amount that was far less than the financial gains experienced by most of the wealthy during the preceding decade. Some observers wondered whether indeed Americans were generous enough, considering the great wealth that had been accumulated in the country. The current generation of rich Americans, according to the *Economist*, lags behind those of a hundred years earlier in contributing early in their lives to good works and in coming forward with original ideas for most usefully putting their money to work. Indeed, this report suggests, the richest Americans may be among the cheapest, noting that the stock market indices have risen more than tenfold in the period since 1980, but charitable giving has only tripled.[17]

In the late 1800s America's richest men were religious and believed that charity was close to godliness. Most of them, especially John D. Rockefeller and J. P. Morgan, were generous contributors to religious organizations, universities, the arts, and social welfare. Andrew Carnegie believed that it was sinful for a man to die rich, and he endeavored to give most of his huge fortune away before his own death. In the early years of the twentieth century, the great corporate founders set up foundations, funded with company stock, to carry on their good works well into the future. Today eight of the top ten wealthiest American private foundations are organizations founded by such men, including the Lilly Foundation ($15.4 billion in 1998), the Ford Foundation, the Robert Wood Johnson Foundation, and the W. K. Kellogg Foundation. Most of these foundations have since become quasi-public institutions, with large publicly visible boards of directors and much reduced family influence. In the 1980s Henry Ford II resigned as a director of the Ford Foundation because of disagreement with its agenda for distributing the money.

The practice of establishing charitable foundations with private wealth continues into the present time. David Packard, who died in the late 1990s, bestowed most of his $9 billion fortune to the David and Lucille Packard Foundation, not to his children, though the children would have important roles in directing the foundation. Bill Gates, a much younger and richer man, has also set up a foundation, which presumably he will add to during the rest of his life. Valued at about $22 billion in 2000, the country's largest foundation, The William H. Gates Foundation held less than a third of Gates's estimated wealth in 1999.[18]

Ted Turner astonished the world with a $1 billion gift to the United Nations in 1997, an event which enabled Turner to chide his fellow billionaires for being both cheap and unimaginative. Turner wanted to help the world solve its problems and "help the poorest of the poor," a very tall order, so he came up with the idea of giving the money directly to the UN, to be paid in ten annual installments of $100 million each. But giving money directly to the UN, to be spent as it decided, posed lots of problems, mainly in ensuring that Turner's money would end up being spent on programs that he approved of. Turner decided to set up a foundation, headed initially by former senator Timothy Wirth, that would allocate money to UN agencies after these had applied to the foundation for grants. This has created an awkward twist to Turner's generosity: Has he in fact managed to redirect the UN's own relief work away from areas and among populations selected by it to those favored by Turner? Is this, some ask, putting the UN's most important activities up for sale to the highest bidder?[19] Such controversies are likely to surround Turner's gift for a long time.

Sometimes foundations focus on much narrower ground of their own choosing, even becoming self-sufficient, non-profit research institutes, such as the Stowers Institute for Medical Research in Kansas City, established in 1987 by James and Virginia Stowers with gifts that had totaled $220 million at the end of 1998. Stowers, seventy-five years old in 1999, was the chairman of American Century mutual funds, and he and his wife and daughter were all cancer survivors. They wanted their money to go to an effective, enduring organization that would study the genetic origins of cancer. The Stowers have four children, but they decided that if they gave it to them, the money would be divided and nothing of great lasting value could ever come from it. The Stowers give several million each year to the institute and manage its affairs very closely, as if it were a corporation. Having taken care to provide for their children already, they intend to leave their entire estate to the foundation when they die.[20]

In the late-1990s many of America's richest families (particularly the new technology millionaires) were comparatively young and had not reached the stages in their lives when they were deciding exactly what was to become of their fortunes. Distributing the money rarely occupies as much of your thoughts as making it does, particularly when you are still making it. And you may not want to give too much of it away until you are sure just how much you might end up with after another twenty years or so of facing the changing fortunes of business and the stock market. But certainly there is a lot of money building up out there to be distributed sometime. Many of the successful technology wizards have said that they never expected to be as rich as the companies they founded have permitted them to be, and they look forward to "giving it all away," someday.

This thought leaves us wondering what the *Economist* has in mind by urging America's newest millionaires to be more imaginative and resourceful in thinking of ways to give away their money. To the extent that imaginative donors like Turner want some control over the ultimate use of the funds, will the attaching of strings become a public policy issue requiring rejections of some gifts? No public institution wants to be dictated to by distant fat cats or their agents, and certainly not from beyond the grave. After all, such public areas are already ones for which elected governments have responsibility for funding. If Bill Gates wants to improve the public schools in America, what can he do?

Could it be that the greater the amount of money going into private foundations to solve big social problems, the greater will be the amount of competition, redundancy, and confrontation that will develop between the foundations themselves, and between them and the public sectors? To avoid these conflicts, which are not likely to be resolved in favor of the foundations, new ideas about how to use the money will certainly be welcome. Maybe the Silicon generation is arriving on the scene at just the right time. Maybe it will be more creative in identifying ways in which to get money to those who need it most, without going through the government. But this is a tall order. You can give libraries or computer equipment to school systems, pay for private schools or colleges for ghetto kids, or send them to camp. But you will not have access to rebuilding the social systems where they have failed unless you become a public administrator yourself. This is frustrating to those who truly want their money to be used effectively, and who believe that by insuring good management and control, the best results will occur. The frustrations drive them to research institutes (mainly medical) where they can function in a controlled, businesslike way. Much of the work done in these institutes, however, duplicates or competes with efforts undertaken in the private sector. But in the long run how well will such foundations do in competing with large public corporations operating at the top of their form? How many great scientific discoveries have come from foundations?

American Principles and the Vast Circulating System

What is odd about our American ideas about wealth is that they are entirely our own. We haven't imported them from anywhere, though we have shopped around and have had many opportunities. They have been formed by our historical experience as an independent, self-created nation, and by economic policies based on free-market economic principles. We understood from the beginning that money was important in a society, but we had to have a system that would both create it and put it to good use. Its creation had to be the result of industry and endeavor, not of privilege or inherited right. Those who would respond to the opportunity to be tested in an open market contest for wealth would make good settlers and founding fathers. These founders of our miraculous modern economic society recognized that the hand of government, easily corrupted, should be light, checked and balanced, and involve term limits. They declared that taxes, the scourge of European life, must originate in a legislature whose membership was determined by universal suffrage. And they insisted that private property involved rights of ownership and that disputes should be settled openly in the courts, under a legal system designed to treat all equally. These basic principles, and a number of others from our democratic free-market origins, set the mold for our future. They were followed unevenly, with many lapses, but they survived and have been polished over the years.

Our history, of course, is more than documents and principles. We the people settled a vast continent, developed our natural resources, and took advantage of the opportunities handed to us and survived our disasters. We developed an internal market for savings, sponsored education and technology, and welcomed immigrants. Our system has been available to anyone who wanted to join it, at least for most of our history. But throughout it all, the basic principles remained paramount. They were elaborated on but never withdrawn. They are what has made us unique, and why our economic system has been so successful, not just in creating great wealth for a few, but in making prosperity available to all and making millionaires out of millions of Americans.

In 1877 Cornelius Vanderbilt, the "Commodore," died and left almost all of his $100 million fortune, then the world's largest, to his son William. Before his death, the Commodore had claimed that he wanted to keep the fortune intact as a "monument to [his] name," and as the only way to keep his controlling interest in the New York Central railroad intact. His will was challenged by the other siblings soon thereafter, and William was accused by them of having unfairly influenced the old man before his death, thus denying the other children their rightful inheritance. A nasty courtroom battle followed, which was daily reported on in the press. The matter was then settled between the family, without changing the distribution of the Vanderbilt fortune very much. During the trial, however, the New York Daily Tribune in December 1877 published an editorial entitled "Founding a Family." The article took the view that there was no greater folly than to try to found a family on the basis of wealth alone. The United States was a country in which men could rise to great wealth faster than anywhere else, and where ancestral wealth is rare, and the one country in the world "in which inherited money has done so little for its possessors. What becomes of the stupendous fortunes of the day? Most of them vanish as quickly as they came." Most of these fortunes indeed involve "a multitude of heirs" and "will be absorbed in the vast circulating system of the country."[21]

Almost unimaginable amounts of money will be passed on during the first half of the twenty-first century. The government will get a share, but it is every wealth holder's objective to minimize it. The fortunes of the previous century, greater than at any time in history, will pass on to subsequent generations and to foundations and other vehicles for good works. Few family business dynasties will survive more than a generation or two, if the historical record is any guide. But the great wealth of money earned at the end of the twentieth century, as at the end of the century before, will still be absorbed into the vast circulating system of the American economy. Some of it will become institutionalized into mighty foundations and relieve the government from some of the costs of performing its public welfare duties, clashing here and there with political interests or those of the contributing family. Some will be diverted into subsidies for a generation or two of family members, but most of it will be finally absorbed into the system entirely; that is, into the markets. There it will contribute to a rising financial supply that will underwrite and bolster the endeavors of new people trying to make their fortunes many years into the future. It's the essence, the strength, and the miracle of our great American wealth culture. Only here do things like this happen.

Hey, it's a wonderful country.

The End of an Era?

The 1990s ended in a burst of stock market excitement, one so intense that it obscured many corrective mechanisms already at work to restore normality. The great wealth of the era of the last two decades of the twentieth century was largely enabled by the stock market, and the market was still hard at work right up to the end. Tech stocks were the darlings, the Internet boom was intact and casting a heavy shadow of neglect over ordinary industrial companies, however well they were doing. It was the time of the quick-rich entrepreneur, and almost no one could get enough. Start-ups, venture capital, private equity deals, and IPOs all were in great demand. Many experienced investors were leery of the market's record-high price levels relative to earnings, dividends, and such things, and claimed never to have seen a market so ready for a crash as this one. Still none but a few of even them wanted to miss out entirely on what had been almost a sure thing for the past several years: investing in NASDAQ stocks. Many of these, like Cisco, Intel, and EMC, were the well-known, conservative stocks of the Internet revolution, but they boomed ahead anyway. But this market was also the place where you could trade in Plug Power, Globespan, Incyte Pharmaceutical, and ITXC, four companies that had each tripled in value in the first two months of 2000 alone. During 1999 the NASDAQ Composite rose by *more than 85 percent*, leaving the "old economy" Dow (+27 percent) and the S&P 500 (+21 percent) well behind. What a way to end a century!

The market, however, was very narrowly drawn in 1999; the top one hundred stocks of the S&P 500 index, for example, accounted for 90 percent of its market capitalization, and the top one hundred NASDAQ stocks returned 102 percent for the year. The excitement out there was undiminished by the news that the computer business was soft, the government was trying to break up Microsoft, oil prices had risen above $30 a barrel again, and, because of inflation concerns, interest rates were steadily being pushed upward by the Federal Reserve.

Indeed, though the technology wave was still building, the rest of the stock market had begun correcting, which many of the rationalist old-timers had been expecting and even welcomed. In 1999 only 50 percent of the stocks included in the S&P 500 went up, and the median (i.e., unweighted) return for the whole group was only 0.4 percent. Even on the red-hot NASDAQ, 48 percent of the stocks included in the composite declined for the year, and among the losers the average decline was 32 percent. Without the strong performers of the technology sector, all of the indices of the market's performance would have rolled back and shown a decline for the year. Even so, the NASDAQ losers included a dozen or so previously hot Internet stocks that were trading in January 2000 at prices 50 percent or more off their fifty-two-week highs. Many of the hot IPOs of 1999 were trading below their offering prices by year end. But life went on in the new millennium much as it had before, at least for a while. The markets were choppy, difficult, and hard to predict. Volatility increased to levels that were scary. The NASDAQ had its best and worst days, and the Dow got back some of the respect it had lost the year before. Cautiously we still invested, merged, acquired, restructured, and bought shares back in the market when their prices got too low. The markets were functioning well, even if half of the participants in it were struggling somewhat.

But the market had passed on to another generation, taking with it some of the hotter ammunition of the last, such as technology, but leaving behind a number of spent shells—including many of the favored concepts and persona of wealth creation and enrichment of the past two decades. Warren Buffett had his worst year ever in 1999, when his Berkshire Hathaway stock fell more than 30 percent. Insurance industry woes were the main reason, especially in the reinsurance sector, but during the year his large holdings in bellwether consumer products companies performed very poorly, especially relative to the S&P 500. Coca-Cola was down 30 percent (a loss for Buffett of $4 billion), and Gillette was down 37 percent (a loss of $1 billion). These companies, not long ago America's star performers, were acting tired and uninspired and needed something. Buffett's large positions, however, were just too big to do much with except wait for things to get better, which is what he did. His large holdings in American Express, however, rose by about 50 percent during the year.

Buffett was not alone among highly visible stock market investors whose portfolios performed poorly during the year. He had plenty of company, including his rival value investor Larry Tisch, whose Lowes Corp. stock was off 70 percent relative to the S&P 500. The hedge fund industry, however, had a pretty good year (the best since 1993), with most funds beating the S&P 500. George Soros's $10 billion Quantum Fund was up 35 percent for the year, though Julian Robertson's Tiger Management lost 18 percent. Both men decided, however, that these markets were too changed from what they knew and announced their retirement from the business.

Most of the deal-doers were quiet in the late 1990s. Stocks were so high they couldn't find deals to do. Not much was heard from Kirk Kerkorian but Carl Icahn scored his coup with Nabisco in June 2000. Ron Perleman spent most of the year trying to sort out the management problems at Revlon, which during 1998 plunged from about $55 per share to a little over $10. In 1999 it opened the year at $16, then skipped up to $32 before plunging again, this time to less than $10 per share. Revlon, which Perleman took public in 1996 at $27 per share, certainly was having a correction.

Many of the tycoons were struggling, too. Among them was Eisner at Disney, where the stock was off 32 percent at its low point in 1999, but recovered (partly on the news that Disney will now have a new president) to end the year off only 18 percent. Doug Ivester, Goizueta's successor as CEO at Coke, struggled hard against earnings declines and resigned prematurely after proposing a harsh program of layoffs to the board; the stock was down 10 percent for the year. At H. J. Heinz where O'Reilly was now chairman only (no longer CEO), the stock was off by 24 percent. Resisting these trends, however, were the perennials Neutron Jack, the Citigroup guys, and Hank Greenberg. GE was up 30 percent for the year (though Jack still failed to make the Forbes 400; Citigroup, still performing well, up 51 percent, though John Reed quit early in 2000. And AIG, somehow exempt from the problems of its industry, saw its stock price rise 30 percent. All of these gentlemen were paid well, of course, but so was David Komansky, CEO at Merrill Lynch, whose bonus and awards of restricted stock and stock options were all doubled from his previous year's compensation. Merrill's earnings per share increased 65 percent during 1999. Its stock, however, was typically volatile. It opened the year at $66 per share, drove up to $100 in March, sank to $64 in July, rose again to $80 in August, then hit $64 again in September, then closed the year at $82, a gain for the year of 28 percent.

The sports and entertainment world remain unchanged— star performers made more money than ever, but not as much as their handlers, and even higher prices were paid for sports teams. However much they made, it still seemed small in relation to the size of giant corporate transactions and the valuations placed by the market on risky companies. On December 31, 1999, Amazon.com (which had never had any earnings) was valued at $23 billion. In January 2000 America Online offered a merger with Time Warner valued at $160 billion, the largest deal ever announced in America. And in early March, 2000 Palm Inc. (the maker of the Palm Pilot) went public with an offering that shot up to $96 per share, where its market capitalization exceeded that of General Motors and its P/E ratio was over 2000. By the end of June, however, the market had taken a second look at these deals. Amazon was worth $11 billion less, AOL's stock (still tied to the Time Warner merger) was down 25 percent, and the Palm stock had dropped by more than two thirds to less than $30 a share.

In early fall of 2000, when this book went to press, the market remained our most important medium. Americans were in tune with its message daily, sometimes more frequently. There were new things to worry about now after all those years of easy money—huge swings in prices, margin calls, and the disappointing performances of several famous money managers. If Buffett and Tisch were doing so poorly, and Soros and Robertson decided to pack it in, maybe it was time to wonder if the market hadn't run out its string.

Perhaps. But over the past twenty years, even substantial corrections (such as October 1987) have been quickly followed by funds flowing in to take advantage of buying opportunities and a fairly quick restoration of the upward trend in prices. The market is now mainly controlled by institutions that need to invest in stocks and among them constitute a vast amount of liquidity. Rather than exit the market, many investment professionals say, just brace yourself for a few shocks every now and then and hang in there. You'll do much better if you do. The market is a wonderful and magical place.

However, on the theory that money is made over the long haul by adapting to the deeper, underlying trends of the economy, we should be wondering about the ability of the market to give us another twenty years like the ones we have just completed. We know that much of the drive in the market of the last twenty years came from steadily lowering interest rates, together with widespread corporate profit growth from productivity improvements, much of which were the result of successful, but one-time, restructuring efforts. Some of the rest of the market performance was attributed to the acceleration in the rate at which new telecommunications technology was being absorbed into industry. And the increasingly global market environment enabled investors from abroad to participate in our thriving market place to a greater extent. But not all of these factors are likely to be as potent in the future as they were over the past twenty years. Indeed, the value of financial assets issued and traded has grown at twice the rate of the real economy for nearly all of these twenty years, and inevitably, the growth rate must slow down to the same rate as the underlying economy itself. Maybe this slowdown in the growth of financial assets will not affect all parts of the world at the same time, but it is likely to descend on America, where we have been ahead of the pack for a long time. If this happens, we may have to start looking around for places where the American experience of the 1980–2000 wonder years might be repeated.

"WE WANT TO BE LIKE YOU"

In 1985 the members of the European Common Market, urged on by Margaret Thatcher and Helmut Kohl, approved radical changes in their methods of economic governance. Each country would give up much of its economic sovereignty in exchange for a real common market, one that could compete with the Americans for world economic leadership. Economic growth was low, unemployment high, and the long-term future of their standards of living was at stake. Too large a commitment to government intervention in the economies, to the economic theories of socialism, and to the power of trade unions had rendered European economic competitiveness ineffective. What was needed was a good dose of Americanism—open markets, optimism, free (if rough) competition, and a major reduction in government economic controls and ownership of assets. They decided to take the medicine.

In 1989 the Berlin Wall was brought down from the inside. The Communist world had imploded, probably not so much from fear of Ronald Reagan's commitment to destroy the "evil empire" with "star wars" and other devices, as from the fact that the economy simply collapsed. After more than seventy years it was then clear that Communism did not work very well as an economic system in a competitive world. If European socialism produced poor results, then Russian Communism produced worse ones. This idea spread also to China, to India, and other parts of Asia, where the constraints of their particular forms of socialism were relaxed so their economies could participate in the higher growth that only seemed possible under a more democratic, free-market capitalistic system.

If we should ever lack confidence in our own methods for generating and distributing wealth in America, we should look around us at a world in which, during the last dozen years, approximately half of the population has chosen—nonviolently—to adopt an economic system based on ours. Not for centuries, if ever, has the world quietly accepted a common system for creating and distributing wealth. And they chose it because they wanted to, because our system, with all its faults, works better than any other to create economic value and wealth.

And it is being emulated. In Europe a decade of deregulation, increased competition, cross-border investing, and a growing awareness of the importance of shareholders insisting on good management and high stock prices has caused an epidemic of restructuring. Over $800 billion of mergers took place in Europe in 1999 (more than in the U.S.), many of them hostile, including the epic struggle for control of (first) Telecom Italia, and (second) Mannesmann, both of which were won by the attacking company. In neither case did the government intervene to prevent the transaction, nor did Mannesmann resort, as it could have, to the "barbed wire" German takeover defenses available to it. In both cases the deals involved a massive exchange of shares and the issuance of several billions of dollars of bond financing. The markets took these all in stride; indeed it was not difficult to do. In 1999 more than a trillion dollars of financing occurred in the international bond market (based in London) and the volume of new international equity issues, a record at over $150 billion, was nearly twice what it had been the year before. Further, a once fledgling market for smaller companies was flourishing, and a venture capital market had emerged. But as far as these had developed, there was still a long way to go. Large numbers of unrestructured and government-controlled companies still remained to be attended to. There were still a vast number of European companies that had not yet been granted access to the capital markets, and many banks, savings institutions, and insurance companies were still operating as they had thirty years before. There was a great deal yet to do; the markets would certainly be busy doing it for another decade.

In Japan, too, big changes were beginning to happen in early 2000. After a decade of denial, the government and business communities began to understand that they needed to restructure their system from top to bottom or else fall hopelessly behind the economies of the U.S. and the EU, now a serious competitive threat to Japan. A number of large Japanese financial companies had failed, and some of these (not all) were allowed to be merged away or liquidated. American firms stepped in at Yamaichi Securities, Nikko Securities, and Long Term Credit Bank to make the investments necessary, and to provide the management, to revive these companies. American managers were put in charge of Mazda, the car company. Nissan tied up with Renault. A number of large industrial companies were shedding subsidiaries (some had as many as one thousand), reducing their work forces, and even repurchasing their own shares. But whereas Europe was already ten years into its major economic reforms to invigorate the private sector, Japan was just beginning. There would be twenty years of restructuring ahead for it, out of which many opportunities such as those that occurred in the United States in its two golden decades should appear.

Emerging markets present restructuring opportunities, too. They come in different sizes and shapes: the least risky are in the larger Southeast Asian countries and Latin America, next the large Asian (China, India) and the better-grade countries of Eastern Europe. The riskiest opportunities, and therefore the most difficult, are in Russia and other countries among the worse off former satellite states. But these struggling countries may represent long-term opportunities of the sort that haven't been seen since America was developed during the nineteenth century. During that time, the United States as an emerging market presented a lot of investment risks. Half the country was thought to be lawless, savage. The other half was largely agricultural. Railroads solved a lot of problems, but they were very expensive and had to be managed well. Corruption was hardly invisible—especially in railroads' dealings with municipalities along their paths. Politics were ineffective, and a massive and vastly expensive Civil War hardly encouraged investors. Still it happened. The United States was developed, capital investment did take root, industry arose. Clearly many of the governments of emerging markets are well aware of what they have to do to set favorable investment conditions, and they have found it possible to attract the capital they have needed. Others, like Russia, with much greater problems, will take longer. But the potential is there to be developed over the next hundred years, and as it happens, especially if it happens according to a free-market capitalistic model, another wave of restructuring, reform, and wealth creation might occur.

There are plenty of opportunities. American wealth creation doesn't have to die out as the boom times come back to normal; it just has to look abroad.

ACKNOWLEDGMENTS

A book like this requires a lot of help. Its inspiration came in a visit from my friend and former Goldman Sachs partner, Corbin Day, in the summer of 1997. Corbin stopped by my house on Cape Cod for a visit. He was on a leisurely cruise up the East Coast to Maine. "Boy," he said to me, "there sure is a lot of money out there. Suddenly everywhere you go there's somebody who just retired at forty-five, building a palace on a golf course or filling up the marinas with an enormous new yacht. Real estate prices, like the stock market, have gone sky high and just about everyone acts rich. Where's it all coming from?" It seemed like an important question. These were not ordinary times; this was not an ordinary bull market. We both knew that. I set out to look into it further.

As I did so, I asked for a lot of help from my colleagues and friends, who spent considerable time and effort helping to review chapters and making suggestions. Among these I want to especially acknowledge are my colleagues at New York University, particularly Dean George Daly, and Professors Martin Gruber, Helen Scott, George Smith, Richard Sylla, Ingo Walter, and David Yermack. Henry Christensen, a tax specialist at Sullivan and Cromwell in New York, and former Goldman Sachs colleagues Robert Friedman and William Landreth, were also helpful. Entrepreneurs Mike Bloomberg, Phil Cunningham, Marc Josephson, Ken Langone, Walt Minnick, Dave Phillips, and Vic Woolley contributed their stories and other insights. And without Catherine Peck and Julia Clarkson, research analysts at the Goldman Sachs business library, I would never have finished the project. Finally my appreciation, too, is expressed to Truman "Mac" Talley, my editor, whose many contributions to this effort over several years were as bold as they were right. My great thanks to all of these friends, and my exoneration from any faults or mistakes in the book, all of which are entirely my own responsibility.

NOTES

Introduction: A Shining City on a Hill

1. Goldman Sachs U.S. Economic Research, "The Consumer Balance Sheet," *The Pocket Chartroom*, December 1999–January 2000.
2. Dinesh D'Souza, "The Billionaire Next Door," *Forbes*, October 11, 1999.
3. Jacob Schlesinger, "Rise in Inequality of Wealth in 1980s Slowed in Early 1990s, IRS Study Shows," *The Wall Street Journal*, March 27, 1998.
4. *Ibid.*
5. Harold Seneker, "Are You Rich Yet," *Barron's*, September 20, 1999.
6. Daniel Patrick Moynihan, *Came the Revolution*, New York, Hartcourt Brace Jovanovich, 1986, p. 154.
7. Michael C. Jensen, Statement before the House Ways and Means Committee of the U.S. Congress, February 1, 1989.
8. The method used for determining merger intensity is to divide the value of completed domestic and U.S. cross-border transactions for the five-year period by the mid-year nominal GDP of the U.S. In 1898–1902, based on data compiled by Ralph Nelson,

the volume of mergers was $6.3 billion, which, divided by the 1900 U.S. GDP of $18.7 billion, was 33.7 percent. The five-year total of mergers done in the U.S. in 1994–1998 was $2.64 trillion, based on data supplied by Securities Data Corp. This, divided by the 1996 nominal GDP of $7.67 trillion, was 34.4 percent.
9. Abraham Bleiberg, "Tech M&A, Size Does Matter," Goldman Sachs Investment Research, June, 1998.

I. The Entrepreneurs

1. Michael Bloomberg, *Bloomberg on Bloomberg*, New York, J. Wiley & Sons, 1997, pp. 1–110.
2. Small Business Administration, "The Facts About Small Businesses, 1997," September 1997.
3. Ron Chernow, *Titan*, New York, Random House, 1998, pp. 72–75.
4. Michael Klepper and Robert Gunther, *The Wealthy 100*, Secaucus, NJ, Citadel Press, 1996, pp. 66–69.
5. Klepper and Gunther, *Op. Cit.*, pp. 130–131.
6. Ron Zemke, *The Service Edge*, New York, NAL Books, 1986.
7. *Forbes*, Oct. 13, 1997.
8. 30.15 percent assuming dividends were reinvested.
9. There is no real agreement on what the premium over the S&P 500 return should be. Some argue that the S&P 500 return should be discounted about 30 percent to reflect the lack of liquidity in the investment. This would lead to a risk premium of 10 percent to 15 percent. Others (Gompers and Lerner at Harvard Business School) argue that if estimates of intrinsic values that increased over the life of the investment, and the benefits of diversification across many different investments, were taken into account, the required premium would be between 5 percent and 10 percent.
10. Small Business Administration, ACE-Net Report, 1998.
11. PricewaterhouseCoopers Survey Research Center quarterly venture capital report, Fourth Quarter, 1998.
12. PricewaterhouseCoopers, October 1999.
13. Jennifer Tung, "I'm Not a Feminist," *The New York Post*, March 25, 1999.
14. Lisa Napoli, "A Focus on Women at iVillage.com," *The New York Times*, August 3, 1998.

2. The Dealsmakers

1. Amy Dunkin and Laurie Baum, "Bergerac's Golden Parachute: The Biggest Ever," *Business Week*, May 5, 1986.
2. Connie Bruck, "How Drexel's Pawns Stormed Corporate America," *The American Lawyer*, April 1988.
3. Ellen Pollock and Martha Brannigan, "The Sunbeam Shuffle," *The Wall Street Journal*, August 19, 1998.
4. Leah Nathans Spiro, "Ron Perelman, the Man Who Collects Companies," *Business Week*, September 11, 1995.
5. Martha Moore, "Tisch Obsessed with Bottom Line," *USA Today*, August 2, 1995.
6. Duff McDonald, "We Size Up Buffett and Tisch in a Battle of Heavyweights," *Money*, December 1997.
7. *Forbes*, December 15, 1997.
8. Judy Brennan, "The Cat's Ninth Life," *Entertainment Weekly*, August 2, 1996; and *Forbes*, December 1997.
9. Christina Binkley and Nikil Deogun, "Playing in Las Vegas: Two Titans in Takeover Drama," *The Wall Street Journal*, February 24, 2000.
10. Riva Atlas, "The Lone Raider Rides Again," *Institutional Investor*, June 1997.
11. Andrew Serwer, "Who's Afraid of Carl Icahn?," *Fortune*, February 17, 1997.
12. Roy C. Smith, *Money Wars*, New York, EP Dutton, 1990, pp. 179–215.
13. Mitchell Pacelle, "LBO Investing for the Merely Rich," *The Wall Street Journal*, August 21, 1998.
14. Smith, pp. 209–210.
15. *Forbes*, October 13, 1997.
16. Shawn Tulley, "Trump: A Ex-Loser is Back in the Money," *Fortune*, July 22, 1996.
17. *Forbes*, October 13, 1997.

3. The Investors

1. The change in market capitalization reflects factors other than price increases. During this time Securities Data Corp. notes

approximately $6 trillion in cash mergers or acquisitions and negative $141 billion of net stock issues (new issues minus corporate repurchases) occurred. These transactions actually reduced the number of shares outstanding in the market by a considerable extent, suggesting that the price increases experienced during the period were considerably greater than 15 percent.

2. Barrie Wigmore, "What is the Real Outlook for the S&P 500?," unpublished paper, July 1998.
3. Duff McDonald, "We Size Up Buffett and Tisch in a Battle of Heavyweights," *Money,* December 1997.
4. James Miller and Leslie Scism, "Buffett's Berkshire to Buy General RE," *The Wall Street Journal,* June 20, 1998.
5. Berkshire Hathaway, Inc., 1999 annual report.
6. In 1998 Berkshire Hathaway announced its $23.4 billion acquisition of General Re, for $276.99 per share, a premium over the closing market price the day before of 23.6 percent. The acquisition, however, was to be in Berkshire Hathaway stock, the first time Buffett had ever used the stock for an acquisition. Some analysts thought the price has high for General Re, but not so high in Buffett's hands or when using his stock.
7. *Ibid.*
8. See Robert G. Hagstrom, Jr., *The Warren Buffett Way: Investment Strategies of the World's Greatest Investor,* New York, J. Wiley & Sons, 1997 and Roger Lowenstein, *Buffett: The Making of an American Capitalist,* New York, Doubleday, 1996.
9. See Edwin Lefevre, *Reminiscences of a Stock Operator,* New York, George H. Doran and Company, 1923 (supposedly about Jesse Livermore), and Bernard Baruch, *Baruch, My Own Story,* New York, Henry Holt & Co., 1957.
10. *Forbes,* October 13, 1997.
11. Goldman Sachs & Co. and Financial Risk Management, Ltd., "Hedge Funds Demystified," July 1998.
12. Jack Willoughby, "The $600 Million Man," *Investment Dealers Digest,* September 12, 1994, and James Glassman, "In One Speculator's Spectacular Fall, a Few Essential Lessons," *The Washington Post,* November 22, 1997.
13. Robert Slater, *Soros,* New York, McGraw Hill, 1996, pp. 1–69.
14. *Wall Street Journal,* May 28, 1975.

15. *Institutional Investor,* June 1981.
16. Slater, *Op. Cit.,* pp. 81–168.
17. Slater, *Op. Cit.,* pp. 1–5.
18. Gretchen Morgenson, "Soros' Losses in Russia Put at $2 Billion," *The New York Times,* August 27, 1998.
19. William Lewis and Joshua Chaffin, "Soros to Cut Back Hedge Fund Action," *The Financial Times,* April 29/30, 2000.
20. Diana B. Henriques, *Fidelity's World,* New York, Scribner, 1995, pp. 1–129.
21. John Train, *The New Money Masters,* New York, Harper & Row, 1989, pp. 192–226.
22. Lynnley Browning, "Lynch Pin," *The Boston Globe,* January 31, 1999.
23. Henriques, p. 349, also Thomas Easton, "Will Fidelity Sit out the Dance?," *Forbes,* May 4, 1998.

4. The Tycoons

1. Kevin J. Murphy, "Executive Compensation," in Orley Ashenfelter and David Cards (eds.) *Handbook of Labor Economics,* Vol. 3, New York, North Holland, 1999.
2. Merrill Lynch & Co., 1999 annual proxy statement.
3. Carol Loomis, "AIG: Aggressive. Inscrutable. Greenberg," *Fortune,* April 27, 1998. Market capitalization at April 1, 2000.
4. Joseph B. Treaster, "Insurers Set $17.8 Billion Stock Deal," *The New York Times,* August 21, 1998.
5. Deborah Lohse, "AIG, SunAmerica Cross-Market Plans Are Under Way," *The Wall Street Journal,* December 31, 1998.
6. Loomis, *Op. Cit.*
7. Charles Gasparino and Paul Beckett, "How John Reed Lost The Reins at Citigroup To His Co-Chairman," *The Wall Street Journal,* April 14, 2000.
8. Ken Auletta, *Greed and Glory on Wall Street,* New York, Random House, 1986, pp. 189–202. And Gary Weiss, "Sandy's Triumph," *Business Week,* October 6, 1997.
9. David Yermack, "Companies' Modest Claims About the Value of CEO Stock Option Awards," *Review of Quantitative Finance and Accounting,* 10, 1998. The author gives credit to Kevin Murphy for suggesting the idea of a reload option as a stock put.

10. Jennifer Reingold, "Nice Option if You Can Get It," *Business Week*, May 4, 1998.
11. Citigroup, 1999 proxy statement.
12. David Greising, *I'd Like the World to Buy a Coke*, New York, John Wiley & Sons, 1997, pp. 1–300.
13. Robert Slater, *The New GE*, New York, Business One–Irwin, 1993, pp. 60–127.
14. General Electric Company, 1999 proxy statement.
15. H. J. Heinz Company, 1999 proxy statement.
16. "Executive Pay" (The 1998 Survey Results), *The Wall Street Journal*, April 8, 1998.
17. "Executive Pay—Special Report," *Business Week*, April 21, 1997.
18. Greising, *Op. Cit.* pp. 89–90.
19. Cendant Corporation, 1998 proxy statement.

5. The Entertainers

1. Diane MacIntrye, *The Silents Majority*, at mdle@primenet.com, 1996–1997.
2. H. W. Brands, *Masters of Enterprise*, New York, Free Press, 1999, pp. 300–301.
3. Harold Vogel, *Entertainment Industry Economics*, Fourth Edition, Cambridge, England, Cambridge University Press, 1998, pp. 65–75.
4. Bernard Weinraub and Geraldine Fabricant, "The Revenge of the Bean Counters," *The New York Times*, June 13, 1999.
5. Lisa Gubernick and Peter Newcomb, "The Richest Man in Hollywood," *Forbes*, December 24, 1990.
6. Vogel, pp. 263–274.
7. W. S. Miller (Ed.), *1998 Inside the Ownership of Professional Sports Teams*, IMR Team Marketing Report, Chicago, 1998, pp. 13–14.
8. K. Jaguar Myers (Ed.), *Sports Market Place*, New York, Custom Publishing, Inc., Spring 1998, p. 32–34, 100–101, 160–163.
9. Brian Garrity, "Sidelined," *Investment Dealers' Digest*, May 17, 1999.
10. Richard Sandomir, "The Jets Fill One Opening: New Owner at $635 Million," *The New York Times*, January 12, 2000.
11. Richard Sandomir, "How Green Is Your Gridiron," *The New York Times*, March 13, 1999.

6. The American Wealth Culture

1. Goldman Sachs & Co., "The Equity Market Fuels Growth," May 1998.
2. Goldman Sachs & Co., *The Pocket Chartroom*, "Issues and Outlook," December 1999/January 2000.
3. Christina Duff, "Rich May Be Different, but Few of Us Either Envy or Resent Their Wealth," *The Wall Street Journal*, March 5, 1998.
4. Federal Reserve Board, *Survey of Consumer Finances*, 1998; John C. Weicher, "The Rich and the Poor, Demographics of the U.S. Wealth Distribution," *Federal Reserve Bank of St. Louis Review*, July/August 1997.
5. *Barron's*, September 13, 1999.
6. Tim Triplett, "The Rich are Even Different from the Rich," quoted in *Marketing News*, August 1, 1994.
7. Lois Carrier and David Maurice, "Beneath the Surface; the Psychological Side of Spending Behaviors," *Journal of Financial Planning*, February 1998.
8. Juliet B. Schor, *The Overspent American: Upscaling, Downshifting, and the New Consumer*, New York, Basic Books, 1998.
9. Josh Maskow, "Poor Representation Creates Voter Apathy," *The Battalion*, Texas A&M University, November 2, 1998.
10. Perot report to Federal Election Commission, 1992.
11. Eliza Newlin Carney, "Rules? What Rules? A Guide to Loopholes," *The National Journal*, May 8, 1999.
12. John Marelius, "The Year of the Millionaires," *The San Diego Union-Tribune*, March 16, 1998.
13. Monica Langley, "Even CEOs Sweat Out Carnegie Hall Tryouts; For the Board That Is," *The Wall Street Journal*, July 30, 1998.
14. Susan E. Tiffet and Alex S. Jones, *The Patriarch: The Rise and Fall of the Bingham Dynasty*, New York, Summit Books, 1991, pp. 364–465.
15. Leslie Wayne, "Zero Is the Verdict in $2 Billion Koch Family Feud," *The New York Times*, June 20, 1998.
16. American Association of Fund Raising Counsel data, as quoted in "Giving Your All?," *The Economist*, May 29, 1999 and Karen

Anderson, "Charitable Giving Surged Again in 1999," *The New York Times*, May 23, 2000.

17. "The Challenge for America's Rich," *The Economist*, May 30, 1998.
18. *Fortune*, March 15, 1999, p. 72.
19. Mary Ann Glendon, "On Abortion, It's Clinton vs. the UN," *The Wall Street Journal*, May 5, 1998.
20. Scott McCormick, "Medical Portfolio," *Forbes*, May 31, 1999.
21. Vanderbilt, *Op. Cit.*, p. 416.

INDEX

Post, Marjorie Merriweather, 133
power and money, 295–304
"Predators' Ball," 128
Presley, Elvis, 263
Price, Michael, 7
Primerica, 223, 224
privatization, 18
Prudential Securities, 189

Quantum Emerging Markets
Growth Fund, 166–67, 170–76,
172
Quantum Fund, 328
Quota Funds, 172

R. J. Reynolds Tobacco Holdings,
108
raiders, 92, 93–110
Rainwater, Richard, 109
Ranieri, Louis, 122
Reagan, Ronald, 14–16, 286, 296,
332
Reaganomics, 1–3, 15–16, 21, 45,
110, 170, 286
and the deficit, 15–16, 17
real estate, 4, 5, 6, 69
investors, 92, 131–36, 262–63
real estate investment trusts
(REITs), 168–69
Redstone, Summer, 280
Reed, John, 7, 221, 225, 239, 329
Regan, Donald, 297
Reichman Bothers, 133
Relecom Italia, 333
reload plans, 226–30
Renault, 334
Republic Industries, 277
Revlon, 96–99, 328
Revlon v. MacAndrews and Forbes, 96–
97
Revson, Charles, 96
Reynolds Tobacco. *See* R. J.
Reynolds Tobacco Holdings;
RJR Nabisco
Rich, Marc, 4, 161
Right Stuff, The (Wolfe), 67–68
Riklis, Meshulam, 125
RJR Holdings, 108
RJR Nabisco, 107–8, 112, 119, 152,
328

See also Nabisco Group Holdings;
R. J. Reynolds Tobacco
Holdings
Robert Wood Johnson Foundation,
318
Roberts, George, 114, 122
Roberts, Julia, 265
Robertson, Julian, 163, 176, 328
Robinson, David, 271
Robinson, Jim, 223, 224
Rock, Arthur, 69–70
Rockefeller, Jay, 299
Rockefeller, John D., 48–49, 55,
317
Rockefeller, Nelson, 297, 299, 313
Rockefeller, Winthrop, Jr., 299
Rockefeller, Winthrop, Sr., 299
Rockefeller family, 6, 76, 305
Rodman, Dennis, 271
Rogers, Roy, 261, 262
Rohatyn, Felix, 110–11
Ronstadt, Linda, 268
Roosevelt, Franklin, 17, 313
Ross, Steve, 268
Roy Rogers Museum, 262
Roy Rogers restaurant chain, 262
Rubin, Robert, 16–17, 297–98
Russia
communism, collapse of, 332
economic development of, 334–
35

S. G. Warburg, 189
S&L (Savings & Loan) crisis, 97–
98, 125
Salomon, Inc., 97, 224
Salomon Brothers, 38–40, 119, 151,
153, 188–89
Salomon Smith Barney, 224
Samuelson, Paul, 157
San Francisco Opera, 302
Scholes, Myron, 164, 245–46
Schor, Juliet, 294–95
Schroeder, Alice, 144
Schumacher, Mike, 270
Schumer, Charles, 302
Schwab, Charles, 6, 65
Schwab, Leslie, 7
Seamans Furniture, 120
Sears Roebuck, 190